Michael J. Miller

The Curious Elephant

Holy Curiosity:
Factoids From the First Century

A compendium of articles discussing the Covenants, the Gospel, the Prophecies, and more from the first century perspective of the Biblical record.

redshoebooks

If the shoe fits, wear it.

Also by Michael J. Miller
The Blind Man's Elephant
The Hijacked Elephant

Copyright © 2008-2011
The Curious Elephant, Michael J. Miller

All Rights reserved under International and Pan-American Copyright Conventions. This book may not be reproduced in part or in whole, in any form or by any means whatsoever without prior written permission of the publisher except in the case of brief quotations embodied in articles, reviews or books when properly credited.

ISBN 978-976-8212-76-4

A redshoebooks publication
www.redshoe.com

Layout & Cover design: Blue-Concepts GmbH
                         www.blue-concepts.com

The redshoebooks' bookmark and redshoe graphics are trademarks of redshoebooks.

Dedication

To whom it may concern

Contents	Page
Forward	21
Introduction	25

Sections

The Covenants	31
The Gospel	85
The Prophecies	123
The Holidays	199
The Blind Man's Elephant	243
The Hijacked Elephant	291
The Great Rebellion: A Summary	319
The Great Britain-US Flow Chart	335
The Bible Books and Versions Abbreviations	347

The Covenants

Mirror, Mirror, On The Wall   Page 33

While we're looking at factoids from the first century, the biggest surprise is the one in Matthew fifteen when Christ said very plainly: *"I am not sent but unto the lost sheep of the House of Israel."* Now lest we think the King James translators made a mistake here, let's take a look at what the other translations say.

Abraham's Seed And Heirs   Page 39

Where did the notion come from that Christians are gentiles? For those of you suggesting that I read John 3:16, please see the chapter *Mirror, Mirror, On The Wall.* The apostles in the first century, Paul in particular, understood the change that took place in the theological landscape with Christ's first coming. Essentially, this is what is missing from modern day Christianity. There is a misconception that Christ came to save all the gentiles of the world. But this was not the first century understanding of the gospel, the change that took place according to the Biblical record.

Tale Of Two Covenants   Page 53

Christ greatly changed the theological landscape in the first century. Christians usually are unaware of exactly what took place. And it's not what is commonly believed. In the first verse of the New Testament we read, "The book of the generation of Jesus Christ, the son of David, the son of Abraham." In Matthew chapter fifteen, Christ said, "I am sent only to the lost sheep of the House of Israel." And in Matthew 5:17, Christ said, "Think not that I am come to destroy the Law, or the Prophets: I am not come to destroy, but to fulfill."

Why Was Jesus Jewish, But Not Moses? Page 63

While the answer to this question is alien to our 21st century, gentile oriented Christian mindset; it was common knowledge among our first century Christian predecessors. The evidence for the veracity of why Jesus was Jewish, but Moses wasn't, is amply found in the pages of the Biblical record, both Old and New Testaments. But, the simple answer as to why Jesus was Jewish is that given our circumstances with the law covenant, there was no other option.

What About Everyone Else? Page 77

As Christ is "Our Redeemer, the LORD of hosts... the Holy One of Israel... the Lord God of Israel... [who] *redeemed His people*" [Isa. 47:4; Luke 1:68], being the son of David, and the son of Abraham [Mat. 1:1] and who was sent only to the lost sheep of the House of Israel [Mat. 15:24], where does that leave everyone else?

The Gospel

What Exactly Is The Gospel? Page 87

I keep reading that Christians need to get back to the gospel. Or that we've gotten away from the gospel. Or that we've got to get the gospel right. But what exactly is the gospel? We are told it's a divine purpose. It's a historical event. Okay, but what is it exactly? It seems there is no end of talk about The Gospel but very little telling us what exactly the gospel is and what specifically it means for those to whom it was delivered. It's almost as if it's kept vague intentionally and that we're just supposed to know what it is through some sort of religious osmosis.

Galilee Of The Gentiles   **Page 93**

Some of you may point out that Christ began his ministry in Galilee of the Gentiles. Wouldn't this mean that Christ was sent to the gentiles after all? One could assume this. But when we let the Biblical record define itself, we find the correct answer.

The Tie That Binds   **Page 97**

The fundamental underlying premise of *The Hijacked Elephant* is that the entire Biblical record is one story written to and about the same people. In it, the analogy is that Christ is the "shoelace that binds both the Old and the New Testaments together." While this may not be news for some, *Yehovah elohiym*, the LORD God of the Old Testament is the same person as Jesus Christ of the New Testament in the first century. It's no accident that the name Jesus means *Yehovah is salvation*.

Christianity Is Not A Surrogate...   **Page 105**

Recently, a well-known author publicly stated that she was quitting Christianity, but not Jesus Christ. Many of those in mainstream Christianity, be they Protestant or Catholic, apparently cannot understand the difference between the two. As one member of a well-known "Christian corporation," aka church organization, wrote in the Christian Post regarding this, "... she still loves Jesus but she doesn't love Christianity. Yet, I know that it is impossible to love Jesus without loving his church." The critical point of understanding is that 21st century incorporated, denominational Christianity is not the church, or *ekklesia* in Greek, as it was intended in the first century.

Heaven Can Wait   **Page 113**

Apparently, there's going to be a lot of lonely Christians wondering where everybody went. And I'm not referring to the "rapture." A survey was conducted recently that showed 21st century Christians, evangelicals in particular, believe good people and people of other religions, after they die, go to heaven. It is astounding that nearly 500 years after the Protestant Reformation, these evangelicals still adhere to the Roman Catholic vision of eternal life rather than God's, as revealed to us from the first century in the Biblical record.

The Prophecies

Is The US In End-times Bible Prophecy?   **Page 125**

"The United States is absent from end-times Bible prophecy." For some reason, many Christian evangelists and pastors in all sorts of forums propagate this observation. But the plain fact of the matter is that it's simply not true. Not by a long shot. This prophetic blindness comes about because of a simple fact we've mentioned many, many times before. If we don't know our place in Biblical history, we can't know our place in Biblical prophecy. The US is not only not "absent from end-times Bible prophecy," but it is at the heart and core of circumstances directly leading to the events in the Apocalypse.

A Funny Thing Happened... **Page 141**

The identity of the fifth empire in Daniel 2 has eluded scholars and historians, with good reason, probably from about the time Daniel actually penned the account. So, I thought I would post an entry, properly cited and sourced, along with some elementary deductive reasoning, to share with others the identity of Daniel's missing fifth empire as it has great relevance to our current day's events. I was a bit taken back when a popular on-line encyclopedia refused to keep my entry posted citing the following reasons.

Ten Horns, Ten Nations **Page 155**

The Middle Eastern nation-state of Israel is only *one of the ten nations of Israel* [prophetically, in Daniel and Revelation, the ten horns] today with a national identity according to what Israel told his twelve sons, including his son Judah, the Jews, in the last days prophecy of Genesis 49.

Apokalypsis **Page 159**

The Book of Revelation was written in the first century, penned by the apostle John. But as we're told in the first verse, it is the "revelation of Jesus Christ, which God gave to him...." The word revelation is the Greek *apokalypsis*. Literally, it means a laying bare, which we can take to mean holding nothing back, showing everything. In this case, it is a book of revealing.

Christ Against Christians? **Page 163**

According to the most common Christian perception of "The Apocalypse," it is a general reference to the end of the world as a judgment upon evildoers while saving those who belong to Christ. Christians, most especially those who consider themselves to be of the conservative, evangelical variety, believe they will be the ones saved or raptured from "The Apocalypse." Of course, in the Book of Revelation it clearly states only 144,000 will be redeemed from the earth. If the world has a population of about seven billion people, our chance is about .000002 to make the cut.

Revelation 17   Page 173

Many devout people assert that Revelation 17 is the most difficult chapter in the Book of Revelation to understand. Yet, like so many things, it is easier to understand when we let the Biblical record interpret itself. Rather than use contemporary events as a prism through which we attempt clarity, we need the correct context. This context is the entirety of the Biblical record, which is one book written to the same people. Grasping this vital principle, our task is made that much simpler.

The Holidays

Peace On Earth?   Page 201

The holiday time of the year is filled with greeting cards that people send to family and friends. Typically, they have tranquil scenes, often with some snow on the front cover or will have a Nativity scene showing the wise men with their gifts as well as some shepherds at the manger. Very often the cards will say, "Peace on Earth," as did the one I got in the mail. Inside it said something about glad tidings, joy and peace on earth at Christmas.

Merry Christmas?   **Page 205**

By the way, Christ wasn't born in December either. What!? Of course, whether or not he was born in December is irrelevant to many folks. Some will say, we can't know his date of birth, so one day is as good or bad as another. This being the case, then we should drop the pretense that Christmas is about celebrating the birth of Christ. It's not. It's all about buying and selling if we're honest with ourselves.

Funny Bunny   **Page 209**

While we're on the subject of holidays not occurring when we think they did, what about Easter? Was Christ resurrected on a Sunday morning? What do the eyewitnesses from the first century say in the Biblical record? When we examine the account closely, we find a very surprising answer. If you truly have a holy curiosity, as Einstein phrased it, then continue reading.

Guess Who's Coming To Supper?   **Page 217**

Christ ate the "Last Supper," with his apostles the night of the Passover. It has become an epochal event in Christianity perhaps best known by Leonardo Da Vinci's popular painting, "The Last Supper." The painting itself has become the focus of many intriguing stories. However, it is best to keep in mind, Leonardo did not make the painting in the first century. He was fifteen centuries too late for that. The painting is a fiction, Leonardo's interpretation. Nothing more.

A Christmas Message Page 225

We want our government leaders to champion our traditional democratic values and culture, the liberty and way of life that strikes a resounding cord within us. Yet if we were told what *we, the people,* needed to do to attain this state of wellness, we'd balk at doing so. Why?... because we've become indifferent. No longer feeling empowered to shape our lives in any meaningful way, we resign ourselves, tolerating lies and fables in place of the truth, most notably at airports, during election years and each year regarding the ever expanding Christmas tradition, which has become so deeply rooted in our society on so many levels.

The Blind Man's Elephant

Atheistic Phone Apps
And Yellow Pencils Page 245

The debate over whether or not God exists has been around for a long time. Now there are phone apps for those who wish to engage in the debate, which usually centers on the idea put forward by atheists that "You can't prove God exists." This in turn usually gets a professed Christian's dander all riled up. The sparks fly from this point forward leading to strife and contention while each participant attempts to prove they are right. It's a bit like debating the outcome of the immovable object versus the irresistible force.

Is Genesis 1 A Jolly Good Myth?   Page 253

There are those who, while believing in a Creator, have a problematic time believing that the account of creation in Genesis 1 is nothing more than a myth; one of the many creation myths found in various cultures. If asked, most often the various reasons put forth usually are not based on any specific criteria or evidence. Most people probably have never really taken the time to carefully look at the specifics of Genesis 1.

Three Creations:
Neanderthal To Adam To Christ   Page 263

In May 2010, scientists came forward proclaiming that some of us are walking around with varying amounts, one to four percent, of Neanderthal DNA. While this may explain what many of us have long suspected about some of our co-workers, this appears to pose a dilemma for Christians who say that Adam was the first man.

Life In The 'hood   Page 269

The latest strategy by those who believe life begins at conception is the drive to create a status designated as "personhood" for embryos. Personhood Kansas was quoted as saying, "As a movement, we know what our goal is: *to have all children in the womb protected by love and law.*" While their motives are likely well meaning and good intentioned... their theology appears to be off center as to when life begins if using the Biblical record as their source text.

Brown Paint: Quantum Potentialities   Page 283

What we observe to be the world, our life or our physical reality is an illusion. As Einstein said, "Reality is merely an illusion, albeit a very persistent one." This comment is based on the way our universe is constructed at the quantum level as it manifests itself in our everyday, 4-D "real" world. Our four dimensional physical universe, three dimensions of space, and only one of time, is fundamentally much different than what we perceive it to be.

The Hijacked Elephant

The Three Dualities In God's Plan   Page 293

Ironically, while Christianity is ignorant of these dualities and, consequently, gives no credence to them, they are more important for Christians than ever before. The primary reason for this ignorance is that we don't know our Biblical identity, as Christ made clear to us in the first century. [Mat. 15:24]. And even though we are ignorant of the duality that Christ has and is fulfilling on our behalf, our continuing refusal to acknowledge our heritage means we will have to "pass through the fire," aka the Apocalypse, for the remnant to reach the third as is made clear in the Biblical prophecies.

What Days Do Christians Need To Observe?   Page 303

If there were days required of us to physically observe, it would be the days given to our ancestors of the House of Israel, and not the counterfeits Christianity blindly accepts today. However, the critical point to acknowledge is that Christ said he came to *fulfill* the Law and the Prophets because he broke the law covenant he made with our ancestors.

The Great Rebellion: A Summary

**Why Is First Century Christianity
More Relevant Than Ever?** **Page 321**

The simple answer is that Christ implemented major theological changes regarding the covenants, which resulted in good news for a specific group of people in our age. This group of people today is largely oblivious to the gravity of their current circumstances due to blithely ignoring their heritage despite the warnings given to them in end-time prophecies.

The Curious Elephant

Holy Curiosity:
Factoids From the First Century

Foreward

The title of this book, *The Curious Elephant,* which completes the Elephant book trilogy, is the logical progression of the titles of the first two books, *The Blind Man's Elephant* and *The Hijacked Elephant*. In all three books the elephant is a metaphor for Christianity with gratitude to John Godfrey Saxe for his 19th century poem, *The Blind Men and the Elephant*.

The subtitle, *Holy Curiosity: Factoids From the First Century* began as the title of a section on our web site. It was somewhat of a response to the main premise of Phyllis Tickle's Book, *The Great Emergence*. Her point is that about every 500 years or so in Christianity, there is a relatively major event resulting in big changes, most recently the Protestant Reformation. Since the advent of Christianity, this would make the Protestant Reformation the third major change.

In this regard, there is something interesting in Peter's epistle. "… knowing this first: that scoffers will come in the last days, walking according to their own lusts… But, beloved, do not forget this one thing, that with the Lord one day is as a thousand years, and a thousand years as one day." [2 Pet. 3:3, 8; see Jude 1:18].

A day with the Lord, according to Peter, is as a thousand years. And we know the Millennium after Christ's return is a thousand year period and is referred to as the "last great day." This is a reference to the Feast of Tabernacles, the last high holy day of the sacred year, aka the Millennium, which occurs prior to the great judgment and the new heaven and Earth. [See Zec. 14:16].

If we make the fairly reasonable assumption that there are seven ages, following the pattern of the Genesis creation of "seven days," [See chapter three *The Blind Man's Elephant*], then the prophetic last days could be the last two thousand years before the Millennium. This would mean that the Christian age, the beginning of the summer harvest marked by Pentecost, the time between Christ's first coming and his second coming, is two thousand years according to our Father's reckoning rather than ours.

The Protestant Reformation was the third of these major events, and history shows us that this began about 1517 with Martin Luther posting his 95 Theses at the Castle Church in Wittenburg. The fourth major event then, if the last days are approximately a 2000 year period, puts us within the time frame of the last of these 500 year major events occuring just before the return of Christ.

As Paul explained, before Christ's return there first has to be a *great apostasia* or falling away from the truth of the Lord. The Protestant Reformation could hardly be seen in this light unless you are a Catholic theologian.

Therefore, it is possible that we are in the midst of that great falling away which is why our current day major event, according to Tickle, is the emerging movement to get back to the basics delivered to us by Christ and his apostles in the first century. Time will tell if this is a plausible premise.

The phrase, holy curiosity, was inspired by Albert Einstein. *"Curiosity has its own reason for existing. One cannot help but be in awe when one contemplates the mysteries of eternity. Never lose a holy curiosity."* The first book, *The*

Foreword

Blind Man's Elephant, addresses a few of the mysteries in science that plague some theologians. Was Adam the first man? Was the Earth created 6000 years ago? And was it created in six 24-hour Earth days? Science says no. Religion says yes. Which is it? Having a holy curiosity helped us arrive at some startling and unexpected answers found in the Biblical record.

The Biblical record also has provided some amazing facts from the first century that have been abandoned and are virtually unknown in Christianity twenty centuries later. The articles that make up the chapters in this book are a result of the research prodded by the motivation imparted by holy curiosity in accordance with 1 John 2:27.

The chapters in *The Curious Elephant* are intended to teach us the primary principles of the word of God in support of the first two Elephant books, *The Blind Man's Elephant* and *The Hijacked Elephant*. The first two books were written to expand our look at Christianity and God's plan contained within the pages of the Biblical record that remain a mystery to so many Christians. They are the defining big pieces of the puzzle, if you will, the quantum theological points that outline the immense and intricate story found in the Biblical record. The chapters in this book provide the foundational and vital pieces of the puzzle, lost since the first century, that will bridge many of the remaining gaps in our knowledge so we can better understand the one big picture that is the Biblical record. In this sense, it is somewhat of a Christian primer redux, both for laymen and Christian shepherds alike.

The Curious Elephant

Introduction

When someone asks me a question relating to one of the Elephant books or the chapters herein, I often have a time of it converging my thoughts and picking a single pathway to a direct answer. The reason is that after close to five decades of study, research and writing, I've grown to realize how entangled everything is in the Biblical record, from Genesis to Revelation. It truly is one story. It's like connecting individual threads in order to make a chenshan. You can show someone a handful of thread, but it tells them nothing about the chenshan, what is it is, what it looks like, etc. You have to give them enough thread so they can envision the big picture that is the chenshan, or Chinese shirt. Otherwise, they have no context for the answer.

Thus, every thought leading to an answer spawns half a dozen more, which likewise propagate until there appears before my mind's eye a vast network of threads, any of which will lead to the answer of the question I have been asked. By then, I likely will have digressed, to a lesser or greater extent, from directly answering the original question in the mind of the questioner. The beauty, therefore, of reading the chapters is that my enthusiastic digressions have been corralled, written down, revised and edited for your reading pleasure. Well, to a certain point at least.

While the chapters in this book started out to be pithy, even in writing the answers tended to swell mysteriously as if digital yeast had been sprinkled into my keyboard. Not including the time ruminating about your own digressions, each chapter can be read in twenty to thirty contiguous minutes or so, unless this is a book-light bedtime read. Then, all guarantees expire when your head touches the pillow.

Riding rogue ponies into the Apocalypse

At its most fundamental level, the story contained in the Biblical record is quite simple to understand as the flow chart at the back of the book shows. It is totally and completely related to the two covenants, the one made with Abraham and his Seed, Christ and the law covenant made with all the children of Israel and the relationship between them both through Christ.

Not understanding our place in Biblical history, we've lost track of who we are and our relationship to both covenants. Perhaps this is why one Christian author made the point that Christians disagree as how to best go about following Christ in our everyday lives. What gets in the way of our understanding are the rogue ponies, the false traditions and fables that have ridden their way into Christianity over the past twenty centuries. This is why part of the subtitle of this book is *Factoids From the First Century*.

The Curious Elephant is devoted to getting us back in sync with Christ's faithful and true teachings from the first century. Many common practices of Christianity today were not recognized or sanctioned by Christ and the apostles, as they did not exist in the first century. And in our ignorance, and our apathy for the love of the truth, we justify our wayward pious actions whether they be of commission or omission. Much of this stems from the fact that over the past two millennia theologians and pastors have gotten away from the truth of what Christ in fact said. Too long we've been riding the rogue ponies toward the sunset that is the Apocalypse. [See Rev. 19:11-16; 16:1-21].

Today, these traditions of men, the fables have more credibility than the truth. We need to let the Biblical record speak for itself. We need to get back to basics. After all, we can't be expected to master the calculus of prophecy when we've flunked the arithmetic of the covenants. And those fundamentals are all found in the Biblical record. The first section of this book, therefore, is comprised of chapters directly relating to the covenants.

The Old Testament [Jewish Bible], as canonized by Ezra after the Babylonian captivity, is comprised of 3 divisions, the Law, the Prophets and the Psalms, with 22 books and occur in an order different than what is found in Christian Bibles. The original order is listed in Appendix One of *The Hijacked Elephant*. By 150 BCE, the Old Testament was considered complete and recognized as such by contemporary scholars and acknowledged by Christ. [See Luke 24:44].

The New Testament was written only by those who walked and talked and were directly taught by Christ in the first century, including the apostle Paul. [See Gal. 1:12]. No other books or writings merit inclusion to the canon of the New Testament organized by the last of the original apostles, John. Thus, the Biblical record is our complete source text.

Our goal, therefore, as Christians in studying and living our faith with a love of the truth is to dutifully separate the Biblical word of truth from the rogue ponies, which is essential in order for spiritual growth to occur. While our natural inclination is to avoid the growing pains associated with this process, we need to be rigorous in our pursuit of the truth. Under the outward guise of zeal for Christ and the truth, we are tempted to keep riding the rogue ponies, following the fables and other similar and comforting opinions to support our personal preferences without accurate Biblical substance to support them.

This duplicity has dire consequences. "There is a way that *seems right* to a man, but its end is the way of death." [Pro. 14:12]. While our traditional beliefs may feel natural because we've ridden them so long now, getting back in the saddle of the Word of God in faith is vital despite any unfamiliar feelings it may initially engender. Faith and works go hand in hand.

Mankind has the proclivity to project onto God our personal, human limitations. And it's because we don't grasp or respect the perspicacity of God, that we tend to heap our human weaknesses and shortcomings on him. Rather than put forth the effort to elevate ourselves to the level and standard established by God, we indolently take the path of least resistance. We filter God through our diminutive selves thereby creating a god in our own image and likeness. Collectively, this tendency has given us a flat Earth, created in six 24 hour days 6000 years ago, which was then placed in the center of our solar system. At one time these beliefs were held sacred. Hindsight has shown us they were nothing more than rogue ponies.

In our study of the Biblical record, it is wise to be mindful of this tendency, and place it aside. It impedes spiritual growth. While we may not understand all that God says or does, some of which, initially may seem contrary to our human reasoning, by living in faith continually seeking light, the first principles of the word of God, understanding and wisdom emerge from our spiritual growth. The more light we gather, the more we grow. For Christians, that Light is the word of God. Each of our lives, then, is a matter of priorities. Spiritual growth versus the cares of this world.

As the apostle Paul notably pointed out, the flesh and the Spirit have opposite polarities. [See Gal. 5:17]. We can't be both hot [*on Sundays and holidays*] and cold [*the rest of the time*] for the word of God. It appears, however, that many people have convinced themselves otherwise. The end result of these compromised efforts is being spiritually lukewarm, which is not a good place to be. [See Rev. 3:16].

Consequently, our modern day version of Christianity has lost its relevancy for many people due in part to our imprudently humanizing the authority and power of God. Yet, when we objectively examine in faith what is written in the Biblical record rather than riding rogue ponies [See Mark 7:6-9], we find a remarkable abundance of relevancy pertaining to our lives in the 21st century.

As always, do not take what you read here at face value either [1 Ths. 5:21]. Our love for Christianity must be a love for the truth not blinded by tradition. Holy curiosity and critical thinking are great tools. But they exist only when used.

You will find some overlap in the chapters. It is such because, when painting the big picture that is Christianity through its various facets, the Light gets refracted into many of those common threads that give us context for the whole.

Biblical quotes are taken from the King James Version [KJV] or the New King James Version [NKJV]. If otherwise, it is noted. The abbreviations for the Bible books, [Mat. for Matthew, Eze. for Ezekiel, etc.] are listed at the back of the book for easy reference. I highly recommend reading the referenced verses in the brackets as you come upon them as they add context and relevancy to the points being addressed.

Also the abbreviation for the Christian Era, CE, is used rather than A.D., Anno Domini, Latin for the year of our Lord, mainly because history scholars are not certain of the year Christ was born except it is not 1 A.D.

A grateful thank you to those individuals who have contributed their ideas and efforts in making this book a reality. And I thank all of you who've given me feedback on the Elephant books as several of the suggestions have been incorporated into this book. Also check out our website periodically for new articles. If you have any comments or questions regarding the Biblical record, please send them to us at ask@redshoe.com.

Michael J. Miller, 2011

The Covenants

Mirror, Mirror, On the Wall

When looking at factoids from the first century, the biggest surprise for most Christians is the one in Matthew fifteen when Christ said very plainly: "*I am not sent but unto the lost sheep of the House of Israel.*" Now lest we think the King James translators made a mistake here, let's take a look at what the other translations say.

My copy of the New King James Version says, "I was not sent except to the lost sheep of the House of Israel." My old copy of the Harmony of the Gospels from 1901 says, "I was not sent but unto the lost sheep of the House of Israel." My Revised Standard Version says, "I was sent only to the lost sheep of the House of Israel."

You can go through all the various translations, the ASV, the NIV, the NLT, etc., and they all are very clear about what Christ said. In fact, the NLT is perhaps the most to the point, when Christ says, "I was sent only to help God's lost sheep—the people of Israel."[1] In this case, the lost people are the House of Israel. These are the ones of Israel who aren't Jewish. See the flow chart at the end of the book.

Now the exclamation point to Christ's statement, for all of you Christians who can't believe you are descendants of Israel through Abraham, is that Christ said this to a gentile woman, meaning a woman of *non-Israelite descent*. As Christ explained it to her, he said, "It is not good that I take the children's bread and throw it to the dogs."

Christ was very clear that he wasn't sent to the gentiles of the world. He was blunt when he used the analogy of dogs in referring to them. Modern day Christianity disagrees with Christ on this point of heritage because we are ignorant of our place in Biblical history.

Of course, right about now, some of you may be thinking, "Before you make an idiot of yourself, consider John 3:16." And so we will. John also essentially makes the same point in chapter four, verse 42. "... we know that this is indeed the Christ, the Savior of the *world*." So let's take a look at what he is saying because it's wholly keyed into the covenants given only to the nations of Israel.

Christ wasn't ambiguous about who he was sent to and neither is the Biblical record. This consistency runs through the entire Bible from Genesis to Revelation. Christianity is confused however because we are pretty much clueless about our history and the relevancy of the covenants. In chapter three of John, Christ was explaining a few things to Nicodemus, a teacher of Israel, because he was unaware of them. Christ essentially said to Nicodemus, "How can you claim to be a teacher of Israel and not know these things?" The same point can be made to Christian teachers today. So Christ told Nicodemus, "For God so loved the *world* that He gave His only begotten Son, [*sent only to the lost sheep of the House of Israel*] that whoever believes in Him should not perish but have everlasting life." [John 3:16]. Who or what is the world here? Most assume Christ and John used it as a reference to people, or mankind. They didn't and it's not.

The English word world used by John is not the Greek word *anthropos*, meaning people or mankind, nor is it *oikoumene*, which is the inhabited Earth. It is *kosmos*, meaning an ordered arrangement or agreement or covenant.

Lest we think the apostles didn't know what they were writing about, take a look at 1 Corinthians 4:9. "For I think that God has set forth us the apostles last, as it were appointed to death: for we are made a spectacle [*theater*] to the world, and to angels, and to men." The word angels here is *aggelos* in Greek and it does mean angels. The word men in Greek here is *anthropos* and it does mean mankind. And the word world here, completely separate from angels and mankind is *kosmos*. Kosmos is not a reference to mankind nor to angels. Compare this to Hebrews 2:5 in reference to angels where the word world is *oikoumene* meaning the inhabited earth.

However, for those who insist upon quoting John 3:16, we must also examine John 3:19 in the same context. We see that the word *kosmos* and the word *anthropos*, used by John just three verses after verse 16, are completely separate and do not have the same meaning as the context clearly shows. "This is the judgment, that the Light has come into the world, and men loved the darkness rather than the Light, for their deeds were evil." [NASB].

If both words, world and men, mean the same thing in context of John 3, then how is it the Light, a reference to Christ, came into mankind and mankind loved the darkness? If this is so, we must conclude that Christ is the author of spiritual darkness. It makes no theological sense. It's contradictory. The words *world* and *men* have two different meanings.

It is consistently clear from this that John very well knew the difference between kosmos and anthropos in the first century as opposed to modern day Christians. The two are not one in the same, and the context here bears this out. John understood the covenants and how they relate to Christians. And what Christ and John meant is all very plain when we understand our place in Biblical history as it relates to the covenants as well.

Correctly understood, the KJV translators could have rendered this verse, "For God so loved *the covenant promises made with Abraham* that He gave His only begotten Son...." In context of the entire Biblical record, John 3:16 is referencing *the full extent and scope of the covenant promises made with Abraham and his Seed, Christ, which are all part of God's plan*. Christ, during his first coming, broke the Mosaic Law covenant made with Israel, and instituted the Abrahamic covenant in its place.

"And I [*God*] *will establish my covenant* between me and you [*Abraham*] and your seed after you...." [Gen. 17:7]. This covenant was not made with the gentiles of the world. It was established with the House of Israel in the first century. The word covenant in Hebrew is *beriyth* and has essentially the same definition as *kosmos* meaning a formal agreement or alliance. God "has in these last days spoken to us by His Son, *whom He has appointed heir of all things*, through whom also He made the worlds..." [Heb. 1:2]. Thus, the kosmos, the scope of the covenant made with Abraham and his Seed, Christ, is rather large and all encompassing. The word *worlds* here, in the Greek is *aion* and refers to ages.

Paul is clear about Christ's role with the new covenant. "Now to Abraham and his Seed were the promises made. He does not say, 'And to seeds,' as of many, but as of one.

'And to your Seed,' who is Christ." "And *if you are Christ's, then you are Abraham's seed* [Greek, *sperma*, meaning semen, hence physical descendants], and heirs according to the promise [*of the new covenant*]." [Gal. 3:16, 29]. There is a reason why Christ's genealogy, his seed line from Abraham, is the first thing we read in the New Testament.

And as Christians are Abraham's seed and heirs according to the promise, then we are not gentiles of the world, as in many seeds, especially as the covenant promises were passed to Isaac, "... in Isaac shall your seed be called" [Rom. 9:7], and then it was passed on to Isaac's son Israel. It is all connected to the Genesis Birthright, which is discussed in detail in chapter six of *The Blind Man's Elephant*. Also see the next chapter, *Abraham's Seed and Heirs.*

Who are the lost sheep of the House of Israel? Christians. At least that's what Christ and the apostles very plainly said. Israel was Abraham's grandson. Israel had twelve sons. They were the children of Israel. And they remained as one nation until just after the death of Solomon because "Solomon did evil in the sight of the Lord, and did not fully follow the Lord, as did his father David." [1 Kng. 11:6].

So the nation of Israel was split into two nations. The descendants of the son Judah, the Jews, became known as the House of Judah. Ten other remaining sons became known as the House of Israel. The one son Levi, was the priesthood, and was found in both Houses. In 732 BCE, God divorced the ten nation House of Israel from the covenant promises because of their gross idolatry, but not the House of Judah. [See Jer. 3:8]. Being divorced, they lost their national identities and covenant promises. They were taken captive and scattered among the regions of the Assyrian empire. Thus, they became the same as any other *gowy*, or gentiles or *people not in the covenant relationship with God*. Again, this history is diagramed in the flow chart at the end of the book.

Because God made a promise to Abraham that was passed on to Isaac and then passed on to Israel, the ten nations of the House of Israel needed to be redeemed, brought back into their covenant relationship or alliance with God. Thus, Christ, the Seed of Abraham, as he said, was only sent to the ten nations of the House of Israel. They were the only ones needing to be redeemed at Christ's first coming because of the covenant promise made by God with Abraham. It's all about the covenant. This is what John is referring to in his chapter three because God sent His only begotten Son only to the lost sheep of the House of Israel.

---

[i] Scripture quotations marked NLT are taken from the Holy Bible, New Living Translation, copyright 1996, 2004. Used by permission of Tyndale House Publishers, Inc., Wheaton, Illinois 60189. All rights reserved.

Abraham's Seed and Heirs

Where did the notion come from that Christians are gentiles? For those of you suggesting that I read John 3:16, please see the chapter *Mirror, Mirror, On The Wall*. The apostles in the first century, Paul in particular, understood the change that took place in the theological landscape with Christ's first coming. Essentially, this is what is missing from modern day Christianity. There is a misconception that Christ came to save all the gentiles of the world. But this was not the first century understanding of the gospel, the change that took place according to the Biblical record.

The focus of the Old Testament was the law covenant made with Moses and the children of Israel. *The focus of the New Testament is the covenant made with Abraham and his Seed, Christ, the root and offspring of David as King of Israel.*

The theological shift made by Christ was his covering the debt of the law covenant by his death and resurrection, thereby initiating his fulfilling of the Law and the Prophets [the first two divisions of the Old Testament] on behalf of the children of Israel. [See Mat. 5:17]. Christ instituted the covenant made with Abraham built on faith and grace beginning with the House of Israel. Consequently, it was not a shift from the Jews to the gentiles of the world. Rather, it was a shift from the House of Judah to the House of Israel who was, for the 700 years or so preceding Christ's first coming, outside the covenant relationship with God.

The very first verse of the New Testament tells us to whom the New Testament is directed, and it's all in the family. "The book of the *generation* of Jesus Christ, the son of

David, the son of Abraham." No gentiles here. Then, just six verses from the end of the New Testament, we read in the book of Revelation, "I, Jesus, have sent my angel to testify to you these things *in the churches.* I am the root and the offspring of David, the bright and morning star." The New Testament is as much for Israel as is the Old Testament. Conversely, the Old Testament is as much for Christians as is the New Testament. It's all one story written to and for the same people. Twenty-first century Christianity misses the mark completely with this pivotal point of understanding.

Gentiles of the world are not considered the children of Abraham, Isaac and Israel [Jacob]. In fact, Biblically, the gentiles would be considered everyone NOT the children of Abraham, Isaac and Israel, all those outside the covenant relationship with God. As the apostle Paul pointed out, Abraham had a son of a bondwoman, and a son of a freewoman, with whom he begat Isaac who begat Israel. Which one is the covenant heir with Christ, those of the bondwoman, the gentiles or those of the freewoman, the nations of Israel? [See Gen. 17:19-21].

In the New Testament, Paul makes our answer abundantly clear. "Nevertheless what does the Scripture say? '*Cast out the bondwoman and her son, for the son of the bondwoman* **shall not be heir** *with the son of the freewoman.*' So then, brethren [*fellow Christians*], *we are not children of the bondwoman* but of the free." [Gal. 4:30, 31]. Or as it reads in the Old Testament, "... for the son of the bondwoman shall not be heir with my son, Isaac." [Gen. 21:10]. And Isaac's son, of course, is Israel.

The Covenants
Abraham's Seed and Heirs

The reference by Paul here is to the Abrahamic covenant, not the law covenant. The son of the bondwoman references the gentiles of the world. And the son of the freewoman is a reference to those with whom the covenant was made, Abraham and his seed, which pre-dated the law covenant by more than 400 years. Paul is telling us that Christians are not gentiles, but literally are the seed line, the children of both Abraham and Isaac, father to Israel. [See Rom. 9:7]. This does not mean we are Jews or those of the House of Judah. Remember, Judah was only one of Israel's twelve sons.

After leaving Egypt, all the children of Israel, including those of Judah, did fall under the legal force of the law covenant. And sin is defined as the transgression of the law. [See 1 John 3:4]. According to the Biblical record, then, the only ones legally to whom sin can be imputed are those under the law covenant. Also, faith is not of the law. Therefore, whatever is not of faith, meaning the faith covenant with Abraham, is of the law covenant whereby sin is imputed. [See Rom. 14:23]. And because of her sins, the House of Israel was divorced from God and the covenant promises of Abraham.

The law covenant was in force at the time of Christ's first coming. By redeeming those under the law, those to whom sin was imputed, Israel, Christ's death and resurrection once again made available the covenant promises given to Abraham, father of the faithful, which are contained in the first division of the Old Testament. As Christ said, he came to fulfill not to destroy.

Paul made the point that Christ came "*to redeem those under the law*, that we might receive the full rights of sons."

[See Gal. 4:1-7]. This is the gospel, or good news, that was preached by Christ. But Christ didn't come to redeem the whole world. Who was under the law, as in the Law and the Prophets? Was it the gentiles of the world or Israel? So whom did Christ come to redeem? Israel. And they were to receive the full rights as heirs according to the promises given to Abraham.

To reinforce this point unequivocally, who does Christ, the Redeemer, say he was sent? Addressing his remark to a *gentile* or non-Israelite woman, Christ said, "I am sent only to the lost sheep of the House of Israel." [Mat. 15:24]. While Christianity tends to ignore this extremely plain statement by Christ today, it is exactly the point Paul made about the son of the bondwoman *not being heir with the son of the freewoman*. If we knew nothing else but this, we would see for whom Christ's first coming is meant.

For an understanding of what was happening at Christ's first coming, we need a brief history lesson. For a more detailed analysis, see chapter six of *The Blind Man's Elephant*. Abraham is the patriarch of Israel through his son Isaac. Israel had twelve sons. Each son had a family that eventually became so numerous that each came to be referred to as a tribe and then as a nation. All Israel, all twelve nations of Israel, came to be united as one under King Saul and then David. David's son Solomon became king upon David's death. But Solomon sort of got off track with his 1000 wives and concubines, not following the ways of the Lord as diligently as his father.

Upon the death of Solomon, God split the twelve nations of Israel into two entities. One nation, Judah, the Jews, became the House of Judah. The nation of Levi was the priesthood in service to God. And the other ten nations of Israel became the House of Israel. If Christ can be believed, this is the same House of Israel Christ said he was *only* sent to in the first century. To visualize this a bit better, see the flow chart at the end of the book.

With this in mind, let's read what it says in Matthew chapter four about Christ's ministry. "And leaving Nazareth, he came and dwelt in Capernaum, which is upon the sea coast, in the borders of Zebulun and Naphtali: That it might be fulfilled which was spoken by Esaias the prophet [Isa. 9:1, 2], saying, 'The land of Zebulun, and the land of Naphtali, by the way of the sea, beyond Jordan, Galilee of the *Gentiles*; The people which sat in darkness saw great light; and to them which sat in the region and shadow of death light is sprung up. From that time Jesus began to preach, and to say, Repent: for the kingdom of heaven is at hand.'" [See Mat. 4:12-17].

Reading this as isolated verses, we could come to the conclusion that Christ came to save the gentiles of the world. This error is primarily due to translating the Greek word *ethnos* as gentiles rather than nations as it was meant originally referencing the divorced condition of the nations of the House of Israel.

Matthew is quoting the Old Testament here. And as this is a quote from the Old Testament, it should give us a big clue as to its original intended audience. A bigger clue is that *both Zebulun and Naphtali are two nations of the House of Israel!* [See Gen. 49]. How is it that this Old Testament *quote* suddenly refers to the *Gentiles* in the New Testament whereas in Isaiah's Old Testament account it reads, "Galilee of the nations" in the context of Israel? The Old Testament, obviously, was not written to the gentiles of the world, but rather it is all about Abraham and Isaac's descendants, *the nations of Israel.*

What got lost in the translation was the fact that the King James translators bought into the notion that as Christians are not Jews, they must be gentiles, and not of Israel. Therefore, Christ had to be the savior of the gentiles, the non-Israelites, of the world. Not understanding the covenant promises and for whom they were meant, this faulty logic guided their translation.

However, from the time of the House of Israel's divorce until being redeemed by Christ more than 700 years later, the House of Israel was indeed as any other heathens or gentiles outside the covenant relationship with God. While this situation made them "gentiles," as far as the covenants were concerned, they were still the children of promise, descendants and heirs of Abraham and Isaac's seed. They were outside the law covenant relationship of Moses because of their adultery, meaning they turned away from God to seek after false gods. "And I saw, when for all the causes whereby backsliding [*House of*] Israel committed adultery I had put her away, and given her a bill of divorce; yet her treacherous sister [*House of*] Judah feared not, but went and played the harlot also." [Jer. 3:8].

The nations of the House of Israel were divorced. The House of Judah, the Jews weren't. Thus, as far as the law covenant relationship, Judah was still in, but the nations of the House of Israel were out. In the book of the prophet Zechariah, in reference to Christ's first coming, it states, "Then I [*Christ*] cut in two my other staff, Bonds, that *I might break the brotherhood* between Judah and Israel." [Zec. 11:14].

The shift or the breaking of the brotherhood, from the Old Testament to the New Testament was a shift from the House of Judah and the law covenant to the House of Israel and the faith covenant of Abraham through his Seed, Jesus Christ. This is the most important fact we can know in order to Biblically understand who Christians truly are in our world today.

The Hebrew word, *gowy* and the Greek word, *ethnos* in reference to the nations of the House of Israel recognizes their divorced state or being outside their covenant relationship with God up to the day of Pentecost in the first century. [See Acts 2:36-38].

Hence, both the Hebrew gowy and the Greek ethnos are oftentimes translated as heathen or gentile, which has led to much confusion. As a result, context is important in determining what is meant provided one understands that the Biblical record is one story written to and about the same people.

Despite their divorce under the terms of the law covenant, the House of Israel was eligible for the promises made to Abraham. "And this I say, that the covenant, that was confirmed before of God in Christ, the law, which was four hundred and thirty years after, *cannot disannul, that it should make the promise* [given to Abraham] *of none effect.*" [Gal. 3:17].

Christ, as the Seed of Abraham, clearly said he was sent only to redeem the lost sheep of the House of Israel with a ransom, his blood and his life to cover our debt to the law covenant. Why does Christianity ignore him? As we read in Luke, Christ said to Zacchaeus, "This day is salvation come to this house, because *he also is a son of Abraham. For the Son of man is come to seek and to save that which was lost.*" [Luke 19:9, 10]. *And it was only the divorced nations of the House of Israel that were lost from their covenant relationship with God.*

Thus, upon Christ's resurrection, the House of Israel was not only reinstated into a covenant relationship with God, it was a better covenant, one built on grace and faith and not one of the law and works of the flesh. "But now has he [*Christ*] obtained a more excellent ministry, by how much also he is the mediator of a better covenant, which was established upon better promises," [Heb. 8:6] promises given to Abraham.

But this was not apparent to those who translated the King James Bible. In the King James Version we read, "And the scripture, foreseeing that God would justify the **heathen** through faith, preached before the gospel to Abraham, saying, 'In you shall all **nations** be blessed.'" "That the blessing of Abraham might come on the **Gentiles** through Jesus Christ; that we might receive the promise of the Spirit through faith." [Gal. 3:8, 14].

First, we need to ask ourselves, how can it be that the blessing of Abraham might come on the Gentiles, the son of the bondwoman, through Jesus Christ when the New Testament scripture plainly says, "*Cast out the bondwoman and her son... [who]* **shall not be heir** *with my son Isaac?*"

The reason for the misunderstanding is that the words *heathen, Gentiles* and *nations* here are all the same Greek word, *ethnos*. It is the same word that was translated gentiles in 'Galilee of the *Gentiles*' in Matthew's Old Testament quote of Isaiah. When we realize that Christ was sent only to the divorced, i.e., lost sheep, the lost nations of the House of Israel, then the word ethnos should read nations in all three examples.

Reading it this way, it is in agreement with the fact that Abraham's heirs are descendants of his son Isaac and his son Israel. "And the scripture, foreseeing that God would justify the nations [*of Israel*] through faith, preached before the gospel to Abraham, saying, 'In you shall all nations [*of Israel*] be blessed.'" "That the blessing of Abraham might come on the nations [*of Israel*] through Jesus Christ; that we might receive the promise of the Spirit through faith." This is consistent with Biblical context and fits perfectly for it is as Christ said, he was sent *only* to the lost nations of the House of Israel and not to all the gentile nations of the world.

In the Old Testament prophesy in Isaiah, Edom [Israel's brother, nee Esau, see Gen. 25:25, 26] is complaining to God about their loss of the birthright inheritance, [i.e., being heirs], "I Edom will mention the loving kindnesses of the LORD and the praises of the LORD, according to all that the LORD has bestowed on us, and the great goodness toward **the House of Israel**, which He has bestowed on them according to his mercies, according to the multitude of his loving kindnesses. For He said, 'Surely they [*House of Israel*] are my people, children who will not lie.' So, *He became their Savior.*" [Isa. 63:7, 8].

And when Christ sent out the twelve apostles, he told them *not to go into the way of the gentiles*, nor any city of the Samaritans, "But rather go to the lost sheep of **the House of Israel**, and preach, saying 'The kingdom of God is at hand.'" [Mat. 10:6, 7]. Christ shows us here that gentiles are those not of Israel.

The House of Israel, Christians, today need to be aware of our true Biblical identity. We are not some group of gentiles who happen to believe in Christ, the very same Christ who said, "I am sent only to the lost sheep of the House of Israel," "... children who will not lie." Who is the liar? Christ or the Antichrist? Yet do Christians believe we are the lost sheep of the House of Israel as Christ said? Then who is it that we believe? [See Rev. 20:2, 3].

Which nations are blessed in Abraham? Is it all the nations of the world, the gentiles or specific nations, as in all the nations of Israel, the children of Abraham and Isaac? When Israel was in slavery in Egypt, we read, "And God heard their groaning, and God remembered his covenant with Abraham, with Isaac, and with Jacob [Israel]." [Exd. 2:24].

This is important for Christians today because as Paul, the apostle to the nations, reminded *the Christians* in the Corinth church in the *first century*, "Moreover, *brethren,* I would not that you should be ignorant, how that *all our fathers* were under the cloud, and *all passed* through the sea; And were *all baptized* unto Moses in the cloud and in the sea; And did *all eat* the same spiritual meat; And did *all drink* the same spiritual drink: for they drank of that spiritual Rock that followed them: and *that Rock was Christ.*" [1 Cor. 10:1-4; see the chapter *The Tie That Binds*].

The Covenants
Abraham's Seed and Heirs

The covenant was not made with all the nations of the world, but only with Abraham, his son Isaac and Abraham's grandson, Israel. And Christ is the Seed of Abraham. "Now to Abraham and *his seed* were the promises made. He said not, And to seeds, as of many; but as of one, And to your seed, which is Christ." [Gal. 3:16].

So who then could these nations be that would be justified through faith, to whom the good news, the same gospel Christ brought to Christians possibly be, "That *the blessing of Abraham* might come on the nations [*ethnos*] through *Jesus Christ*; that we might *receive the promise of the Spirit* through faith." [Gal. 3:14].

Our answer is found in both the Old and New Testaments. "And I [*God*] will establish my covenant between me and you [*Abraham*] and your seed after you *in their generations for an everlasting covenant*, to be a God unto you, and to your seed after you. And God said unto Abraham, You shall keep my covenant therefore, you, and your seed after you in their generations." [Gen. 17:7-9]. The covenant promises made with Abraham and his generations, are between God and Abraham's descendants through Christ. No one else is included. So then who would that apply to today, the children of the bondwoman, gentiles of the world or the nations of Israel, Abraham's generations?

Who are Christians according to the word of God? We find our answer in the New Testament, "*And if you are Christ's, then you are* **Abraham's seed, and heirs according to the promise.**" [Gal. 3:29]. The word seed here is the Greek, *sperma*, which means physical seed, hence Abraham's generations or descendants. It is not a metaphorical reference to gentiles of the world.

Remember, the children of the bondwoman, gentiles, are not considered heirs. The children of Abraham, Isaac and Israel are. It's just as it was stated in Genesis. God established his covenant between *Abraham and his generations, including Christ*, for an *everlasting* covenant. An everlasting covenant would include 21st century Christians. Those descendants of the House of Israel who have repented, changed, and have received the promise of the Spirit of God are considered heirs, for they are Christ's. This is what separates the House of Israel from everyone else in this age.

The ethnos, the nations in the New Testament that Christ, as the seed of Abraham came to redeem are the lost sheep, the lost nations of the House of Israel just as Christ said. And when Christ said to the gentile woman that he was only sent to the lost sheep of the House of Israel, the gentile woman replied, "Lord, help me." And what was Jesus Christ's response to this gentile woman? "But He answered and said, "It is not good to take the children's bread and throw it to the dogs." [Mat. 15:26].

Christ was not sent to save the gentiles of the world. Christians are the children of the House of Israel, the sons of Abraham. The shift from the Old Testament to the New was a shift from the House of Judah to the House of Israel until Christ's second coming, when a new covenant will be made with both the House of Judah and the House of Israel, their brotherhood mended. [Eze. 37:16-28; Heb. 8:8].

The Covenants
Abraham's Seed and Heirs

There is a reason why the Christian Bible contains both the Old and New Testaments, after all.

Perhaps the questions we need to be asking are, "Why do we think we are gentiles rather than who we really are?" "Where did this idea come from?" "And in whose interest is it to keep us from knowing the truth?" The startling answers to these questions can be found in *The Blind Man's Elephant* chapter six, The Genesis Birthright.

The Tale of Two Covenants

Christ greatly changed the theological landscape in the first century. Christians usually are unaware of exactly what took place. And it's not what is commonly believed. In the first verse of the New Testament we read, "The book of the generation of Jesus Christ, the son of David, the son of Abraham." In Matthew chapter fifteen, Christ said, "I am sent only to the lost sheep of the House of Israel." And in Matthew 5:17, Christ said, "Think not that I am come to destroy the Law, or the Prophets: I am not come to destroy, but to fulfill."

Taken together this seems very "Jewish." However, with the exception of the reference to David, none of it is Jewish, although it is all of Israel. Abraham was Judah's progenitor, and therefore he wasn't Jewish. The patriarch Israel, being Judah's father, also wasn't Jewish. The nations of the House of Israel are Israel *minus* the Jews. The Jews are the House of Judah. And the Law and the Prophets, which are two of the three major divisions of the Old Testament, were for all Israel, not just for Judah or the Jews.

Most Christians have been taught that the Old Testament is for the Jews and the New Testament is for Christians, who supposedly are some unrelated, yet amalgamated group of gentiles. However, this is not the case. If you haven't already done so, for a more complete understanding of this subject, read *Abraham's Seed and Heirs*. In fact, the entire Biblical record, both testaments are for the same people. If you'd like a full explanation of this, see chapter six, *The Blind Man's Elephant* and specifically *The Hijacked Elephant*. It is no accident the Christian Bible contains both the New

Testament and the Jewish Bible or the Old Testament. This is exactly as it should be for Christians are the lost sheep of the House of Israel. The Old Testament is our book too.

Therefore, it greatly helps all Christians to understand how the Old Testament flows into the New Testament, which is all about fulfilling the Law and the Prophets as Christ said. None of this makes sense until we realize we are descendants of our patriarch Israel. Not understanding this, we ask why rather than how. "Why is Christ fulfilling all that Old Testament stuff? Christianity has nothing to do with that."

However, the contrary is true. Christ said, "These are the words which I spoke to you while I was still with you, that all things must be fulfilled which were written in the Law of Moses and the Prophets and the Psalms concerning Me." [Luke 24:44]. This is another way to say what is written in the entire Old Testament concerns Christ. In this sense, the Old Testament is a very Christian book, as one should expect with Christ being sent only to the lost sheep of the House of Israel.

Christianity is based on the Old Testament regarding the Law and the Prophets for a reason. In fact, the two great commandments of Christianity, to love God with all our heart, mind and soul and to love our neighbor as ourselves, have their basis in the Old Testament. As Christ said, "On these two commandments hang all the Law and the Prophets." [Mat. 22:40].

Why, then, is the entire foundation of Christianity a carry over from the Old Testament? Because the New Testament is the beginning of the fulfilling of the promises made to

Abraham as recorded in the Old Testament, hence the very first verse of the New Testament above. The promises made to Abraham comprise the Abrahamic covenant, which was made with Abraham and his Seed, Christ. [Gal. 3:16]. And the Abrahamic covenant is found in the Book of the Law, the same book in which the Mosaic covenant or the law covenant made with Moses and all the children of Israel is found.

However, the Abrahamic covenant is found before we find the law covenant in the Old Testament Book of the Law. Why? It's because the law covenant was added as a temporary bridge to get us from the time after Abraham to Christ. "Wherefore the law was our schoolmaster to bring us to Christ, that we might be justified by faith." [Gal. 3:24]. A key point should not be overlooked in what the apostle Paul is saying here to Christians, "The law was our[s]...." He is telling us that our ancestors were under the law covenant and it brought us, Christians, nee children of the House of Israel, to Christ.

The only people under the law covenant in the Book of the Law were *the children of the House of Israel*, who today are Christians, and those of the House of Judah who still look to the old covenant. However, about 700 years prior to Christ's coming, the nations which comprised the House of Israel were divorced by God, cast out of the covenant relationship, because of their blatant disregard of their law covenant obligations. "And I saw, when for all the causes whereby backsliding [*House of*] Israel committed adultery I had put her away, and given her a bill of divorce...." [Jer. 3:8]. This is why Christ said, "I am sent only to the lost sheep of the House of Israel." Christ came to redeem us and in so doing is fulfilling the promises given to Abraham.

Let's take a look at the process from the Book of the Law that lead to Christ's ending one covenant and beginning the fulfillment of the second in the first century. It will help us understand what it truly means being a Christian.

A key point of understanding for Christians is that *the law covenant was not made with the patriarch Israel, but with Moses and all the children of Israel.* Moses, by the way, was not Jewish. He was of the tribe or nation of Levi, which became the priesthood for all Israel including Judah. The law covenant was added 430 years after the promise of the Abrahamic covenant. Therefore, the covenant made with Isaac and Israel was that of Abraham, and not Moses. *The two covenants are mutually exclusive of each other* as the apostle Paul makes abundantly clear. The descendants of Abraham through Isaac are beholden to only one of them. Christ, in his prerogative, took the entirety of the old one upon himself, and has given us a completely new one in its place as promised. Thus, Christ's "fulfilling the Law and the Prophets."

The Seed of Abraham, Christ, therefore, purposefully subtracted us, and our ancestors in the first century from the law covenant equation by breaking the law covenant. While the observing of the holy days ordinances delivered by Moses was an integral part of the law covenant, it is null and void, as is any required observance on our part. However, Christ fulfilling these days is the blueprint for all the major events of Christianity including Christ's second coming. *The Hijacked Elephant* goes into great detail explaining this. Devoid of this understanding, Christianity wanders aimlessly not knowing who we are and where we are in the great scheme of things. As a result, we have followed after falsehoods and lies oblivious to the consequences of our ignorance. [See the chapters *Merry Christmas?*, *Funny Bunny* and *Revelation 17*]. In large part, Christianity has lost its relevancy to our daily lives due to our ignorance.

But the Abrahamic covenant coming to fruition for Christians was only possible once the law covenant made with Moses and the children of Israel was terminated. Christ did this as the prophecy concerning Christ's death and the breaking of the law covenant in the book of the prophet Zechariah, chapter eleven is clear, "And I took my staff, Beauty, and cut it asunder, that **I might break my covenant which I had made with all the people. And it was broken in that day**: and so the poor of the flock that waited upon me knew that it was the word of the LORD. And I said unto them, If you think good, give me my price; and if not, forbear. So **they weighed for my price thirty pieces of silver**." We find confirmation of this for Christians in the New Testament gospel of Matthew, "Then was *fulfilled* that which was spoken by Jeremy[1] the prophet, saying, And they took the thirty pieces of silver, the price of him that was valued, whom they of the children of Israel did value...." [Mat. 27:9].

How is it that the Old Testament prophecy in the book of Zechariah foretold this specific event about Christ if Christians are mere gentiles? Why would a "Jewish" prophet in the "Jewish" Bible include a prophesy about a "gentile" savior that is not recognized by Judaism as foretold by the prophet Isaiah? [Rom. 11:8; Isa. 29:10]. It makes no sense, unless... Christians are not gentiles. The fact is, we are descendants of the House of Israel, and as such we are children of Israel. And Christ said, "Think not that I am come to destroy the Law, or the Prophets: I am not come to destroy, but to *fulfill*." Christ fulfilled that which was written by the prophet Zechariah exactly as he said.

The Law and the Prophets, the first two divisions of the Old Testament, are significant for Christians today. The Book of the Law *contains both* the promises of the Abrahamic covenant, which is applicable for Christians today and the Mosaic law covenant, which was applicable to our ancestors of the House of Israel as well as to those of the House of Judah. But as Christ said, "I am only sent to the lost sheep of the House of Israel."

When Christ said he came to fulfill the Law and the Prophets, this includes both his breaking the law covenant on our behalf, as we just read, *and* giving Christians a better covenant built upon better promises according to the covenant made with Abraham. The two are tied together. Thus, both covenants have relevance for Christians.

Christ broke the law covenant, the legal contractual obligation that required our ancestors, the children of Israel, to keep ordinances of the law. As prophesied, Christ broke that contract and took over our responsibility to the law. Christ paid off our bad debt [sin] with his death. Christians repent of their sins when they accept Christ's sacrifice on their behalf. It is no coincidence, then, that in the New Testament we read, "... for sin is the transgression of *the law*." [1 John 3:4]. Again, that which we read in the New Testament is tied to that of the Old Testament. The law covenant was binding only on the children of Israel. In place of our old debt, Christ has given us our new covenant based on faith rather than on the works of the law, thereby making us debt free or free from the penalty of breaking the law, which is sin, which results in death. [See 1 Cor. 15:56].

By fulfilling the Law and the Prophets, Christ fulfilled the old covenant Passover, the Days of Unleavened Bread, and Pentecost, which was marked by the receiving of the Holy Spirit on the very first day of Christianity. It is no coincidence either that on that Pentecost day the apostle Peter, the same Peter to whom Christ said "And I also say to you that you are Peter, and on this rock I will build my church, and the gates of Hades [*death*] shall not prevail against it," stood up and addressed his remarks to... "*all the House of Israel.*" [Acts 2:36-38].

Christ is still fulfilling the days given to all the children of Israel in the Book of the Law. Originally, these days were days given to all the children of Israel to observe under the contractual terms of the law covenant. Now as Christ said, he is fulfilling the Law including these days on our behalf. It is these days that have great relevance for Christians rather than the counterfeits celebrated today. [See *The Hijacked Elephant* for details].

The annual holy day in the Law next observed after the day of Pentecost is the day of Trumpets. Most Christians probably have never even heard of this day. Yet it is the day that Christians look forward to and is written about in great detail in the Book of Revelation. And who is it that will *fulfill* the Day of Trumpets? The answer is Christ. "And I saw the seven angels which stood before God; and to them were given seven trumpets." [Rev. 8:2]. This day marks the return of Christ to Earth at his second coming preceded by the blowing of trumpets. [See chapter five, *The Hijacked Elephant* for a thorough explanation].

All of those 144,000, which Christians talk about all the time, are only from the nations that are comprised of the children of Israel. "And I heard the number of those who were sealed. One hundred and forty-four thousand of all the tribes of *the children of Israel* were sealed: of the tribe of Judah twelve thousand were sealed; of the tribe of Reuben twelve thousand were sealed; of the tribe of Gad twelve thousand were sealed; of the tribe of Asher twelve thousand were sealed; of the tribe of Naphtali twelve thousand were sealed; of the tribe of Manasseh twelve thousand were sealed; of the tribe of Simeon twelve thousand were sealed; of the tribe of Levi twelve thousand were sealed; of the tribe of Issachar twelve thousand were sealed; of the tribe of Zebulun twelve thousand were sealed; of the tribe of Joseph twelve thousand were sealed; of the tribe of Benjamin twelve thousand were sealed." [Rev. 7:4-8; see Gen. 49 for a listing of the children of Israel as nations in the last days].

The law covenant was made only with the children of Israel. Christ broke that covenant and is fulfilling its obligation on our behalf. Thus, it is important to distinguish between the Abrahamic covenant and the law covenant contained in the Book of the Law. The Abrahamic covenant was made with Abraham and his Seed, Christ. The law covenant that was later added was made with the children of Israel. "What purpose then does the law serve? It was added because of transgressions, [*not an everlasting covenant as it had a timing factor*] until the Seed [*Christ*] should come to whom the promise was made; and it was appointed through angels by the hand of a mediator." [Gal. 3:19]. Christ broke one covenant, paid our debt and gave us a better one. He is fulfilling that which is written in the Book of the Law concerning both covenants.

The Covenants
The Tale of Two Covenants

So, which one do we have today? The covenant of Abraham and his Seed, Christ, as it was set forth in the Old Testament and was brought to fruition for Christians in the New Testament. But, both testaments have relevance for Christians today. To fully understand the new covenant, we need to understand the old covenant realizing that, at one time, our ancestors lived under its veil. Thus, we have a liberty in Christ they never had under the law covenant.

As Paul explained it to the Christians in Corinth, "Therefore, since we have such hope, we use great boldness of speech unlike Moses, who put a veil over his face so that the children of Israel could not look steadily at the end of what was passing away [*the law covenant*]. But their minds were blinded. For until this day the same veil remains unlifted in the reading of the Old Testament [*Jews of the House of Judah*], because the veil is taken away in Christ. But even to this day, when Moses is read, a veil lies on their heart. [*See Isa. 29:10*]. Nevertheless when one turns to the Lord, the veil is taken away. Now the Lord is the Spirit; and where the Spirit of the Lord is, there is liberty" rather than bondage to sin. [2 Cor. 3:12-17].

Thus, in Christ the veil of the old covenant and sin was taken away 2000 years ago for us and the light of the new covenant [See 1 John 1:7] took its place as promised in the Law and the Prophets for the House of Israel, in the generation of Jesus Christ, the son of David, the son of Abraham.

---
[1] "Perhaps the true explanation is the following, from LIGHTFOOT: "Jeremiah of old had the first place among

the prophets, and hereby he comes to be mentioned above all the rest... because he stood first in the volume of the prophets... therefore he is first named. When, therefore, Matthew produces a text of Zechariah under the name of JEREMY, he only cites the words of the volume of the prophets under his name who stood first in the volume of the prophets." *Jamieson, Fausset and Brown, commentary David Brown, Chapter 27 Matthew.*

Why was Jesus Jewish, But Not Moses?

While the answer to this question is alien to our 21st century, gentile oriented Christian mindset; it was common knowledge among our first century Christian predecessors. The evidence for the veracity of why Jesus was Jewish, but Moses wasn't, is amply found in the pages of the Biblical record, both Old and New Testaments. But, the simple answer as to why Jesus was Jewish is that given our circumstances with the law covenant, there was no other option.

Understanding this comment means understanding the relationship between the Mosaic law covenant made with *all* the children of Israel and the Abrahamic covenant made with Abraham and his Seed, meaning Christ. It also means understanding Christ's central role with both covenants. In fact, it's all about the covenants. The Biblical record is divided into two sections, the Old Covenant and the New Covenant, for a reason. Yet, it's all one book written to the same people… all Israel. And it means we Christians today most likely don't know our Biblical identity. And when we don't understand these things, we really can't truthfully understand the Biblical record, our personal interpretations to the contrary.

Because we've lost sight of our Biblical identity, we don't understand the covenants and how they relate to us. And we don't realize how fundamental the roles of the covenants are in Christianity and how the gospel is tied to them. If we did, then it would be common knowledge as to why Jesus needed to be a physical descendant of David, a descendant of Judah.

The very first verse of the New Testament or New Covenant provides us with some insight. Matthew one, verse one reads, "The book of the generation of Jesus Christ, the son of David, the son of Abraham." In other words, *the seed line of Christ* is directly from David, a son of Israel, in turn directly from Abraham, a progenitor of Israel. Hence, Christ as Abraham's seed is the mediator of the new covenant, the one for Christians in this age. [See Gal. 3:16; Heb. 12:24].

According to the *promise* given to Abraham, his Seed Christ established *the new covenant* with *the House of Israel*. "Therefore let all the House of Israel know... the promise is unto you and your children..." which would be us today. [See Acts 2:36-39]. With his death and resurrection, Christ ended one covenant and initiated the other... ultimately, for the same people, all Israel. [See Rom. 11:26; also the flow chart at the end of the book for a quick overview].

One thing is clear. Knowing Christ was physically a descendant of the House of Judah does not mean a "Jew came to save the Gentiles." Rather it means Christ, as the Seed of Abraham, came to save all Israel; the House of Israel first and the House of Judah second. In terms of our understanding, as has been pointed out in the chapters here and in the previous Elephant books, Abraham, Israel and Moses were not Jewish.

Jews are physical descendants of one of Israel's twelve sons, Judah. Both Abraham and Israel were Judah's progenitors. Moses, the "lawgiver," was not Jewish. He was a descendant of Levi, a brother of Judah. [See 1 Chr. 23:13]. In a very extended sense, Moses was Judah's nephew, not his son. So, while Moses was not a descendant of Judah, he was a descendant of Israel, who in this extended scenario would be Moses' grandpa.

The first king of all Israel was Saul. Saul was not Jewish either. He was a descendant of Israel's son Benjamin, also a brother of Judah. The apostle Paul, author of most of the New Testament, was a descendant of Benjamin too and therefore was not Jewish, or descended from Judah by birth. While those who are adherents to Judaism are referred to as Jews today, our discussion here is strictly of one's physical lineage, not choice of religion.

David, who succeeded Saul as king of all the nations of Israel, was a descendant of Judah, and therefore was Jewish. Solomon, as David's son, also was a descendant of Judah and was Jewish. However, after his death, all twelve nations of Israel were split into two kingdoms: the House of Judah, the Jews; and the House of Israel, the rest of the sons of Israel except those of Levi. The Levites were the priesthood for both the Jews of the House of Judah, and for Israel of the House of Israel. The apostle Paul, a Benjamite, notes, "For it is evident that our Lord arose from Judah, of which tribe Moses [*a Levite*] spoke nothing concerning priesthood." [Heb. 7:14]. Both Houses were governed by the law covenant delivered by Moses from Mt. Sinai to the children of Israel. [Exd. 24:3-8].

When this split between the Houses of Judah and Israel occurred, Rehoboam, a son of Solomon became the king of the Jews or the House of Judah [1 Kng. 11:43]. Jeroboam, a descendant of Joseph, the tribe of Ephraim, one of Israel's other twelve sons, became king over ten nations of Israel, or the House of Israel. "And it came to pass, when all Israel heard that Jeroboam was come again, that they sent and called him to the congregation, and made him king over all Israel: there was none that followed the house of David, but the tribe of Judah only." [1 Kng. 12:20]. As we can see, the Jews were a small minority of all Israel. The same holds true today.

By way of historical clarity, the house of David is the kingly line of Judah. The house of Joseph, through his son Ephraim, is the kingly line of Israel to this day. [See the chapter, *Is The US In End-times Bible Prophecy?*].

This split arrangement lasted for a couple of centuries or so until the House of Israel became so idolatrous that God divorced them. [See Jer. 3:6-8]. They were taken captive by the Assyrians and dispersed throughout the Assyrian empire. It was then that they lost their claim to their covenant inheritance. And they lost their national identities. It wasn't until the twelfth or thirteenth centuries CE [Christian Era] that the national identities of the House of Israel began to emerge once again. But we get ahead of ourselves here. [See the chapter, *Ten Horns, Ten Nations*].

By 730 BCE or thereabouts, the nations of the House of Israel disappeared into obscurity, forgotten by name, but not deed, in the history books. They were a people who sat in darkness, lost and estranged from the covenant promises made with Abraham millennia earlier. [See the chapter, *Galilee of the Gentiles*]. This left only the House of Judah, the Jews, as the legal heirs to both the law covenant and the promises of the Abrahamic covenant.

Consequently, the only participants in the law covenant at Christ's first coming, and the only people of Israel still legally entitled, was the house of David, or Judah. In order for the House of Israel to be redeemed, only someone bound by the law covenant could fulfill its terms on behalf of the divorced House of Israel. Of course, that left only Judah. Thus Christ, in the flesh, had to be a son of David [See Rom. 1:1-3], a descendant of the House of Judah or Jewish in order to be savior of the divorced, lost sheep of the House of Israel. This need not be the case if Christ was sent to save the gentiles of the world, which he wasn't. In the larger scheme of things, Christ was an Israelite. These events were driven by the covenants, which are part of the kosmos or God's plan for all Israel.

At the coming of Christ in the first century, the entire theological landscape regarding both the law covenant and Abrahamic covenant dramatically changed, as did the roles of the House of Judah and the divorced House of Israel. [For details, see chapter six *The Blind Man's Elephant*].

Christ broke the law covenant. "And I took my staff, **Beauty, and cut it in two, that I might break the [*law*] covenant** which I had made with the people [Hebrew, *'am, kinsmen of Israel*]. And it was broken in that day. And the LORD said to me, "Throw it to the potter"-that princely price they set on me. So I took the thirty pieces of silver and threw them into the house of the LORD for the potter. Then I cut in two my other staff, **Bonds, that I might break the brotherhood between Judah and Israel.**" [Zec. 11:10-14]. It remains this way theologically today between the Jews and Christians.

With the law covenant broken, Christ's resurrection marked the beginning of the Abrahamic covenant with the House of

Israel. Also at this time, the bonds of brotherhood between the House of Judah and the House of Israel were broken. It was the House of Israel only at Christ's first coming that was redeemed, which is why Christ clearly said, "I am not sent except to the lost sheep of the House of Israel." [Mat. 15:24]. The time for the House of Judah will be at Christ's second coming. [See Eze. 37:16, 17, 22; Heb. 8:8].

Paul explains the broken brotherhood relationship between the House of Judah and the House of Israel metaphorically. "And if some of the branches [*House of Judah*] be broken off, and you, being a wild olive tree [*the divorced House of Israel outside the covenant*], were grafted in among them, and with them partake of the root and fatness of the olive tree [*the Abrahamic covenant promises*]; Boast not against the branches [*the House of Judah*]. But if you boast [*House of Israel*], you bear not the root, but the root you. You will say then, The branches were broken off, that I might be grafted in. Well, because of unbelief they [*the House of Judah, see John 12:37-41*] were broken off, and you stand by faith. Be not highminded, but fear: For if God spared not the natural branches, take heed lest he also spare not you."

"Behold therefore the goodness and severity of God: on them [*the House of Judah*] which fell, severity; but toward you [*the House of Israel*], goodness, if you continue in his goodness: otherwise you also shall be cut off. [*See the chapters Christ Against Christians and Revelation 17*]. And they [*the House of Judah*] also, if they abide not still in unbelief, shall be grafted in: for God is able to graft them in again. For if you [*the House of Israel*] were cut out of the olive tree which is wild by nature [*being divorced*], and were grafted contrary to nature into a good olive tree: how much more shall these, which be the natural branches, be grafted into their own olive tree? "

Paul continues, explaining the mystery and to whom he has been referring. "For I would not, brethren, that you should be ignorant of this mystery, unless you should be wise in your own conceits; that *blindness* **in part** *is happened to Israel*, [*the one-twelfth House of Judah part*] until the fullness of the nations [*Greek, ethnos*] be come in. And so, *all Israel* shall be saved: as it is written, There shall come out of Sion [*Jerusalem, the city of David*] the Deliverer [*Christ; see Mat. 1:1*], and shall turn away ungodliness from Jacob [*all Israel*]: For this is my covenant to them, when I shall take away their sins." [Rom. 11:17-26; see Eze. 37:17].

If we are still unsure that this is referring to the Houses of Judah and Israel, i.e., all Israel, rather than the Gentiles, then a simple equation can remove our doubts. We know that Christ broke the law covenant and the brotherhood between Judah and Israel. The part of Israel that is blind to Christ to this day is Judah, the Jews. And as Paul wrote, Judah plus X [the fullness of the nations] equals *all* Israel. Therefore, the House of Judah plus the nations of the House of Israel equals all Israel. Judah plus the Gentiles do not equal all Israel. This fits perfectly with what Christ said. "I am not sent except to the lost sheep of the House of Israel."

A part of Israel is blind to Christ. This is the House of Judah because "of their unbelief." "What then? [*all*] Israel has not obtained that which he seeks for; but the election [*the House of Israel*] has obtained it, and *the rest* [*the House of Judah*] *were blinded*. (According as it is written, [*in the Old Testament*] God has given them [*the House of Judah*] the spirit of slumber, eyes that they should not see, and ears that they should not hear;) unto this day. [See Mat. 13:25-30]. And David says, Let their table be made a snare, and a trap, and a stumblingblock, and a recompence unto them: Let their eyes be darkened, so that they do not see, and bow down their back always." [Rom. 11:7-10 from Isa. 29:10; see Psa. 69:22, 23, 35].

The word election, *ekloge*, a noun or the word elect, *eklektos*, an adjective in Greek means chosen. God chose Abraham as the father of the faithful. His Seed was Christ. The House of Israel was chosen by Christ to be his people. [See Isa. 63:7, 8]. And we know all Israel are God's chosen people, including the House of Israel. "For you are a holy people to the LORD your God; *the LORD your God has chosen you to be a people for Himself, a special treasure above all the peoples on the face of the earth.*" [Deu. 7:6].

Disregarding our unique and blessed relationship with our LORD, we've been duped into forsaking it, believing we are an amalgamated group of Biblical vagabonds, commonly known as Gentiles. The Gentiles of the world, however, were never under the law covenant. While it was true, we were divorced from God and lost any claim to the promised covenant inheritance due to our being divorced according to the terms of the law, scattered among other peoples of the world without an identity, the fundamental point of the New Testament is that *Christ as the son of Abraham, changed all that in the first century.*

Our Lord Jesus Christ gave his life to redeem us, the House of Israel. He gave us a new covenant as promised because we were "chosen to be a people for Himself." [See Gal. 3:13, 4:4, 5; Mat. 15:24]. This is a major theological point of Biblical understanding completely lost on modern day Christianity. This is the good news, the gospel. When we don't understand this change in the covenants meant for us, we don't understand the gospel. [See 2 Cor. 4:3, 4].

Why, then, have we, the House of Israel, Christians, not chosen to claim our rightful heritage as God's own children, a "peculiar people?" [Tts. 2:14, Exd. 3:10]. And in who's best interest is it, that we remain blinded to it, at our own peril, as Judah is to Christ? [Read chapter six in *The Blind Man's Elephant*]. The answers to these questions are vital for us given the path we have chosen to walk.

Those who still look to the old law covenant as binding to any degree are blinded. But the election are those of the House of Israel who have obtained the promises of the new covenant upon the death and resurrection of Christ, by which we have received the Holy Spirit. And we know that on the first day of Christianity, only those of the House of Israel were promised the Holy Spirit. [Acts 2:36, 38].

Where did events stand 2000 years ago? The House of Israel was divorced. The House of Judah, still under the law covenant, was the sole repository of the new covenant *promises*. Due to the divorced House of Israel needing to be redeemed, Christ broke the law covenant and is fulfilling its terms on our behalf. [Read *The Hijacked Elephant* for details]. Christ also broke off the natural branches, the House of Judah, who were given "eyes that slumber" because of their unbelief when he broke the bonds of brotherhood between them and the House of Israel. [See the flow chart].

The sheep of the House of Israel today, Christians, have a new covenant with God, the covenant made with Abraham, the father of the faithful and his seed, Christ.

The apostle Paul explains in the New Covenant book of Hebrews. "But now has he [*Christ*] obtained a more excellent ministry, by how much also he is the mediator [*1 Tim. 2:5*] of a better covenant, which was established upon better promises. For if that first [*covenant*] had been faultless, then should no place have been sought for the second. For finding fault with them, he said, Behold, the days come, says the Lord, when I will make a new covenant with the House of Israel and with the House of Judah..." [Heb. 8:6-8, see 9:15].

"Not according to the [*law*] covenant that I made with their fathers in the day when I took them by the hand to lead them out of the land of Egypt; because they continued not in my covenant, and *I regarded them not*, said the Lord." [Heb. 8:9]. As a result, the House of Israel was divorced, while the House of Judah was taken into captivity for seventy years by the Babylonians.

"For this is the covenant [*Abrahamic covenant*] that I will make with **the House of Israel** after those days, said the Lord; I will put my laws into their mind, and write them in their hearts: and I will be to them a God, and **they shall be to me a people**:" [Heb. 8:10; see Isa. 63:8, Christ here refers to the House of Israel as "my people"]. Paul makes the point that it is with the children of the House of Israel only, after Christ broke the law covenant, that the new covenant came into force. The time is not yet for the House of Judah as they remain blinded and estranged from the Abrahamic covenant and the House of Israel.

But when the time is come, "None of them shall teach his neighbor, and none his brother, saying, 'Know the LORD,' for all shall know Me, from the least of them to the greatest of them." [Heb. 8:11]. This will occur when the brothers, the House of Israel and the House of Judah, both are partakers of the new covenant, their bonds of brotherhood once again renewed.

Ezekiel provides more details. "As for you, son of man, take a stick for yourself and write on it: 'For **Judah** and for the children of Israel, his companions.' Then take another stick and write on it, 'For **Joseph**, the stick of Ephraim, and for **all the House of Israel**, his companions. Then **join them one to another for yourself into one stick**, and they will become one in your hand."

"And when the children of your people speak to you, saying, 'Will you not show us what you mean by these?'—say to them, 'Thus says the Lord GOD: "Surely I will take the stick of Joseph, which is in the hand of Ephraim, and the tribes of [*the House of*] Israel, his companions; and I will join them with it, with the stick of [*the House of*] Judah, and make them one stick, and **they will be one in My hand**. And the sticks on which you write will be in your hand before their eyes." This will occur after the return of Christ.

After the events of the Apocalypse have been accomplished, "Then say to them, 'Thus says the Lord GOD: "Surely I will take the children of Israel from among the nations, wherever they have gone, and will gather them from every side and bring them into their own land; and I will make them one nation in the land, on the mountains of Israel; and one king shall be king over them all [*David; Christ is king of kings, Rev. 17:14]; they shall no longer be two nations, nor shall they ever be divided into two kingdoms again.* They shall not defile themselves anymore with their idols, nor with their detestable things, nor with any of their transgressions; but I will deliver them from all their dwelling places in which they have sinned, and will cleanse them. **Then they shall be My people**, and I will be their God. And David, my servant, shall be king over them...." [Eze. 37:16-24]. After all, the New Testament is "The book of the generation of Jesus Christ, the son of David, the son of Abraham." [See the chapter, *The Tie That Binds*].

As Paul continues in Hebrews, "For I will be merciful to their unrighteousness, and their sins and their iniquities will I remember no more. In that he says, A new [*covenant*], he has made the first old. Now that which decays and waxes old is ready to vanish away." [Heb. 8:12, 13; Jer. 31:31-34].

Today, twenty centuries removed, we are ignorant of all this and are not continuing in his goodness, which is why we Christians don't know why Christ had to be Jewish in the flesh. Nor do we understand the importance of the covenants and Christ's role with them. The House of Israel has regressed. Theologically and spiritually, we are no more mature than babies, unable to recognize the truth of our first century heritage.

"For though by this time you ought to be teachers, you need someone to teach you again the first principles of the oracles of God; and you have come to need milk and not solid food. For everyone who partakes only of milk is unskilled in the word of righteousness, for he is a babe.

But solid food belongs to those who are of full age, that is, those who by reason of use have their senses exercised to discern both good and evil." [Heb. 5:12-14].

What About Everyone Else?

As Christ is "Our *Redeemer*, the LORD of hosts… the Holy One of *Israel*… the Lord God of *Israel*… [*who*] *redeemed His people*" [Isa. 47:4; Luke 1:68], being the son of David, and the son of Abraham [Mat. 1:1] and who was sent only to the lost sheep of the House of *Israel* [Mat. 15:24], where does that leave everyone else?

Well that's a good question. Mankind was created in the image and likeness of God. This is a reference to the spirit of man. And the spirit of man is the common denominator among *all men*. [See chapter one, *The Blind Man's Elephant*].

And what do we read about all men in the New Testament? "For it is for this we [*Paul and the other apostles*] labor and strive, because we have fixed our hope on the living God, who is the Savior of all men, especially believers. [1 Tim. 4:10, NASB].

It is important to point out here that in the KJV English text, as well as in most other translations it reads "the living God." However, in Greek it reads, the God of the living. Theologically, this is a key difference. It speaks to the resurrection from the dead rather than making the point that God is alive. Christ made this same point when addressing the Sadducees, who believed there is no resurrection.

"But concerning the dead, that they rise, have you not read in the book of Moses, in the burning bush passage, how God spoke to him, saying, 'I am the God of Abraham, the God of Isaac, and the God of Jacob'? 'He is not the God of the dead, but *the God of the living*. You are therefore greatly mistaken [*about there being no resurrection*].'" [Mark 12:26, 27].

We should keep in mind that the Old Covenant ended with Christ's death [Zec. 11:10-13], but the New Covenant began with his resurrection from the dead to life. The wages of sin is death, but the gift of grace is life. [See Rom. 6:23]. This is the hope upon which Christianity is built. "... that having been justified by His grace we should become heirs according to the hope of eternal life." [Tts. 3:7]. Thus, our Father is the God of the living or eternal life.

The reference to the God of the living here in Greek is *theos zao*, *theos* being God, *zao* being living. The Savior of all men reads, "*soter pas anthropos*." *Pas anthropos* means all men or each man. *Soter* is the word for savior.

Now as we read above, Christ was sent only to the lost sheep of the House of Israel to redeem those who were under the law covenant and to institute the Abrahamic covenant. This is a fairly specific assignment for a specific group of people. It is one that precludes a lot of the world's anthropos. And to some people, not understanding this, it strikes them as being unfair.

However, the key to understanding this is that Christ was sent. And he was sent only to the House of Israel, not to all mankind. So who could send him? As the Biblical record makes clear, God the Father is the head of Christ [1 Cor. 11:3]. Therefore, Christ was sent by God the Father.

The Abrahamic covenant is a specific agreement made with one person that is intended for his Seed, Christ, and Abraham's generations according to that covenant. It says nothing about everyone else. And neither is everyone else bound by this covenant.

Let's go over to Matthew 16:13. Christ is with his disciples. "When Jesus came into the coasts of Caesarea Philippi, he asked his disciples, saying, 'Who do men say that I, the Son of man, am?'"

They answered Christ giving him different answers. "And they said, 'Some say that you are John the Baptist: some, Elijah; and others, Jeremiah, or one of the prophets.'"

So then Christ asked them who they thought he was. That's when Peter stood up and replied, "You are the Christ, *the Son* of God of the living."

This is a very important answer. Peter said Christ was the **Son** of the God of the living. He did not say Christ was the God of the living. While Christ may have been God incarnate and he is living, in contrast to God the Father, Christ is the Son of God of the living.

The Son of God of the living in Greek reads **hulos** *theos zao*. Christ is the Son of the God of the living whereas God the Father is the God of the living or *theos zao*. Did Peter get this wrong? No.

"Jesus answered and said to him, 'Blessed are you, Simon Bar-Jonah, for flesh and blood has not revealed this to you, but *My Father* who is in heaven.'" So it was God the Father making the point that Christ is *the Son* of God of the living.

Our point is that Christ is the Son of God the Father. Christ was sent only to the lost sheep of the House of Israel. Who is the savior of all men, especially believers? *The God of the living* who *is our Father.* This means that all men, not just those of Israel, will be judged in the great resurrection and will have the opportunity for eternal life... *living* forever.

And who was it that sent Christ just to the House of Israel in the first century? It was God the Father, "savior of all men, especially believers." And when we pray, to whom did Christ instruct us to address our prayers? Our Father in heaven. Asking what? His kingdom come. And? Our Father's will be done on Earth as it is in heaven.

While Christ has a particular relationship to Abraham and David, it is our Father in heaven who is the savior of all men. Except for Christianity, all the monotheistic religions of the world look to God. In this case, it's God our Father. Only Christianity looks upon Christ as divine because Christ redeemed Israel or only those who were under the first covenant. And even this does not yet apply to the House of Judah until Christ's return.

While it is true that Christ is the mediator between God the Father and men, and all things will be given to him, within context of both the law and the Abrahamic covenants, Christ was sent only to redeem Israel. [See Heb. 12:24]. It is important for us to grasp the fundamentals of both covenants in order to understand the Biblical record correctly.

The law covenant, or the first covenant, was only made with Moses and the children of Israel, and they were the only people redeemed by Christ. "And for this reason He is the Mediator of the new covenant, *by means of death, for the redemption of the transgressions under the first covenant*, that those who are called may receive the promise of the eternal inheritance." [Heb. 9:15]. Eternal life is available to all men. The eternal inheritance is of the promises given to Abraham and his Seed, Christ. "For if the inheritance is of the law, it is no longer of promise; but God gave it to Abraham by promise." [Gal. 3:18].

In Revelation, however, the great judgment day is for all men. "And I saw the dead, small and great, standing before God [*theos*], and books were opened. And another book was opened, which is the Book of Life. And the dead were judged *according to their works,* by the things which were written in the books." [Rev. 20:12].

All Israel, however, has been justified *by grace*, not by our works, through our Redeemer, Christ on our behalf as promised in the Abrahamic covenant. The apostle Paul made this point, "... being justified freely by His grace through the redemption that is in Christ Jesus [*for the transgressions under the first covenant*]... And if by grace, then it is no longer of works [Greek, *ergon*, actions, deeds]; otherwise grace is no longer grace. But if it is of works, it is no longer grace; otherwise work is no longer work." [Rom. 3:24, 11:6; see Rom. 4:4, 6; 11:26].

The reason that all men die, at least once, goes back to the days of Adam and Eve. "But of the tree of *the knowledge of good and evil* you shall not eat, for in the day that you eat of it you shall surely die." [Gen. 2:17]. And it came to be, so all men shall be judged according to their works, having done good or evil. Only the descendants of the father of the faithful Abraham, Isaac and Israel have the covenant exemption available to us through our *Redeemer,* Christ. Redeem [Greek, *exagorazo*] means to buy back by payment of a price that which was lost.

And Christ was sent by God the Father to redeem... "the lost sheep of the House of Israel."

As the judgment day concerns the dead, and as all men die, as Paul pointed out, "And as it is appointed unto men once to die, but after this the judgment..." [Heb. 9:27], those who don't pass muster here will suffer the eternal second death. "But the fearful, and unbelieving, and the abominable, and murderers, and whoremongers, and sorcerers, and idolaters, and all liars, shall have their part in the lake which burns with fire and brimstone: which is *the second death*." [Rev. 21:8]. A side note, this lake of fire results in death, non-existence, not an eternal burning in hell fire.

Therefore, all men will have their day to stand before God and be judged according to their works. All men will have the chance to have eternal life when found written in the book of life. And it is God the Father who will do this as the savior of all men, the God of the living.

Through Christ, the Son of the God of the living, we have a special covenant relationship with Abraham as his heirs, sons and daughters that is unique among men. Christ, as Abraham's seed redeemed us from under the curse of the law covenant, or the penalty of the second death. We are justified by grace no longer to be judged by our works. As Paul said, 'And so all Israel shall be saved: as it is written, There shall come out of Sion a Deliverer and shall turn away ungodliness from Jacob [*Israel*]."

Lacking understanding of the role of the covenants and Christ's role in them as the Son of the God of the living, as well as our Father's role as the savior of all men, especially believers, we have lost this critical understanding that Christ and the apostles delivered to our ancestors of the House of Israel in the first century. Instead, we've been riding those rogue ponies.

Nevertheless, we need to be very mindful of an important point lest we become complacent and lukewarm in our faith. As we read in Isaiah, "Do not let the son of the foreigner who has joined himself to the LORD Speak, saying, 'The LORD has utterly separated me from His people;' Nor let the eunuch say, 'Here I am, a dry tree.' ... Even to them I will give in My house and within My walls a place and *a name better than that of sons and daughters*; *I will give them an everlasting name that shall not be cut off.*" [Isa. 56:3, 5]. The God of the living is the savior of all men just as Paul said.

To answer our initial question, "What about everyone else?" Everyone else is in good hands if they so choose.

The Gospel

What Exactly Is The Gospel?

I keep reading that Christians need to get back to the gospel. Or that we've gotten away from the gospel. Or that we've got to get the gospel right. But what exactly is the gospel? We are told it's a divine purpose. It's a historical event. Okay, but what is it exactly? It seems there is no end of talk about *The Gospel* but very little telling us what exactly the gospel is and what specifically it means for those to whom it was delivered. It's almost as if it's kept vague intentionally and that we're just supposed to know what it is through some sort of religious osmosis.

So let's change that and directly look into exactly what the gospel means and its implications. Matthew mentions the word gospel the first time in the New Testament. The Greek word for gospel is *euaggelion,* which means good tidings or good news.

What is the good news we need to get back to? What is the good news we've got to get right? What is the divine purpose of this good news and at what historical event was this good news delivered, by whom to whom?

Let's go to the verses in Matthew chapter four where Christ is delivering the good news.

"Now when Jesus heard that John had been put in prison, He departed to Galilee. And leaving Nazareth, He came and dwelt in Capernaum, which is by the sea, in the regions of Zebulun and Naphtali: that it might be fulfilled which was spoken by Isaiah the prophet saying, 'The land of Zebulun and the land of Naphtali, By the way of the sea, beyond the Jordan, Galilee of the nations: The people who sat in darkness have seen a great light, And upon those who sat in the region and shadow of death Light has dawned.' From that time Jesus began to preach and to say, Repent, for the kingdom of heaven is at hand... And Jesus went about all Galilee, teaching *in their synagogues*, preaching *the gospel of the kingdom*, and healing all kinds of sickness and all kinds of disease among the people." [v.12-17, 23]. Not only did Christ physically heal the sick, he spiritually healed the wound suffered by the people in the land of Zebulun and Naphtali.

Let's take it one step at a time. Christ left Nazareth when John the Baptist was put into prison. And he went to Galilee of the nations. Where exactly in Galilee? Christ went to Capernaum by the sea, on the northwestern shore of the Sea of Galilee, in the regions of Zebulun and Napthali. Why there? Because they were the people who sat in darkness, the same people who sat in the region and shadow of death.

Who are these people Zebulun and Naphtali and why were they sitting in darkness, in the shadow of death to begin with? And why did Christ single them out to begin his ministry, to be a great Light, "the bright morning star," to them? The answers to these questions give us our answer to what is the gospel or good news.

First off, Zebulun and Naphtali are two sons of Israel, the House of Israel to be specific. They are not Jews, or descendants of Judah. You can read about them in Genesis 49 concerning them as nations *in the last days,* which means they are still around as Christian nations in the 21st century even though, most likely, they are oblivious to their identity as Zebulun and Naphtali. [See the chapter *Ten Horns, Ten Nations*].

Why were they sitting in darkness in the first century, in the early days of the Roman Empire? Well, they were, along with their eight other brothers of the House of Israel, divorced from God as we can read in Jeremiah 3:8. Being put away for their idolatry and other sins, they were cast out of the covenants: one made with Abraham and the law covenant made with all the children of Israel given on Mt. Sinai. Once outside the covenants, they were lost, sitting in darkness in the shadow of death.

But why did Christ begin his ministry here, teaching and preaching *the gospel in their synagogues,* in the land of Zebulun and Naphtali, and not some place else like the churches of the gentiles? The synagogues [Greek, *synogoge*] were places of worship for those of Israel, which is why descendants of the House of Israel would be found there initially. Once the gospel was understood to be for the House of Israel in this age, eventually Christians moved away from the synagogues. The apostle to the nations, Paul, explains, "As He says also in Hosea [*a prophet to the nations of Israel, not the gentiles of the world*]: 'I will call them My people, who were not My people And her beloved, who was not beloved. And it shall come to pass *in the place where it was said to them,* 'You are not My people,' There they shall be called sons of the God of the living.'" [Rom. 9:25, 26; see Hos. 1:6, 10; also Mark 12:27]. "Them" here is a reference to the House of Israel, not the gentiles of the world.

The reason why Christ began his ministry in that place was that when the LORD God divorced the House of Israel, they were taken captive by the Assyrian king, Tiglathpileser and dispersed throughout the Assyrian empire. [See Jer. 5:15; 2 Kng. 15:29]. And the very first place from which the children of the House of Israel, and not the gentiles of the world, were taken captive by the Assyrians was in Galilee of the nations of Zebulun and Naphtali. And as it was prophesied in Hosea, the first of the Assyrian period prophets, *in the place where the sons of the House of Israel were first taken captive was the first place they would be called the sons of the God of the living*, no longer in the shadow of death. Thus, the Light, Jesus Christ delivered the gospel, the good news first to them rather than to others of the House of Israel.

Later, when Christ began sending out his apostles to preach the gospel, he sent them to the lost sheep of the House of Israel and not to the gentiles. [Mat. 10:5-7]. And Paul was sent to travel the road to Europe, including as far as current day England, delivering the gospel, as promised by the prophets in the Old Testament, to the lost nations [*ethnos*] of the House of Israel. [Rom. 1:1-3].

So what is the good news, the gospel? Well, the bad news was that for more than seven centuries all the House of Israel, beginning with Zebulun and Naphtali, were divorced from God. [See the flow chart at the end of the book]. They were cast out of the covenant relationships with God. Spiritually, they were dead before God. There was no hope for them. From this condition, they got the good news delivered to them by Christ in person. The House of Israel was now given a new covenant; a covenant built on the better promises of Abraham and his seed, Christ, based in faith and grace not on the works of the law covenant. They were to have access to the Spirit of God being called sons of the God of the living. This is the good news, the gospel, delivered by Christ who was sent only to the House of Israel.

Is this *the gospel* being preached today? Hardly. While the tenured evangelists and pastors bemoan the state of Christianity among our youth today, claiming they hold the theological high ground, these same pastors and ministers don't even know or understand what the gospel is, to whom it was delivered by Christ and why. It doesn't get any more basic than this in terms of understanding first century Christianity. When we step off the path delivered by Christ, no matter where we go from there, we are not where we need to be. Christians are the children of Abraham, Isaac and Jacob.

This is why Christ began his ministry in Galilee. This is the good news he preached first to Zebulun and Naphtali. This is why Christ said, "*I am sent only to the lost sheep of the House of Israel.*" [Mat. 15:24]. The lost sheep of the House of Israel were the only ones divorced, told by God, "You are not my people." They were the only ones cast out of the covenant relationships with God and therefore sat in darkness in the shadow of death. They were the only ones who needed redeeming. And to them Christ said, "Repent [*change your ways*], for the kingdom [*royal power and authority*] of heaven is at hand [*through the Spirit of God*]." And this all began on that first day of Christianity, Pentecost, a fulfilling of the high holy day of Israel, when Peter stood up and said to 'all the House of Israel,' "Repent, and let every one of you be baptized in the name of Jesus

Christ for the remission of sins and you shall receive the gift of the Holy Spirit." [See Acts 2:36-38].

The gospel, the good news was delivered by Christ to the House of Israel in Galilee, where the Assyrians, seven centuries earlier, first took them captive. These people are our Christian ancestors. And they are nations today according to the prophecy given by Israel to his twelve sons in Genesis forty-nine.

It is correct that we've gotten away from understanding what the gospel is and for whom it is meant. And yes we need to get the good news right. After all, if evangelists and pastors don't know for whom the gospel is meant, and what it means, how can they preach the gospel delivered by Christ in the first century?

As the apostle Paul told the church in Galatia, "I am amazed that you are so quickly deserting him who called you into the grace of Christ, to a different gospel... as we've said before, so I say again now, if any man is preaching any other gospel to you contrary to what you received [*from the apostles, in the Biblical record for us today*], he is to be accursed!" [Gal.1:6, 9 NASB].

The good news as first delivered by Christ, is for the people who sat in darkness. Since the first century, the children of the House of Israel were called the sons of the God of the living [Mark 12:27]. We are no longer divorced. We no longer sit in the shadow of death. Now, we Christians just need to realize who we truly are in order for us to fully understand the gospel delivered by Christ and the apostles in the first century. [See the chapter *Abraham's Seed and Heirs*].

Galilee of the Gentiles

Some of you may point out that Christ began his ministry in Galilee of the Gentiles. Wouldn't this mean that Christ was sent to the gentiles after all? One could assume this. But when we let the Biblical record define itself, we find the correct answer.

Unfortunately, the King James translators, who bought into the false notion that Christ was sent to the gentiles of the world, not understanding that Christ was sent only to the lost sheep of the House of Israel, translated the Greek word *ethnos* as heathens, nations, people, and gentiles. In some verses the same word *ethnos* is translated as two different words in English [see Gal. 3:8], which totally changes the intent and meaning of the verse. It can be confusing.

As the book, *The Hijacked Elephant* makes abundantly clear, the Bible is one book written to the same people. Thus, the word *ethnos* primarily references the nations of Israel. When the apostle Paul, a descendant of Israel's son, Benjamin, says he is the apostle to the gentiles, the word used is *ethnos.* Correctly understood, Paul is the apostle to the nations. Which nations? It's the nations of the House of Israel, the same nations to whom Christ was sent. [See 1 Cor. 10:1-4; Mat. 15:24].

The nations [*gowy*, OT; *ethnos*, NT] of the House of Israel remained in their divorced state, or "gentile" state, if you like, only until the death and resurrection of Christ. Once this took place, major changes were implemented among the nations of Israel. [See the flow chart at the end of the book; also chapter six, *The Blind Man's Elephant*].

When we fully realize this, it unlocks an understanding of the Biblical record that's been lost from the first century.

The Matthew four reference to Galilee of the *gentiles* actually is a quote from Isaiah 9 in the Old Testament. In Isaiah 9 it says, Galilee of the *nations*. Nations is the Hebrew word *gowy*, which is equivalent to *ethnos*. "Nevertheless the dimness shall not be such as was in her vexation, when at the first he lightly afflicted the land of Zebulun and the land of Naphtali, and afterward did more grievously afflict her by the way of the sea, beyond Jordan, in *Galilee of the nations.* The people that walked in darkness have seen a great light: they that dwell in the land of the shadow of death, upon them has the light shined." [Isa. 9:1, 2].

The entire context of this Old Testament passage, paraphrased in Matthew, concerns the *nations of Israel*, not the gentiles of the world. Just to make this clearer, who are these "gentiles" of Galilee, Zebulun and Naphtali? If we go over to Genesis 49, we see Israel talking to his twelve sons telling them what shall befall them *as nations in the last days*, meaning they are identifiable nations today. And whom do we find among Israel's sons here? Zebulun and Naphtali, neither of which are "gentiles of the world."

Why, then, did Christ begin his ministry at this place in Galilee? It fulfilled *Israel's* Old Testament prophecy of Hosea, chapter one. Hosea was the first of the Assyrian period prophets. As Paul, a descendant of the House of Israel's son Benjamin, not Judah, the Jews, told the Christians at Rome, "And it shall come to pass, that *in the place* where *it was* [732 BCE, the time of the Assyrian captivity] said unto them, You are not my people; there shall they be called the children of the God of the living... For as many as are led by *the Spirit of God*, they are the sons of God." [Rom. 9:26]. That place was Galilee of the nations of the House of Israel where Christ began his ministry, sent by our Father only to the lost sheep of the House of Israel.

As we read in Luke when Christ began his ministry, "Then He [*Christ*] went down to Capernaum, a city of Galilee, and was teaching them on the Sabbaths." "He said to them, 'I must preach the kingdom of God to the other cities also, because *for this purpose I have been sent*.' [See Mat. 15:24]. And He was preaching in the *synagogues of Galilee*." [Luke 4:31, 43, 44]. The gentiles of the world would hardly be found in the synagogues of Israel's historical land on the Sabbaths. But you would find those descendants of the House of Israel to whom Christ was sent.

The first day of Christianity was Pentecost about 2000 years ago when our Father sent the Holy Spirit in Christ's name. As we read in Acts 2:36ff, the apostle Peter, upon whom Christ built his church, addressed his remarks that day, not to the gentiles of the world, but to *all the House of Israel*. Peter told them to repent, be baptized and receive *the Holy Spirit of God.* Are we to believe our Father and Peter got this wrong? It is not coincidence that Pentecost was the summer harvest high holy day of... Israel. It was for the twelve sons of Israel, and not just Judah, the Jews, all of which has absolutely nothing to do with the "gentiles of the world."

The Tie That Binds

The fundamental underlying premise of *The Hijacked Elephant* is that the entire Biblical record is one story written to and about the same people. In it, the analogy is that Christ is the "shoelace that binds both the Old and the New Testaments together." While this may not be news for some, *Yehovah elohiym*, the LORD God of the Old Testament is the same person as Jesus Christ of the New Testament in the first century. It's no accident that the name Jesus means *Yehovah is salvation*.

First, let's take a look at what the apostle John tells us in his gospel. "**No one has seen God at any time**; the only begotten God, who is in the bosom of the Father, He has explained Him." [John 1:18 NASB; 1 John 4:12]. John is telling us that no man has ever seen God the Father except Christ, the only born Son who took the form of a man in the first century. [John 1:14]. As Paul explained, "Let this mind be in you, which was also in Christ Jesus: Who, being in the form of God, thought it not robbery to be equal with God: But made himself of no reputation, and took upon him the form of a servant, and was made in the likeness of men: And being found in fashion as a man, he humbled himself, and became obedient unto death, even the death of the cross." [Php. 2:5-8].

We know from the apostle John's account that no man has seen God the Father at any time. We know that God the Father is the head of Christ. [1 Cor. 11:3]. We know that Christ was God, but took the form of man. And we know that God the Father sent him to redeem the lost sheep of the House of Israel and to atone for the transgressions of all Israel including the House of Judah. [See Mat. 15:24; Rom. 11:26, Heb. 8:8].

Paul also tells us in his letter to the Corinthian church that Christ was with the children of Israel in the Old Testament or Jewish Bible. "Moreover, brethren, I would not that you should be ignorant, how that all our fathers were under the cloud, and all passed through the sea; And were all baptized unto Moses in the cloud and in the sea; And did all eat the same spiritual meat; And did all drink the same spiritual drink: for they drank of that spiritual Rock that followed them: and that Rock was Christ." [1 Cor. 10:1-4].

We know that prior to taking on the form of man, Christ was God. Remember, *elohiym*, the word for God in Hebrew, is a noun like the word family meaning there is more than one person in the God family as in "Let *us* make man in *our* image and likeness...." So we know there are at least two members of the God family. God the Father, and his "firstborn" son [as a man], Jesus Christ.

And we know there are other sons of God as well as we can read in Job 38:7 when "... all the *sons of God* shouted for joy." Or in the days before Noah, [Gen. 6:2], "That the *sons of God* saw the daughters of men that they were fair; and *they* took *them* wives of all which *they* chose." The daughters of men in Hebrew are *bath adam*; and *ben elohiym* are the sons of God.

The "sons of God" is not a reference to angels as many suppose. As we read in the Book of Hebrews, "For to which of the angels said he at any time, 'You are my Son, this day have I begotten you?' And again, 'I will be to him a Father, and he shall be to me a Son?'" [Heb. 1:5]. So we see elohiym, the word for God, is similar to our word family. One family, many members. One God, many members with Christ being the firstborn of all the sons of God.

The elohiym or God family also includes *twenty-four elders*, as we read, "And round about the throne were twenty-four seats: and upon the seats I saw twenty-four elders sitting, clothed in white raiment; and they had on their heads crowns of gold. And out of the throne proceeded lightnings and thunderings and voices: and there were seven lamps of fire burning before the throne, which are the seven Spirits of God." [Rev. 4:4-5].

Elders here is *presbyteros*. It is an adjective. It is describing members of elohiym. The word seats in verse four in Greek is *thronos.* And as each of these elders has a crown, it describes a senior, royal position within the elohiym family. Thronos is the same word used by Christ in telling the twelve apostles with him on the last Passover night, "You shall sit upon twelve thrones, judging the twelve tribes of Israel."

Thus, in addition to the Father, and Jesus Christ, plus the other sons of God, whose number we don't know, there are at least twenty-four elders who comprise elohiym. And this does not include those who can become the sons of God. [See John 1:12; Rom. 8:14, 19; 1 John 3:1, 2]. Overall, then, in order there are elohiym, angels [Heb. 2:5-7], mankind and creatures.

Mankind's dilemma therefore, is do we seek the higher plane of God's existence available to us, or do we follow the lower crowded path seeking the riches of this reality? [See the chapters *Brown Paint: Quantum Potentialities* and *Heaven Can Wait*].

Now, if no man, or adamkind, has seen God the Father at any time, who could possibly be the LORD God of the Old Testament that appeared to Abram?

"And the **LORD *appeared* to Abram**, and said, 'To your seed will I give this land: and there he built an altar to the **LORD, who *appeared* to him**.'" The word LORD here in Hebrew is *Yehovah*. Who is Yehovah? Well, we know it wasn't God the Father as no man has seen him. And we know, according to the apostle Paul, that Christ was that spiritual Rock that was with the children of Israel when they came out of Egypt.

And we know that when Moses was told to bring the children of Israel out of Egypt, Moses asked, "What is the name of him who sent me? What shall I tell them? Thus shall you say to the children of Israel, The LORD [*Yehovah*] God [*elohiym*] of your fathers, the God of Abraham, the God of Isaac, and the God of Jacob, has sent me [*Moses*] to you [*the children of Israel*]...." [See Exd. 3:13-16].

Moses was sent to lead the children of Israel out of Egypt by the same LORD, Yehovah that appeared to Abram. "Come now, therefore, and I will send you [*Moses*] to Pharaoh that you may bring *my people, the children of Israel*, out of Egypt." [Exd. 3:10].

According to Paul's first letter to the Corinthian church, we know Christ was that spiritual Rock for the children of Israel when they came out of Egypt. It was *Yehovah elohiym* in the Old Testament who called all Israel *his people* and was with them when leaving Egypt. Jesus [Greek, *Iesous, Jehovah is salvation*] in the New Testament was sent to redeem his lost children of the House of Israel in the first century. [Mat. 15:24].

The personage we know as Jesus Christ in the New Testament was the Yehovah of the Old Testament. The LORD God of Israel is Christ. The Biblical record is one book written to and for the same people.

Now when we read the words, LORD God, in the Old Testament we know it is a reference to Christ. And it sort of puts the Old Testament into a new light with a new relevance. It binds the old with the new as it was intended to be from the first century.

We see that it was Yehovah, Christ who made the heavens and the earth. "These are the generations of the heavens and of the earth when they were created, in the day that the LORD [*Yehovah*] God made the earth and the heavens…" [Gen. 2:4].

It was Christ who made the garden of Eden. "And the LORD God planted a garden eastward in Eden; and there he put the man whom he had formed." [Gen. 2:8].

It was Christ who created woman. "And the rib, which the LORD God had taken from man, made he a woman, and brought her unto the man." [Gen. 2:22].

And it was Christ who kicked Adam and Eve out of the garden. "Therefore the LORD God sent him forth from the garden of Eden, to till the ground from whence he was taken." [Gen. 3:23].

It was Christ who instituted the three times of the year Israel was to keep a feast. They are the same three times Christ is fulfilling on behalf of the House of Israel now. [See *The Hijacked Elephant*]. "Three times in the year shall all your men children appear before the LORD God, the God of Israel." [Exd. 34:23].

When the children of Israel, led by Joshua, entered into the land promised by Yehovah to Abraham, it was Christ who commanded him. "So Joshua smote all the country of the hills, and of the south, and of the vale, and of the springs, and all their kings: he left none remaining, but utterly destroyed all that breathed, as the LORD God of Israel commanded." [Jos. 10:40].

And when David was made king over Israel, it was by the hand of Christ, the LORD God of Israel. "And Nathan said to David, 'You're the man.' [*That's what it says*]. Thus says the LORD God of Israel, I anointed you king over Israel, and I delivered you out of the hand of Saul...." [2 Sam. 12:7].

Now look at what Christ tells Christians in the New Testament Book of Revelation. "I, Jesus [*Jehovah is salvation*] have sent my angel to *testify to you these things in the churches*. I am the root and the offspring of David, and the bright and morning star." [Rev. 22:16; See Mat. 22:42-45; Hos. 3:5].

Why is this important for Christians to know? Because Christ is the bridge between the old Israel and the new Israel. He is the tie that binds both together. This fact should be known in all the Christian churches. And it is important enough that Christ himself sent his angel to make a point of it to the churches. But where is this knowledge taught today?

As A.R. Fausset explains in the *Jamieson, Fausset and Brown Commentary*, "Root of David, as being Jehovah; the offspring of David as man. David's Lord, yet David's son." In other words, as Yehovah, Christ was David's root as he established the house of David, anointed him king over all Israel. And as the person of Jesus, he was King David's descendant and king of all Israel. As we read in John's gospel, "Nathanael answered and said to him [*Jesus*], Master, you are the Son of God; you are the King of Israel." [John 1:49].

And when the children of the House of Israel were divorced, taken captive by the Assyrians, it was the LORD God, Christ who did it. "I [*Yehovah*; See Jer. 3:6] saw, when for all the causes whereby backsliding [*House of*] Israel committed adultery I had put her away, and given her a bill of divorce; yet her treacherous sister [*House of*] Judah feared not, but went and played the harlot also." [Jer. 3:8].

And when it came time to redeem the divorced, or lost sheep of the House of Israel, it was Yehovah, Christ who said, "I am not sent except to the lost sheep of the House of Israel." Yehovah divorced the House of Israel and Yehovah, as Christ, paid the ransom with his blood, to redeem the children of Israel. "For what the law could not do, in that it was weak through the flesh, God sending his own Son in the likeness of sinful flesh, and for sin, condemned sin in the flesh… And being found in fashion as a man, he humbled himself, and became obedient unto death, even the death of the cross." [Rom. 3:8; Phi. 2:8].

We Christians need to fully come to the realization that the Biblical record is one story written to and for the same people. Yehovah is salvation. Jesus Christ is the one binds the entirety of the Biblical record together. And as Christians, his people, it's time we leave the darkness and acknowledge the good news, the great light he brought to us, the House of Israel beginning in the first century. [See Mat. 4:16].

Christianity Is Not A Surrogate For Christ

Recently, a well-known author publicly stated that she was quitting Christianity, but not Jesus Christ. Many of those in mainstream Christianity, be they Protestant or Catholic, apparently couldn't discern the difference between the two. As one member of a well-known "Christian corporation," aka church organization, wrote in the Christian Post regarding this, "... she still loves Jesus but she doesn't love Christianity. Yet, I know that it is impossible to love Jesus without loving his church." The critical point of understanding is that 21st century incorporated, denominational Christianity is not the church, or *ekklesia* in Greek, as it existed in the first century.

Christ said, "Render therefore to Caesar the things that are Caesar's, and to God the things that are God's." [Luke 20:25]. Therefore, we need to ask the question, "Is a government issued corporate charter Caesar's or God's?" And we know from the Biblical record that "no one can serve two masters." [Mat. 6:24]. Therefore, it appears our author simply made her personal choice to follow Christ rather than the religious corporate establishment.

Incredible as it may seem, according to the World Christian Encyclopedia there are more than 30,000 Christian denominations today... all from one Christ. [See the chapter *Peace on Earth?*]. Paul addressed this same point when he wrote to the Christians in Corinth. "Is Christ divided? Was Paul crucified for you? Or were you baptized in the name of Paul?" [1 Cor. 1:13]. Of course, the resounding answer is No! But, we hear people say all the time that they are Catholics, or Lutherans or Anglicans or Baptists or Seventh

Day or... the list goes on and on and on. Therefore, what is divided here, Christ or Christianity?

We have a dilemma. Which one is *the church*? Do we embrace all 30,000 plus denominations equally even though they all disagree with each other on what Christianity is even though each claims to have the truth? Christ said, "If a kingdom is divided against itself, that kingdom cannot stand." [Mark 3:24]. Does this mean the kingdom of God will not stand because "Christianity," the 30,000 or so Christian churches, or churchianity, are divided against each other? No, of course not. Holistically, it does mean that Christianity as we know it today will not stand. [See Rev. 6:17; also the chapter *Christ Against Christians?*].

When this author said she was quitting Christianity, she was referring to churchianity, the 30,000 or so man-made religious organizations, not the Christianity of the Biblical record from the first century delivered by Christ. What she was returning to was the one-on-one relationship with God the Father through Christ. It is as she said. She left the Christian organizations for Christ. The two are not synonymous.

There is only one body of Christ. "... so we, being many, are one body in Christ, and *individually* members of one another." [Rom. 12:5]. The key word is individually. True Christianity is an entity of one, the individual [Greek, *heis*], as in you or me. The apostle Paul pointed out, "Now you are the body of Christ, and members *individually*," not denominationally. [1 Cor. 12:27]. Thus, it is the individual as in *indivisble*, that comprises the ekklesia and not the 30,000 plus denominations as in *divisible*. A collection of *individuals* make up the one body of Christ. [1 Cor. 12:18-20]. No denomination makes up the one body of Christ.

The ekklesia, the church are those individuals united in the body of Christ by the Spirit of God. Therefore, the true church is a Spiritual entity headed by Christ. "But *one and the same Spirit* works all these things, distributing to every *individual* purposefully." [1 Cor. 12:11]. Simply stated, man-made church organizations are not the ekklesia. Individuals have the Spirit of God; church organizations do not. The body of Christ is made up of individuals with the Spirit of God, not the multitude of incorporated denominations with charters, constitutions and by-laws.

In terms of our faith and salvation, there is only one mediator between any Christian and God, and that is Christ. No man or organization can step in between the two. This relationship is governed by the Spirit of God, which abides in us. The key to understanding the role of the "church" today is understanding a fundamental point of Christianity delivered to the church in the first century. "For there is one God and one Mediator between God and men, the *man* Christ Jesus." [1 Tim. 2:5].

The reason it says the *man* Christ [Greek, *anthropos*] is to make clear now that while Christ is not on Earth, no man can claim to stand in for him and put himself between us and Christ. No one can do that. *No one.* That's why the true church, the ekklesia follow Christ and not some corporate organization regardless of how long that organization has been in existence. Christ is still the head of his church. No one on Earth is his surrogate.

Individually, we are led by the Spirit on our path to God. "But the anointing [*God's Spirit*] which you have received from Him abides in you, and you do not need that anyone teach you; but as the same anointing teaches you concerning all things, and is true, and is not a lie, and just as it has taught you, you abide in Him." [1 John 2:27]. The point made is that no man other than the one who was the man Jesus Christ is our mediator. No man, or religious organization can say they mediate for us on our behalf to God. If they do, they're lying. And God is not the author of a lie.

A mediator is one who is the means of communication between two parties as would be the case of a person negotiating an agreement on behalf of another person, or in the case of Christians, a covenant, which would be the Abrahamic covenant made with Abraham and his Seed, Christ. [See the chapter *Abraham's Seed and Heirs*]. "But now he has obtained a more excellent ministry, inasmuch as he is also *mediator* of a better covenant, which was established on better promises." [Heb. 8:6].

Of course, many will point out that Paul outlined the qualifications for a bishop or overseer. "This is a faithful saying: If a man desires the *position of an overseer* [bishop, Greek, *episkope*] he desires a *good work*." [1 Tim. 3:1]. Thus, they could claim this would imply a church organization. But this is not what Paul was implying. First of all, the emphasis here is on *the work* involved, not the office, authority or title so to speak.

Today, twenty centuries removed, the word *episkope* or overseer has evolved into that of the formal title of Bishop, a high ranking official in a religious organization complete with appropriate ceremonial regalia including pointy hats, ornate robes and gold rings. This is not what Paul had in mind for an overseer of the ekklesia. He was talking about the labor or work involved, more akin to a shepherd in the fields tending to and protecting the sheep. Normally there aren't too many fancy robes and gold rings out there. Bottom line, there is no authority over a Christian except Christ and our Father. "For you were bought at a price; therefore glorify God in body and in spirit, which are God's." [1 Cor. 6:20].

Most likely Paul had the example of his own labor in mind when he wrote to Timothy. Someone humbly laboring to spread the gospel to the nations of Israel [See the chapter *What Exactly Is The Gospel?*], comforting and guiding them and working, in Paul's case as a tentmaker if need be. This position or work locally would be like that of an elder. As Paul wrote to Titus, "For this reason I left you in Crete, that you should set in order the things that are lacking, and appoint elders [*presbyteros*] in every city as I commanded you- if a man is blameless, the husband of one wife [*it's okay to be married*], having faithful children not accused of dissipation or insubordination. For an overseer [*episkopos*] must be blameless, as a steward of God, not self-willed, not quick-tempered, not given to wine, not violent, not greedy for money...." [Tts. 1:5-7].

The office of a bishop or elder, therefore is like being a shepherd of someone else's [Christ's] flock versus being an official in an institutionalized church hierarchy. The only one with authority over the flock is the person that owns the flock. And Christ bought us with his blood. "You are bought with a price; be not the servants of men." [1 Cor. 7:23].

The apostle Peter pointed out what the true church is like. "For you were like sheep going astray, but have now returned to the Shepherd and Overseer of your lives." [1 Pet. 2:25]. The point made by Peter is that our Shepherd and Overseer is Christ, our mediator and not one of the 30,000 or so denominations that constitute "Christianity." *Christianity is not a surrogate for Christ.* We cannot abdicate our individual Christian responsibility to a church organization with its corporate charters and by-laws. And neither can any church organization abrogate Christ's authority as our mediator and Shepherd.

The purpose of the first century apostles, pastors, overseers, etc., was to spread the gospel, the good news, and nurture each person, for the Spirit of God is not the domain of any organization. "And He Himself gave some as apostles, some prophets, some evangelists, and some pastors *[shepherds]* and teachers, for the *equipping of the saints [See Eph. 6:11]*, for the *work of ministry*, for the *edifying of the body of Christ*, till we all come to the *unity of the faith* and of the *knowledge of the Son of God*, to a perfect man, to the measure of the stature of the fullness of Christ; that we should no longer be children, *tossed to and fro and carried about with every wind of doctrine*, by the trickery of men, in the cunning craftiness of deceitful plotting but, *speaking the truth in love, may grow up in all things into Him who is the head--Christ.*" [Eph. 4:11-15].

Paul was writing to the ekklesia in Ephesus about 60 CE during his first imprisonment in Rome. The phrase, "... for the work of ministry, for the edifying of the body of Christ" does not mean forming organizations each with their different doctrines. For the work, [Greek, *ergon*] means laboring to help each person in their relationship, not with an organization, but with God. The ministry, [Greek, *diakonia*] refers to that which is in service to God. Edifying the body of Christ, [Greek, *oikodome*] literally means to build up or to promote the spiritual growth of each individual, and not an organization. We do not need to go through a church organization to reach God.

Wedging church organizations and hierarchies between individuals and Christ is not a function of the true church. The true church is a Spiritual entity, the body of Christ, with one mediator for all Christians, Jesus Christ. The church is the family of God, an unincorporated family. And as individual Christians, therefore, we grow spiritually at different rates. Denominationally, this has led to more than 30,000 churches. Individually, it means we grow into the truth at our own pace within the body of Christ through the Spirit of God. [See Mark 4:8].

Paul delivered these teachings in the first century. With Paul, as well as the other apostles, their labor was in service to God, to spread the good news to all the nations of the House of Israel until all individuals come into *the unity of faith*. In other words, until all the nations of the House of Israel heard *the same message*, not 30,000 plus versions of it. Christ is not divided. Christianity is.

With so many of these church organizations today claiming to be the true church, intolerant of others, it is difficult for us to realize we are the ekklesia, each one of us individually, not denominationally. We don't need to belong to a denomination to be a Christian. Many of these "true churches" tell us that if we leave their organization, we are leaving our chance for salvation and attaining the kingdom of God. This is pure hogwash, bunkum and codswallop. When any organization uses fear as a motivator to prevent us from going directly to God through Christ, they are not telling the truth. The only true church organization is each one of us individually led by the Spirit of God, with Christ as our mediator to our Father.

So when the author said she was leaving Christianity for Christ, she was leaving the divided, religious corporate structure for going directly to our Father in heaven with Christ as the mediator exactly as it tells us in the Biblical record. The ekklesia are each of us who individually do likewise, diligently seeking the truth with a pure heart, being taught of the Spirit, walking the narrow path that leads to life. "For there is *one God* and *one Mediator* between God and men, the *man* Christ Jesus." [1 Tim. 2:5]. Not even "Christianity" can take His place.

Heaven Can Wait

Apparently, there's going to be a lot of lonely Christians wondering where everybody went. And this is not a reference to the "rapture." A survey[1] was conducted recently that showed 21st century Christians, evangelicals in particular, believe good people and people of other religions, after they die, go to heaven. It is astounding that nearly 500 years after the Protestant Reformation, these evangelicals still adhere to the Roman Catholic vision of eternal life rather than God's, as revealed to us from the first century in the Biblical record.

The idea of being good, which most of us would hasten to say we are despite Mark 10:18, and then after dying, floating off to heaven to live happily ever after all sounds well and good. But there is a slight hitch in this. After our last breath, when we depart our "dust" vehicle that's taken us through life on this Earth, our "soul" doesn't go to "heaven" to live there "happily ever after," well at least not that place in the clouds or wherever it is that we are supposed to merrily cavort with beautiful blonde harp playing angels while gazing into the face of God.

There are two problems with this idea of "going to heaven" to live happily ever after according to the Biblical record. First, the heaven that Christian's believe we are going to for all eternity, is not going to last for an eternity. It's temporary. We read in the book of Matthew, Christ said, "*Heaven* and earth *will pass away*, but my words will by no means pass away." [Mat. 24:35].

The apostle Peter also tells us the same thing. "But the day of the Lord will come as a thief in the night, in which *the heavens will pass away* with a great noise, and the elements will melt with fervent heat; both the Earth and the works that are in it will be burned up." [2 Pet. 3:10].

Second, the kingdom of God is coming to Earth, at least according to the Biblical record. But since when do we Christians pay heed to what it says? [See the chapter *A Christmas Message*]. So, it turns out that God is coming to Earth, we're not going to heaven. How do we get things so backwards?

If Christians believe they will be in heaven, they are going to miss out on the kingdom of God and the new Jerusalem, which will be on Earth. Granted it is a new Earth, but Earth nevertheless. Let's read it straight from the source and then we'll look at where the confusion about this originates.

We find revealed in the appropriately named book of Revelation, "Now I saw a new heaven and a new earth, for the *first heaven* [*this is the one we presently experience and expect to go to after death by being good*] and the first earth had *passed away*. Also there was no more sea. Then I, John, saw the holy city, New Jerusalem, **coming *down out of heaven*** [*the new one*] from God, prepared as a bride adorned for her husband. And I heard a loud voice from heaven saying, "Behold, *the tabernacle of God is with men, and He will dwell with them, and they shall be His people. God Himself will be with them and be their God.*" [Rev. 21:1-3, emphasis added].

So if Christians are going to be in heaven, and the new Jerusalem is coming down out of heaven to Earth, and God's tabernacle is here on Earth and he will dwell with mankind on Earth, and be their God, it figures to be pretty lonely up there in heaven especially as the heaven that now exists, where Christians are figuring to go for an eternity, will have passed away too. Do these Christians pass away as well with the old heaven? I guess this theological dilemma puts them in what, limbo?

While the kingdom of God is referred to as the *kingdom of heaven* in the gospels [Mat. 3:2 et al.], we've seen that God's dwelling place is coming down from the new heaven to the new Earth. Until this happens our Father is still in the temporary heaven, "Let your light so shine before men, that they may see your good works and glorify your Father in heaven." [Mat. 5:16].

The whole idea of living for an eternity in the heaven where our Father currently resides, beginning for Christians with the resurrection of Christ, is contrary to what the Biblical record tells us. [See related chapters *Funny Bunny* and *Guess Who's Coming To Supper?*]. This should come as no surprise. After all, when we recite the Lord's Prayer does it not say, "Our Father in heaven, to your kingdom we go…?" Or does it say, "Our Father in heaven, *your kingdom* **come**…?" God is bringing his kingdom here, that is to a new Earth; we're not going there.

The word used for heaven in the New Testament is the Greek *ouranos.* It is the starry universe or what we call the sky. It's the same word, essentially, as the name of the planet Uranus, named after the Greek god that is the "godification" of the sky. It's what we see if we go to one of those planetarium light shows that project the stars onto a domed ceiling. It's also the place of God's temporary habitation *at this point in time.*

The modern concept of partying for all eternity in Heaven, that extraterrestrial paradise with harp playing angels, where ecstasy is not only legal, but is absolutely expected, are fictions brought over from the Roman Catholic Church.

To wit, "By virtue of our apostolic authority, we define the following: According to the general disposition of God, the souls of all the saints... and other faithful who died after receiving Christ's holy Baptism (provided they were not in need of purification when they died,... or, if they then did need or will need some purification, when they have been purified after death,...) [*this is a reference to the Roman Church idea of blemished souls doing time in purgatory, perhaps for eating meat on a Friday, before moving on to heaven, provided they get there before it passes away*] already before they take up their bodies again and before the general judgment - and this since the Ascension of our Lord and Savior Jesus Christ into heaven - have been, are and will be in heaven, in the heavenly Kingdom and celestial paradise with Christ, joined to the company of the holy angels. Since the Passion and death of our Lord Jesus Christ, these souls have seen and do see the divine essence with an intuitive vision, and even face to face, without the mediation of any creature.

"This perfect life with the Most Holy Trinity - this communion of life and love with the Trinity, with the Virgin Mary, the angels and all the blessed - is called "heaven." **Heaven is the ultimate *end*** and fulfillment of the deepest human longings, the state of supreme, definitive happiness."

[*Catechism of the Catholic Church*, Second Edition, Part One, Section Two, Chapter Three, Article 12, II. Heaven. Emphasis added].

The first thing we could point out is that this is strictly an idea invented by the Roman Catholic Church. "By virtue of *our* apostolic authority, *we define* the following...." The Roman Church also defines, "**Heaven is the ultimate *end*** and fulfillment of the deepest human longings, the state of supreme, definitive happiness." But, actually, according to the Biblical record, they aren't the first to have this idea that going to heaven is the ultimate end, a fulfilling of one's deepest longings. "How you are *fallen from heaven*, O Lucifer, son of the morning! How you are cut down to the ground, You who weakened the nations [*of Israel*]! For you have said in your heart: '*I will ascend into heaven,* I will exalt my throne above the stars of God....'" [Isa. 14:12, 13].

As noted above, however, by virtue of God's authority, he has defined the fullness of the kingdom of God as being on the new Earth where God will dwell with us as we've just read in Revelation. What we choose to believe depends on whose authority we choose to place our faith. From the survey of Protestant evangelicals, it appears most side with the Roman Church.

If the Roman Catholic Church wishes to wrongly invoke Mat. 18:18, "Assuredly, I say to you, whatever you bind on earth will be bound in heaven, and whatever you loose on earth will be loosed in heaven," even though they are not the "you" mentioned in Matthew, there is still the one big no-no mentioned in the book of Revelation. "For I testify to everyone who hears the words of the prophecy of this book: If anyone adds to these things, God will add to him the plagues that are written in this book; and if anyone takes away from the words of the book of this prophecy, God shall take away his part from the Book of Life, from the holy city, and from the things which are written in this book." [Rev. 22:18, 19; also Mat. 18:6].

The Roman Catholic Church is clear, "Heaven is the ultimate end…." The book of Revelation is clear. "Then I, John, saw the holy city, New Jerusalem, **coming *down* out of heaven** [*the new one*] from God, prepared as a bride adorned for her husband. And I heard a loud voice from heaven saying, "Behold, *the tabernacle of God is with men, and He will dwell with them, and they shall be His people. God Himself will be with them and be their God.*" It appears the Roman Catholic Church doctrine, by virtue of their apostolic authority, is the antithesis of those things that are written in the book of Revelation by virtue of God's authority.

So what's really going on according to the Biblical record? Resurrections… from the dead, not the living in heaven. There are two of them. The word resurrection, Greek *anastosis,* means a raising up. But if we're already raised up and running around heaven, why would we need to go back to being dead to be raised up again at a resurrection, and this time on a new Earth when supposedly heaven is the ultimate end? It makes no sense from the point of view of God's authority and the Biblical record.

We read in Revelation, "And they lived and reigned with Christ for a thousand years. But *the rest of the dead did not live again* until the thousand years were finished. This is the first resurrection. Blessed and holy is he who has part in the first resurrection. Over such the second death has no power, but they shall be priests of God and of Christ, and shall reign with Him a thousand years." [Rev. 20:5, 6]. This resurrection is at Christ's second coming when he will reign on this Earth for a period of 1000 years of peace. But how is it possible that the rest of the dead did not live *again*, apparently not just in heaven but anywhere, for at least 1000 more years? Weren't these good dead folks supposed to be alive and in heaven? The answer is simple. We remain asleep in Christ, not alive in heaven, at the death of our mortal flesh.

Again, who is it that said in his heart, "*I will ascend into heaven,* I will exalt my throne above the stars of God…?" [Read *The Hijacked Elephant* beginning in chapter six for details of the resurrections].

The apostle Paul explains it for us. "But I do not want you to be ignorant, brethren, concerning those who have fallen asleep [*meaning those who have died in the flesh*], lest you sorrow as others who have no hope [*of life after physical death*]. For if we believe that Jesus died and rose again, even so *God will bring with Him those who sleep in Jesus*. For this we say to you by the word of the Lord, that we who remain alive until the coming of the Lord will by no means precede those who are asleep. For the *Lord Himself will descend from heaven* with a shout, with the voice of an archangel, and with the trumpet of God. [*This is the second coming of Christ.* See chapter five, *The Hijacked Elephant* for details]. And the *dead in Christ will rise first*. Then we who are alive and remain shall be caught up together with them in the clouds to meet the Lord in the air. [Greek, *aer meaning air not heaven*]. And thus we shall always be with the Lord." [1 Ths. 4:13-17].

Paul makes it clear that at Christ's return, the *dead* in Christ shall *rise* first, not *descend alive* from heaven. Then those who remain alive on Earth at that time will join up with Christ. By definition, if we are alive in heaven, we can't be dead and rise from the Earth at Christ's return. It's plain that by Paul's authority from Christ, he is telling us we are not alive in heaven after we die. We are asleep in Christ. The Greek word for sleep is *koimao* and means to cause to sleep. *Then* at Christ's return, the dead, who were asleep shall awaken, raised up to immortality, not joined again to our former mortal body.

The apostle Paul further explains the first resurrection. "Now this I say, brethren, that flesh and blood cannot inherit the kingdom of God; nor does corruption inherit incorruption. Behold, I tell you a mystery: We shall not all sleep, but we shall all be changed—in a moment, in the twinkling of an eye, at the last trumpet. For the trumpet will sound, and *the dead will be raised incorruptible*, and we shall be changed. For this corruptible must put on incorruption, and this mortal must put on immortality. So when this corruptible has put on incorruption, and this mortal has put on immortality, then shall be brought to pass the saying that is written: 'Death is swallowed up in victory." [1 Cor. 15:50-54].

At the second or great resurrection, we read, "The sea gave up the dead who were in it, and Death and Hades [*the grave, hell*] delivered up the dead who were in them. And they were judged, each one according to his works." [Rev. 20:13]. Again, if we're alive in heaven, the ultimate *end*, supposedly we've already been judged as "good," then what are we doing then coming back to be raised from the dead, from our grave? This makes no sense if we're already alive in heaven. But it makes complete sense when we sleep in Christ at the death of our mortal bodies awaiting the resurrection to immortality in the spirit at his return. Our souls don't come back and reunite with our mortal bodies. There's no need. The kingdom of God is of the spirit, not the flesh.

As Paul said, flesh and blood, our mortal bodies, cannot inherit the kingdom of God. We put on new immortal, non-fleshly bodies *after* we are raised from the dead or sleep. And this only occurs either at the first resurrection at Christ's return, which has not yet occurred or at the great resurrection after Christ's return and after more than a thousand years into our future when heaven will have passed away.

At death, we don't go to heaven, alive in that ultimate celestial paradise living happily ever after. Rather, at death we leave our mortal bodies and our spirit returns to God who gave it. We are dead, or asleep, in Christ until his return or until the great day of judgment that is the second resurrection.

As a group, it seems that we Christians are illiterate in our spiritual understanding of the Biblical record, which plainly tells us the dead are asleep, not frolicking in heaven. The apostle Peter stood up on the first day of Christianity and explained that even our patriarch David, of whom Christ said he was his son [Mat.1:1; also Rev. 22:16], "… he is both dead and buried, and his tomb is with us to this day." [Acts 2:39]. The point Peter is making is that if anyone deserved to have been resurrected at that time, it would have been David, a man after God's own heart [Acts 13:22]. And Peter is saying this after the death and resurrection of Christ.

Where are our shepherds to guide us to the truth? The dead will rise, as in wake up, "changed in the twinkling of an eye," with Christ first at his second coming. This is hardly the image we have of those who have died and "gone to heaven." Supposedly, they are eternally awake, playing harps with angels and looking at God's face, even as we speak.

According to the Roman Catholic Church, by virtue of their apostolic authority, "*Since* the Passion and death of our Lord Jesus Christ, these souls *have seen and do see* the divine essence with an intuitive vision, and even face to face…." I guess they forgot to tell our Father in heaven to tell Christ who told John about this when he jotted down the book of Revelation long after Christ's death, oh, and *resurrection from the dead*. [See John 20:17].

I don't know about you, but when I go to sleep, I don't tend to see much, not even my wife's face, which is right next to me. Personally, I look forward to the return of Christ, whether I'm asleep or alive in the flesh at that time. Heaven can wait.

---

[1] See *Christian Post* article, *Most Evangelicals Believe Good People are Heaven-Bound,* 17 December 2010.

The Prophecies

Is The US In End-times Bible Prophecy?

"The United States is absent from end-times Bible prophecy." For some reason, many Christian evangelists and pastors in all sorts of forums propagate this observation. But the plain fact of the matter is that it's simply not true. Not by a long shot. This prophetic blindness comes about because of a simple fact we've mentioned many, many times before. If we don't know our place in Biblical history, we can't know our place in Biblical prophecy. The US is not only not "absent from end-times Bible prophecy," but it is at the heart and core of circumstances directly leading to the events in the Apocalypse.

Naively, the US is largely funding, both in theological and financial terms, the Antichrist's emergence that we read about in Revelation 13. We're immersed in the process to such an extent that if we recognized, from the true Biblical persepective, what we see and hear in the news daily, it would stagger our senses. [Read the chapter *Revelation 17*].

If you read chapters five and six of *The Blind Man's Elephant,* the answer to the US identity and current circumstances are readily apparent. If you read any number of the website articles in *Holy Curiosity: Factoids From the First Century,* the answer is provided within them as well. In fact, a collective reading of these articles should paint a very good big picture for you. And it all goes back to our pivotal statement made by Christ to a gentile woman. "I was not sent except to the lost sheep of the *House of Israel*." As Christ said, "The House of Israel are my people." [Eze. 34:30].

If we merely accepted Christ at his word here, instead of misinterpreting John 3:16 [See the chapter *Mirror, Mirror On The Wall*], we would be on the path to understanding the United States place in Biblical prophecy. Not only would we look at our history books a whole lot differently, but there would be a groundswell resulting in sweeping changes made to the existing modus operandi of government and financial institutions. But we don't and our shepherds who sweep away Christ's clear statements errantly tell us, "The United States is absent from end-times Bible prophecy." [See Jer. 10:21; Eze. 34:2].

When we provoke our holy curiosity and are willing to maintain an open mind and learn, the Biblical record provides us answers. Although already known by some, the US in Biblical prophecy is Manasseh, the son of Joseph, the son of Israel, of the "lost sheep of the House of Israel." Joseph, through his son Ephraim, is the kingly line of the House of Israel to this day. [1 Kng. 11:31; 12:20]. Manasseh, through Joseph, is one of the ten nations of Israel in the last days with a national identity according to the end-time, or last days, prophecy in Genesis 49.

It is interesting to note that there are a couple cities in the US with the name Manassas, the Greek form of Manasseh, one of which is in the Commonwealth of Virginia, as is Jamestown, the first English/House of Israel settlement in the US. Manassas is located less than 30 miles southwest of the US capital, Washington, D.C. There is one other, a rather small town with a population of about 100 in Georgia. And there is a small town in Colorado established in 1879, spelled Manassa that was named for the son of Joseph. The "Manassa Mauler," aka Jack Dempsey of boxing fame, was born there.

However, from what I can determine, the geographic name Manassas appears no place else in the world.

The Confederate ship CSS Manassas was built in 1855 in Medford, Massachusetts before her days, perhaps ironically, as an ironclad in the Civil War. In terms of prophetic consequence for the end-times, the US was to remain as a *single* great nation as we'll see. Thus, the US not getting split into two nations as a result of the civil war is significant.

There are numerous prophecies, both Old and New Testaments that apply to the House of Israel in the end-times. The current Middle Eastern nation-state of Israel, Judah, the House of Judah in the Biblical record, is only one of the ten nations of all Israel with a national identity today. But when we reject Christ's plain statement in Matthew 15, and the Biblical history that supports it, we deceive ourselves to our detriment. The unwitting, self-inflicted result is that we are fallen prey to the largest identity theft in history.

It's been said, the best place to hide something is in plain sight. And our Biblical identity is right there in front of us in the pages of the Biblical record. Yet we Christians don't see it because we've decided, for some strange reason, to reject the truth that Christ unambiguously gave us. We've abandoned the love of the truth. [See 2 Ths. 2:10-12].

As noted, the US is, prophetically, the nation of Manasseh, one the two sons of Joseph whom his grandfather Israel blessed and made firstborn among their brothers of the House of Israel in the last days. The entire chapter of Genesis 48 prophecy is all about the US, a *single* great nation, and his brother Ephraim, a *multitude* of nations, the

British Commonwealth, the kingly line of the House of Israel in the end-times. A cursory scan of today's headlines for the US and Great Britain brings this into focus, particularly with recent events of the past decade in the Middle East.

The two brothers, the US and the Great Britain, are recipients of the birthright inheritance giving them preeminence over all their brothers of Israel who are nations in the end-times as well. Let's take a look at the events of Genesis 48 that took place more than 3000 years ago.

In verse one we read, "Now it came to pass after these things that Joseph was told, 'Indeed your father is sick'; and he took with him his two sons, Manasseh and Ephraim."

Israel was the father of Joseph, of recent Joseph and the Technicolor Dreamcoat fame. Joseph's two sons were Manasseh and Ephraim. Manasseh was the elder son. As Israel was near death, Joseph took his sons Manasseh and Ephraim to visit their grandfather Israel.

Then in verses two through four, "And Jacob was told, 'Look, your son Joseph is coming to you'; and Israel strengthened himself and sat up on the bed. Then Jacob said to Joseph: 'God Almighty appeared to me at Luz in the land of Canaan and blessed me, and said to me, 'Behold, I will make you fruitful and multiply you, and I will make of you a multitude of people, and give this land to your descendants after you as an everlasting possession.'"

It is true that the population of the nations of Israel today likely number in the one billion to two billion people range. But, occupying the land as an everlasting possession will come into effect at Christ's second coming, after the horrendous events of the Apocalypse. "But I will gather *the remnant* of My flock out of all countries *where I have driven them*, and bring them back to their folds; and they shall be fruitful and increase." [Jer. 23:3; see the chapter *Christ Against Christians?*].

In verses five and six, "And now your two sons, Ephraim and Manasseh, who were born to you in the land of Egypt before I came to you in Egypt, are mine; as Reuben and Simeon, they shall be mine. Your offspring whom you beget after them shall be yours; they will be called by the name of their brothers [*Ephraim and Manasseh*] in their inheritance."

Reuben and Simeon were the natural born first and second sons of our patriarch Israel. But for the sake of the birthright inheritance and events in Biblical prophecy, Ephraim and Manasseh took their place.

Verse seven, "But as for me, when I came from Padan, Rachel died beside me in the land of Canaan on the way, when there was but a little distance to go to Ephrath; and I buried her there on the way to Ephrath (that is, Bethlehem)."

Israel is telling his son Joseph that he buried his mother just outside Bethlehem. Israel had twelve sons that grew to become nations by four different wives, Leah, Zilpah, Bilhah, and Rachel, who was Israel's first love. Rachel bore Israel two sons, Joseph and Benjamin. The apostle Paul was a descendant of Israel's son Benjamin. The first king of all Israel was Saul, also a descendant of Benjamin.

Verses eight through twelve, "Then Israel saw Joseph's sons, and said, 'Who are these?' And Joseph said to his father, 'They are my sons, whom God has given me in this place' [*Egypt*]. And he said, 'Please bring them to me, and I will bless them.' Now the eyes of Israel were dim with age, so that he could not see. Then Joseph brought them near him, and he kissed them and embraced them. And Israel said to Joseph, 'I had not thought to see your face; but in fact, God has also shown me your offspring!' So Joseph brought them from beside his knees, and he bowed down with his face to the earth.'"

In verses thirteen and fourteen we read, "And Joseph took them both, Ephraim with his right hand toward Israel's left hand, and Manasseh with his left hand toward Israel's right hand, and brought them near him. Then Israel stretched out his right hand and laid it on Ephraim's head, who was the younger, and his left hand on Manasseh's head, guiding his hands knowingly, for Manasseh was the firstborn."

This is the beginning of the significance of the US and Great Britain in Biblical prophecy including events in the end-times.

Verses fifteen and sixteen, "And he blessed Joseph, and said: 'God, before whom my fathers Abraham and Isaac walked, The God who has fed me all my life long to this day, The Angel who has redeemed me from all evil, Bless the lads; *Let my name be named upon them, and the name of my fathers Abraham and Isaac*; And let them grow into a multitude in the midst of the earth." [Deu. 33:17].

As the eldest brothers, and recipients of the birthright inheritance, according to the inheritance laws Ephraim and

Manasseh would receive fifty percent of the inheritance. As a side note, at the close of WW2, the US controlled about fifty percent of the world's wealth. The remainder of the Genesis birthright inheritance was divided equally among all other brothers. This economic factor has had implications for us in the end-times. And in these times, which country has the world's number one economy? However, due to our lack of knowledge [See Hsa. 4:6, *some things never change*], this is becoming less so daily.

Despite China's recent overtures, echoed by many other G20 countries and the IMF due to the US lack of concern for "sensible fiscal policy," the US dollar remains in use as the world's number one reserve currency. The question is for how much longer?[1]The British pound preceded the dollar as the world's reserve currency beginning in the 19th century. It remained so until the middle of the 20th century. Today, the pound is the world's third most popular reserve currency behind the euro, which is the currency of many of the other sons of Israel who are nation-states today.

It's also important to note that with Ephraim and Manasseh, Israel's name was to be named upon them. This is a reference to the blessing and promises of the birthright Israel received from God through his fathers, Abraham and Isaac. And it is Christ who is the Seed of Abraham, to whom the covenant promises were given. As we read in verse one of the New Testament, "The book of the genealogy of Jesus Christ, the Son of David, the *Son of Abraham*:" And in Gal. 3:16, "Now to Abraham and his Seed were the promises made. He does not say, 'And to seeds,' as of many, but as of one, 'And to your Seed,' who is Christ."

Ephraim and Manasseh, sons of Joseph, were blessed to become the firstborn of all the sons or nations of Israel *by birthright* through Christ in the end-times. "The oldest son of Israel was Reuben [*France*]. But since he dishonored his father by sleeping with one of his father's concubines, *his birthright was given to the sons of his brother Joseph*. For this reason, Reuben is not listed in the genealogy as the firstborn son. It was the descendants of Judah that became the most powerful tribe and provided a ruler for the nation [*until the death of Solomon when Jeroboam, a descendant of Joseph became king of Israel excepting the house of David*], but *the birthright belonged to Joseph*." [1 Chr. 5:1, 2 NLT; also see 1 Kng. chapters 11, 12. Emphasis added. Also see the flow chart at the end of the book].

As Abraham's Seed is Christ, Christians have the name of Abraham, Isaac and Israel upon them. Yet, we just don't get it even though Christ plainly said he was sent only to the House of Israel, of which both Ephraim and Manasseh are first among their brothers. Our Biblical identity is hiding in plain sight. It's in our own history books[2] [*go to chapter endnote*] and we still don't see it.

Take a step back and think about it. What two nations, in existence today, have been at the pinnacle of world events for the past 200 years and are considered kin? One caveat. None of these blessings are open-ended in that they are guaranteed to last forever. Our neglect in guarding our inheritance will catch up with us according to prophecies in both the Old and New Testaments.

Verses seventeen and eighteen, "Now when Joseph saw that his father laid his right hand on the head of Ephraim, it displeased him; so he took hold of his father's hand to remove it from Ephraim's head to Manasseh's head. And Joseph said to his father, 'Not so, my father, for this one is the firstborn; put your right hand on his head.'"

Our patriarch, Israel, knew something that his son Joseph did not. And it is in effect to this day for us in Biblical end-time prophecy more than 3000 years later.

We read in verses nineteen and twenty, "But his father refused and said, 'I know, my son, I know. He also *shall become a people* [Hebrew, *'am*, *nation*], and *he also shall be great*; but truly his younger brother shall be greater than he, and *his descendants shall become a multitude of nations*.' So he blessed them that day, saying, 'By you Israel will bless, saying, 'May God make you as Ephraim and as Manasseh!' And thus he set Ephraim before Manasseh. Then Israel said to Joseph, 'Behold, I am dying, but God will be with you and bring you back to the land of your fathers.'"

That day Israel made Ephraim the elder son in terms of inheritance. Manasseh became the second born, brother of Ephraim, the sons of Joseph. The birthright resides with them to this day. This is significant for end-time prophecies concerning all the nations of Israel especially Ephraim and Manasseh. As we read above, Manasseh would become a great nation. But his elder brother Ephraim would become a multitude of nations.

Again, what great professed Christian nation today has an 'elder' brother who comprises a multitude of nations? There is only one answer. It is the United States, the most powerful single nation in the world's history, who, by the end of World War 2 controlled about fifty percent of the world's economic assets. The largest empire the world has ever seen, otherwise known as the British Empire, is now the Commonwealth of Nations. Currently, there are a multitude of more than 50 member nations of the British Commonwealth stretching around the globe.

The last war fought between Manasseh and his brother Ephraim, the War of 1812, officially ended with the Treaty of Ghent in December 1814. The British reached their empire "superpower" status the next year, 1815. Israel's blessing upon the lads had come to fruition. This de facto recognition of Great Britain's standing took place at the Congress of Vienna, guided by British Lord Castlereagh, to reestablish the map of Europe, most likely unknowingly for all his Christian brother's nations in the aftermath of the French Revolution and the Napoleonic wars. This was the beginning of *Pax Britannica* [Keep in mind the prophecies of both Daniel and Revelation speak of *ten* identifiable nations of Israel in the end-times; see the chapter *Ten Horns, Ten Nations*].

In addition to all its other many remarkable world shaping achievements, some of which include the vulcanizing of rubber, the invention of the electric motor, jet propulsion and the discovery of DNA more recently, which nation took the lead and gave us the King James Bible four hundred years ago? Prophetically, it was Ephraim, elder brother to Manasseh. The Genesis Birthright resides with these two brothers as prophesied by the blessings of Israel upon his grandchildren.

Read chapter five of *The Blind Man's Elephant* for a startling detailed look at Daniel's chapter two prophecy concerning the critical role of Ephraim [Great Britain] and to a lesser extent Manasseh [the US] in fulfilling one of the most significant and important of the end-time Biblical prophecies less than a century ago. As we read in the last chapter of Daniel, "And he [*God*] said, "Go, Daniel, for the words are closed up and sealed till *the time of the end*." The US and Great Britain are in end-time Biblical prophecies in a big way. And the fulfillment of Daniel's prophecy by Great Britain and the US can be easily verified in history books and encyclopedias.

But why is it that we've missed seeing this? The story goes back to the Genesis Birthright, and the struggle between Israel and his brother Edom. Again this is all explained in great detail in chapter *six* of *The Blind Man's Elephant*.

Perhaps an allegory will help us understand our situation a bit better. Imagine a wealthy heir, who at birth is stolen away. Their most trusted servant tells the parents that their baby has died. All the while, the child who was given away by the servant is completely unaware of his true identity. The couple, dying childless as they understand it, leaves their estate to their most trusted servant instead. In the meantime, the heir grows up thinking he is a just another guy with no inheritance.

When the false new heir is revealed, will the true heir oppose it? No, because he believes he is not the rightful heir. He thinks he's a "gentile" because his true identity has been stolen. Is it in the interest of the deceitful servant to make known to the legitimate heir, his true identity? No, of course not. It's the same for the Antichrist, the false prophet of Revelation. So then, which brother nations are the true heirs to the birthright according to the Biblical record?

Christians, the House of Israel including Manasseh, today need to be aware of our true identity. We are not some group of "gentiles" who happened to believe in Christ, the very same Christ who said, "I was sent *only to* the lost sheep of the House of Israel." Who is the liar? Christ or the Antichrist? Yet do Christians believe we are the lost sheep of the House of Israel as Christ said? Then, who is it we are following? It doesn't get any simpler than this.

While our ignorance comes with great peril, the greater sin is refusing the truth. Not knowing we are Manasseh or Ephraim, of the House of Israel, we are deceived. "For those who are such do not serve our Lord Jesus Christ, but their own belly, and by smooth words and flattering speech deceive the hearts of those without guile." [Rom. 16:18].

This deception has caused us to walk away from the words of Christ. "But **they** [*House of Israel*] **rebelled and grieved His Holy Spirit** [See *Pentecost, Acts 2:36-38*]; So *He turned Himself against them as an enemy,* and **He** [*Christ*] **fought against them**" [Isa. 63:10], which leads us right back to Revelation 13. But when we are led to believe we are not in the end-time Biblical prophecies, we ignorantly walk down the wrong paths.

It is the hand of Edom, Babylon the Great, Israel's brother, in these end-times that "... is *granted to him* [*by Christ*] to make war with the saints and to overcome them," exactly for this reason. [Rev. 13:7]. But when the day of reckoning comes about due to our ignorance, we will be asked, "Why do you cry about your affliction? Your sorrow is *incurable*. Because of the multitude of your iniquities, because your sins have increased, I [*our Lord and Savior Jesus Christ*] *have done these things to you.*" [Jer. 30:12-15]. This is a prophetic reference to the future time of Jacob's or Israel's trouble, aka, the events of the Apocalypse.

In our ignorance, we will ask, "What did we do?" We are deceived daily by the Antichrist into rebellion against Christ and our Father in heaven with severe consequences. We are blindly led astray thinking we are on the right track. "For there shall arise false Christs, and false prophets, and shall show great signs and wonders; insomuch that, if possible, they shall deceive the very elect." [Mat. 24:24]. It is a great wonder that we have been deceived about our truthful Biblical identity and inheritance especially in light of plain statements made by Christ. We have turned to become anti-Christian Christians.

Therefore in our apathetic ignorance, we don't know our place in Biblical history, and we don't know our place in Biblical prophecy. Instead we need to renew ourselves in the knowledge of the truth that we "… should no longer be children, tossed to and fro and carried about with every wind of doctrine, by the trickery of men, in the cunning craftiness of deceitful plotting, but, speaking the truth in love [See the chapter *A Christmas Message*] may grow up in all things into Him who is the head—Christ…" [Eph. 4:14,15].

Knowing our true Biblical identity is foreign to our current understanding. And not without reason, for the spirit of the Antichrist has been at work since Christ's first coming. This is why Paul, the apostle to the nations [Greek, *ethnos*], the House of Israel, warned the Christians at Ephesus to put on the whole armor of God for "we wrestle not against flesh and blood, but against principalities, against powers, against the rulers of the darkness of this world, against spiritual wickedness in high places."

Knowing who we are is a vital piece of armor. Lacking this, we are vulnerable to every deceit. We need to heed the apostle James' advice, "... be doers of the word, and not hearers only, deceiving yourselves." [James 1:22]

Instead of walking in holy curiosity, the path Christ set before us 2000 years ago in the first century, we are foolishly following spiritual detours guided by the false light of the Antichrist. And major among these detours is the belief that "The United States is absent from end-times Bible prophecy."

It's time we start taking Christ at his word. Then make the necessary changes so we "will understand righteousness and justice, equity and every *good path*." [Pro. 2:9].

---

[1] "Just 10 years ago, the U.S. economy was three times the size of China's." [WSJ, 25 April 2011]. Beginning with George Bush's presidency and its expanded military spending in 2001, and subsequent banking fiasco, in the short span of 15 years China will have surpassed the US economy according to an IMF forecast. This threatens the US dollar's privileged status in international markets for the first time since the US economic hegemony was attained at the end of WW2. It will mark the end of the "Age of the American Empire," the United States' descent from atop the world a mere 70 years ago.

[2] For a look at the history of Great Britain read the excellent book by Arthur Herman, *To Rule The Waves, How the British Navy Shaped the Modern World.*

Interestingly enough, Herman quotes US Senator Henry Cabot Lodge in a meeting with his congressional colleagues regarding Lodge's observations of Britain's dominant sea power, its role in the world, and its implications for the US: "*We are a great people*; we control this continent, we are dominant in this hemisphere: we have too *great an inheritance* to be trifled with... It is ours to guard and extend." [page 472; also *Speeches and Addresses 1884-1909,* Henry Cabot Lodge. Emphasis added]. Lodge is acknowledging the divine origin of the United States as beneficiary of a great inheritance to be guarded and extended. [See Eph. 1:11].

For a fascinating look at how Manasseh, the US emerged to become a separate great nation from his elder brother Ephraim, Great Britain, read David McCullough's *1776* and his insightful book, *John Adams.*

McCullough makes a poignant statement about John Adams that is so apropos here, "There's a line in one of the letters written by John Adams where he's telling his wife Abigail at home, "We can't guarantee success in this war [*of independence from Great Britain*], but we can do something better. We can deserve it." Think how different that is from the attitude today when all that matters is success, being number one, getting ahead, getting to the top. However you betray or gouge or claw or do whatever awful thing is immaterial if you get to the top. That line in the Adams letter is saying that *how the war turns out is in the hands of God.* We can't control that, but we can control how we behave." [See http://www.realclearpolitics.com/Commentary/com-4_18_05_DM.html] Emphasis added.

The first time the United States joined forces with Great Britain as a military ally they defeated Germany and the Ottoman Empire in WW1. [For the significance of Daniel's prophecy regarding this, see chapter five *The Blind Man's Elephant*]. In the aftermath of World War 1, the US four star Admiral Hugh Rodman characterized the relationship between the US and Great Britain as one of "brotherhood" and "national kinship." [*The United States in the First World War: an encyclopedia*, p.758, Venson and Miles]. The second time they joined forces, by the middle of WW2, the United States strength as a naval power emerged to replace Great Britain. *Pax Americana* replaced *Pax Britannica* by war's end. Prophetically, however, it's all in the family as Joseph's sons exactly as it says in Genesis 48.

What other nations, much less Christian nations, in world history perfectly fits the description of Israel's laying his hands on the two brother's heads saying, *Let my name be named upon them, and the name of my fathers Abraham and Isaac*, regarding the prophecy of God's promises of inheritance? None. It all goes back to the Genesis 48 prophecy regarding these two brothers, national kin of Israel in the end-times.

A Funny Thing Happened...

The identity of the fifth empire in Daniel 2 has eluded scholars and historians, with good reason, probably from about the time Daniel actually penned the account. So, I thought I would post an entry, properly cited and sourced, along with some elementary deductive reasoning, to share with others the identity of Daniel's missing fifth empire as it has great relevance to our current day's events. I was a bit taken back when a popular on-line encyclopedia refused to keep my entry posted citing the following reasons.

They said it "... does not publish original thought." I don't know whose original thought this was, but I got the feeling immediately that this wasn't meant as a compliment. Nevertheless, I optimistically took it as one, thank you very much. However, aren't all thoughts original to mankind's consciousness at one time? The Biblical record was original. Some of it is still to occur. Even $E=mc^2$ was an original thought about one hundred years ago even though it was based on established fact that had been around billions of years, i.e., the universe. And most certainly, the identity of Daniel's fifth empire didn't originate with me. It's plastered all over the history books. Pointing it out can hardly be considered original.

Therefore, it begs the philosophical question, when does a thought cease being original? It appears in the case of a popular on-line encyclopedia that original thoughts cease to be original after passage of an undetermined period of time and garners approval of a sufficiently large, unknown number of non-original thinkers. Herdapedia™. As of this writing at the end of 2009, there are no on-line matches on the Internet for Herdapedia™. Another original thought. I'm plagued.

A popular on-line encyclopedia noted on-line, "All material... must be attributable to a reliable, published source." I wasn't sure if I should believe them on this one. Oxymoronically, [it's not an original word... I googled it], being published on-line is not sufficient to qualify as a reliable source according to the on-line comment made by the publisher of this popular on-line encyclopedia.

And what are we to make, then, of all these, heretofore, respected print periodicals now on-line? Are they suddenly unreliable? Or are they reliable only if they quote their printed selves? And can we trust something with such an editorially incestuous bias?

It also states that, "Changes made to it should reflect consensus." Taken to a logical deduction, if the herd consensus was 1+1=3, say a flat Earth, and you came along with 1+1=2, a spherical Earth, you'd be out of luck just like the Columbian Nunez discovered when he attempted to climb Mount Parascotopetl.

Imagine a group of people standing on a beach noticing all the water along the shore retreating. They stand there pondering this event they've not seen before. You come along with the original thought, from their perspective, that a tsunami is causing this, and they should leave the beach immediately and run for the hills! They thank you, but say any change in their location will be determined by consensus, if not a really big wave. Thin the herd.

My reason for bringing this up is that if you want to learn something "new and original," even if completely valid and properly cited, you won't find it on a popular on-line encyclopedia even when attributed to a reliable, published source directly related to the topic. You will find consensus error, however, not attributed to a reliable, published source, as we'll see.

The chapter below, ever so briefly posted on a popular on-line encyclopedia, extensively quotes a reliable, published source commonly referred to as the Old and New Testaments, aka the Bible. I thought it to be directly related to the Biblical identity of the fifth empire in the book of Daniel. It also quotes a reliable published source from 1917 whose copyright ended in 1998 dealing with said empire; cites Sir Isaac Newton and includes general common knowledge found in numerous allegedly reliable, published history texts of "Western Civilization," with which the fifth empire was directly involved, all to no avail.

A popular on-line encyclopedia's action to remove the article is particularly puzzling especially in light of the fact that the seemingly "original thought" by Mormons, Jehovah's Witnesses, Seventh Day Adventists and non-cited, reliable [?], published [?] "numerous Jewish scholars," whoever they might be, on the same subject, are included. Heck, my information even agrees with these numerous Jewish guys, whoever they are, as to the number of empires. I thought that I should just write, "According to numerous Jewish scholars," in front of everything a popular on-line encyclopedia determined to be "original."

I don't even know who checks facts and then deletes contributions. I can't image a person verifying the entire article for consensus in mere minutes. Maybe it's a computer. Did you know in numerology that the word "computer" adds up to 666? It's not my original thought in case you were wondering.

A popular on-line encyclopedia also states, "Articles may not contain any new analysis or synthesis of published material that serves to advance a position not clearly advanced by the sources," even when said published material in a popular on-line encyclopedia is in error in relation to preponderant other published source material?

But what about original thought advanced by the sources that have been forgotten over time? Nope. No original thoughts about original thoughts allowed.

The qualifying caveat here is that the position must be *clearly* advanced by the source. This is very strange in that the analysis presented here is exactly what was advanced both by John and Daniel in the Biblical record, a reliable, published source. Although, in all fairness, the book of Daniel does state, "And he [*God*] said, Go your way, Daniel: for the words are closed up and sealed till *the time of the end*," which in context appears to be an original thought obviously not clearly advanced until now. They got me.

As for you, the reader, I leave it up to you to make up your own mind whether this is reliable information. No claims can be levied that this published source is Herdapedia™. Instead, you've entered the OTZ, the Original Thought Zone. Think for yourself and enjoy.

Daniel's Missing 5th Empire

There is general agreement [nearly all Biblical scholars including those reliable published sources such as Nelson's Dictionary Articles, the scholarly commentaries of Matthew Henry, and Jamieson, Fausset and Brown, and Adam Clarke et al] regarding the identity of the first four empires mentioned in Daniel's chapter 2 prophecy, regarding the dream he interpreted for King Nebuchadnezzar of Babylon in the second year of his reign, about 602 BCE.

They are the Babylonian, Persian, Greek and Roman empires. It is the fifth empire that has been difficult to pin down with vague and uncertain guesses as to its identity abounding. And there is debate over whether or not there are five, and not four empires mentioned. However, Daniel 2, a reliable published source is very clear and precise in its identifying the fifth empire exactly in accordance with the *theological* arrow of time. See chapter five in *The Blind Man's Elephant* for additional details.

Sir Isaac Newton recognized the connection between Daniel's book and the New Testament's book of Revelation in his book, *The Prophecies of Daniel and The Apocalypse*, 1733. Most of the key information leading to the positive identity of the fifth empire is contained in Daniel 2, but also in the book of Revelation, chapter 17. In verse seven we read, "And the angel said unto me, Wherefore did you marvel? I will tell you the mystery of the woman, and of the beast that carries her, which has the seven heads and ten horns." Then in verse ten, we read, "And there are seven kings: five are fallen, and one is, and the other is not yet come...."

The woman in verse seven is the city Jerusalem according to John. Jerusalem has relevance to both the seven heads and the ten horns. In context of Revelation 17, the beast is a historical/prophetical reference to all seven empires, five of which are fallen from the time frame of the sixth empire, or the "one is" empire whose "deadly wound was healed" as stated in Revelation 13. After the sixth empire, a seventh will follow at some future date. Daniel 2's empires are the five that are referred to as fallen in Revelation 17.

This beast also has ten horns that carry Jerusalem. The ten horns are the ten nations of Israel in the last days from the time perspective of Revelation 17, which is the time of the sixth, "one is," empire. The sixth empire of Revelation, also referenced in Daniel 7, has not yet made its official appearance on the world's stage, when the Lamb, Christ, opens the sixth seal mentioned in Revelation 6, verse 12. The ten horns are the same ten nations of Israel in Genesis 49 when Israel is telling his twelve sons what shall befall them. According to Israel, two of his twelve sons, Simeon and Levi, are scattered among the nations of their brothers in the last days. Hence, there are ten nations, not twelve.

The current nation-state of Israel is one of the ten nations of Israel. They are the nation of Judah mentioned in Genesis 49, verses 8-12. Together with the nine other nations of Israel, they make up the ten horns according to Revelation 17. Jerusalem, as is commonly known, is of tremendous importance for all the nations of Israel. The process of ten nations of Israel having national identities again began during the Roman Empire according to Daniel. "The fourth beast [*Rome*] shall be the fourth kingdom upon earth... and the ten horns out of this kingdom are ten kings that shall arise…." [Dan. 7:23, 24].

Daniel 2 concerns itself with the "five are fallen" from our current day point of view. The deadly wound of empire number five was inflicted by a "stone." We read in Daniel 2, verse 34, "You saw until that a stone was cut out without hands, which struck the image upon his feet, that were of iron and clay, and broke them to pieces." This is not a reference to the end of the fourth empire or Rome. This is a specific reference to the fifth empire that is fallen.

Indeed, Daniel's chapter 2 description does show us five empires. In verses, 32, 33 we read, "This image's head was of fine gold [*1st empire*], his breast and his arms of silver [*2nd empire*], his belly and his thighs of brass [*3rd empire*], his legs of iron [*4th empire*], his feet part of iron and part of clay [*5th empire*]. As we read then in Daniel 2, verse 35, "Then was the iron [*Roman, 4th empire*], the clay [*5th empire*], the brass [*Greek, 3rd empire*], the silver [*Persian, 2nd empire*], and the gold [*Babylonian, 1st empire*], broken to pieces together, and became like the chaff of the summer threshing floors; and the wind carried them away, that no place was found for them: and the stone that smote the image became a great mountain, and filled the whole earth." So we can clearly see there are five empires mentioned in Daniel 2. And "Western Civilization" history books show this to be reliable and true.

Concluding there are only four empires [our 1+1=3 example above] in Daniel 2 cannot be attributed to the Biblical record. The evidence shows the idea of only four empires is consensus error clearly not advanced by the reliable, published source. Rhetorically, wouldn't we be correct to point out that this should be classified as original thought?

The stone that smote the fifth empire is a reference to the end of the image in the last days, the "deadly wound" inflicted less than one hundred years ago by the nations of Great Britain and the US. [See the chapter *Is The US In End-times Bible Prophecy?*]. The stone here is a reference to Israel's grandsons, Joseph's sons in Genesis 49, verse 24, "But his bow abode in strength, and the arms of his hands were made strong by the hands of the mighty God of Jacob; (from there is the shepherd, *the stone of Israel*)...." Both Great Britain and the US have been the shepherds of their brother nations for the past 200 years.

To discover the identity of the missing fifth empire, we need to look at the first four and note their common characteristics. Basically, they were all dictatorial, were the mightiest military of their day, all would be considered non-Christian, and most tellingly, at the zenith of their power, they would control the territory that included the two most prominent cities in Biblical prophecy, Babylon and Jerusalem which can be readily determined from any historical maps of these empires. The Babylonian, Persian, Greek and Roman empires all shared these characteristics.

What empire that had all these shared traits and followed Rome? It was the Ottoman Empire. The Ottoman Empire fulfilled the detailed descriptions in Daniel 2. In fact, it was the Ottoman Sultan Mahomet II that put an end to the Roman Empire in 1453 when the last Roman Emperor,

Constantinus XI was deposed at Constantinople according to reliable, published sources.

In Daniel 2, there are exact descriptive elements of this fifth empire. In verses 42, 43 we read, "And as the toes of the feet were part of iron, and part of clay, so the kingdom shall be partly strong, and partly broken. And whereas you saw iron mixed with miry clay, they shall mingle themselves with the seed of men: but they shall not cleave one to another, even as iron is not mixed with clay."

It should be noted that this portion of Daniel's description is in reference to the toes and not the entire foot. Anatomically, we have ten toes. Thus, Daniel is telling us that this fifth empire will have ten notable men, or in the case of the Ottoman's, ten notable sultans. British Lord Eversley wrote a thorough history of the Ottoman's, *The Turkish Empire, From 1288 to 1914*. His work was published in 1917. Lord Eversley states, "Solyman was the last of the first *ten* Ottoman sultans, who, succeeding one another from father to son, in rather less than 300 years, raised their empire from nothing to one of the most extended in the world."

Eversley adds, "With one exception, they were all able generals and habitually led their armies in the field. They were all statesmen, persistent in pursuing their ambitious aims. Many of them were addicted to literary pursuits, were students of history and even had reputations as poets. In spite of all these softening traits [*miry clay*], there was in nearly all of them a fund of cruelty [*iron mixed with miry clay*]. It may be doubted whether, in the world's history, any other dynasty has produced so long a succession of [*ten*] men of such eminent and persistent qualities." Emphasis and [ ] added.

The second portion of Daniel's description of these ten toes is, "... they shall mingle themselves with the seed of men: but they shall not cleave one to another, even as iron is not mixed with clay." These ten were unique in Ottoman history in that each sultan killed off his brothers so that he, and he alone, produced the next sultan. The ensuing sultan in turn killed off all his siblings, so that he, and he alone carried on the bloodline. This occurred with these ten sultans, or toes if you will, toe after toe after toe.

But the prophecy in Daniel 2 uses the analogy of ten toes, or sultans, not eleven, twelve or more. Was Daniel 2 correct? A remarkable event took place with toe number ten, Sultan Solyman. Before his death, Solyman killed all his sons so that the bloodline of the first ten sultans stopped with him. There was a major rupture between these first ten sultans and those who followed. As Lord Eversley remarked, "If the persistency of type and high qualities of the first *ten* sultans was remarkable, no less so was the break which occurred in their successors down to the present time [*1914*]. One is tempted to question whether the true blood of the Ottoman race flowed in the veins of these 25 degenerates." Emphasis added.

As noted above, the stone that Nebuchadnezzar saw strike the image comprised of five empires, struck the image on its feet, not its toes.

While this is strong evidence, not only for five empires, but that the Ottoman's were indeed the fifth empire, the Ottoman's controlled the territory, which included both Babylon, or its ancient site, and Jerusalem.

The more telling aspect of the theological arrow of time regarding Daniel's prophecy is the duration of the great image Nebuchadnezzar saw in his dream. Recall, he saw only until *the end of the fifth empire*. Therefore, a timing element is involved. The timing elements are mentioned in Daniel as well.

The first involves Nebuchadnezzar himself. It is found in chapter 4, verses 16 and 17 of Daniel. "Let his heart be changed from man's, and let a beast's heart be given to him; and let seven times pass over him… *the intent that the living may know that the most High rules in the kingdom of men*, and gives it to whomsoever he will, and sets up over it the basest of men."

A time, Biblically speaking, is reference to a year. Thus, seven times here meant that Nebuchadnezzar would live as a beast for seven years. The base unit of a year is the day. A Babylonian year is 360 days. Seven times 360, then, equates to a prophecy covering 2520 years, "the intent that the living may know that the most High rules in the kingdom of men, and gives it to whomsoever he will…." The image of five empires in Daniel 2 was meant to last for 2520 years into Daniel's future.

There is a second prophecy that also tells us that the five empires are numbered. It is found in Daniel 5, verses, 25-28, "And this is the writing that was written, MENE, MENE, TEKEL, UPHARSIN." All these are units of monetary weight. Mene is fifty shekels. Tekel is one shekel. And upharsin is twenty-five shekels. This adds up to 126 shekels. But the base unit is not the shekel, but the gerah. There are twenty gerahs to the shekel. Thus, 126 shekels times twenty equals

2520. It is the same number concerning Nebuchadnezzar "that the living may know that the most High rules in the kingdom of men, and gives it to whomsoever he will...."

The message of Daniel 2 with the five empires is that those of us living in these times should be aware that God rules in the kingdom of men, contrary to popular consensus, and gives it to whomsoever he chooses. And to emphasize this point, we are given an exact time frame for these five empires, established and brought down by God. There is a sixth "one is" empire about to emerge, by the hand of God just as these five had previously.

We read above in Daniel 2, verse 34, that Nebuchadnezzar "... saw until that a *stone* was cut out without hands, which struck the image upon his feet, that were of iron and clay, and broke them to pieces." We read in Genesis 49, "But his bow abode in strength, and the arms of his hands were made strong by the hands of the mighty God of Jacob; (from there is the shepherd, the *stone* of Israel:)" Who is this *stone* of Israel?

As the dream of Nebuchadnezzar came to him in the second year of his reign, about 602 BCE, all we need to do is fast forward 2520 years to the time when he saw a stone smite the image on its feet. It brings us to the year 1918. This was the year the Ottoman Empire was finished, their military strength was broken, and the territory containing both the ancient site of Babylon and Jerusalem passed out of their hands becoming known as British Palestine. Think Lawrence of Arabia.

If you'd like to know more about the fifth empire and the Biblical record's identity of the emerging sixth empire not posted on an on-line source, read *The Blind Man's Elephant,* chapters five and six.

Ten Horns, Ten Nations

The Middle Eastern nation-state of Israel *is only one of the ten nations of Israel* [prophetically, in Daniel and Revelation, the ten horns] today with a national identity according to what Israel told his twelve sons, including his son Judah, the Jews, in the last days prophecy of Genesis 49.

The process of ten nations of Israel having national identities again began during the Roman Empire. It fulfilled a prophecy in the book of Daniel. "The fourth beast [*Rome*] shall be the fourth kingdom upon earth... and the ten horns *out of* this kingdom *are ten kings that shall arise*...." [Dan. 7:23, 24]. The ten horns are separate from the seven heads mentioned in Revelation 17. Rome was the fourth of the five heads in the Babylonian king Nebuchadnezzar's dream as explained by Daniel to him. Also, the ten horns should not be confused with the ten toes of the fifth kingdom in Daniel 2.

As intended, the process of the sons of Israel becoming nations once again was set in motion by Christ's death and resurrection in accordance with the Genesis 49 prophecy. After the fall of what was the western empire of Rome, the area became the geographical home to nine of the ten nations of Israel. The successor to the fourth beast in Nebuchadnezzar's dream, the fifth head or empire did not rule this territory except for that of the current day nation-state of Israel. [See the chapter *A Funny Thing Happened*...].

The Frankish empire's Treaty of Verdun in 843 CE opened the way for the establishment of France, Israel's son Reuben, and the nations of Western Europe, eventually including Germany and Italy. The Norman invasion in 1066 up to the Magna Carta in 1215 led to the establishment of England, one son of Joseph, Ephraim and the British Empire. All these are indigenous Christian nations.

The eastern leg of the Roman Empire, the fourth empire of Daniel 2, lasted until 1453 in Constantinople. But it was the western leg of the Roman Empire that gave rise to the nations of the House of Israel. Christ said at his first coming that he did not come to bring peace on Earth but a sword. The nation-building history of Europe is the history of the nations of the House of Israel fighting each other in wars that eventually led to our modern nation-states today.

By the beginning in the 14th century, we see more clearly the emergence of the Nordic countries especially Denmark, as well as the Spanish, the Portuguese, the Dutch, the French and the English. During this period of nation-building and the quest for building empires, it was the ever-changing alliances and wars between these nations with access to the sea more than the relatively landlocked countries in central Europe that spread their trading enterprises all over the world just as the prophecies of Genesis said they would.

After centuries of struggles and nearly constant wars, the bid for establishing a world empire finally came down to the French and the English. France is the nation of Reuben while the British are a son of Joseph, specifically Ephraim as we see in Genesis 49. Reuben was the firstborn son of Israel by his wife Leah. When Isaac was about to die, he asked Joseph to bring his children, Manasseh and Ephraim, to him. Isaac blessed both of them, and even though Ephraim was the younger, he was blessed to take the place of Reuben as Israel's firstborn. [Gen. 48:16,18-20; also see the chapter *Is The US In End-times Bible Prophecy?*].

Thus Ephraim, who we know today as the English, was elevated to the position of firstborn among his brothers passing over Reuben. When it came to the 17th and 18th century, it was these two brothers, Reuben and Ephraim who fought long and hard to establish a world empire. But as the Genesis birthright prophecies made clear, Ephraim was blessed as the firstborn among all his brothers. And finally, it was the British Empire who reigned supreme at the Congress of Vienna in 1815 after defeating the Corsican Napoleon Buonaparte [his surname spelling at birth, but was later changed in 1796] and his Continental System, which had been aimed at thwarting Britain's trade in Europe. The British and their allies restored the Bourbon monarchy to France at the end of the revolution that had begun in 1789.

The description in the last days prophecy of Genesis 49 regarding Judah, the Jews, the nation-state of Israel partially says, "Judah is a lion's whelp…." This means Judah is a lion's cub or was born of a lion. After World War I, the British Empire captured a large portion of the Ottoman Empire in the Middle East, which became known as British Palestine. After World War II, a portion of this British territory became the Jewish nation-state of Israel. The historic symbol of the British Empire, Israel's son Joseph, is a standing lion. Judah's national identity was born of a lion exactly as our patriarch Israel said.

The Jews, the House of Judah, descendants of Israel's son Judah, are a one-twelfth part of all Israel today. Nine other sons of Israel currently have national identities just like the Jewish nation-state of Israel. The US and nations of Europe are among them. The descendants of Israel's other two sons, Levi and Simeon, according to Genesis 49 are scattered among the ten nations of their brothers. The Antichrist will rule over the ten nations of Israel before being destroyed. [See Rev. 17:12, 16. Obadiah v.18]. It's all about the Genesis Birthright.

We are blind to all this because Christians refuse to believe Christ when he plainly said, "I am not sent except to the lost sheep of the House of Israel." We need to move past the Antichrist myth that we are just a bunch of gentiles. Christians are not gentiles, at least according to Christ and God the Father who sent him. We are descendants of our patriarchs, Abraham, Isaac and Israel, as was Christ, the Seed of Abraham.

Apokalypsis

The Book of Revelation was written in the first century, penned by the apostle John. But as we're told in the first verse, it is the "revelation of Jesus Christ, which God gave to him…." The word revelation is the Greek, *apokalypsis*. Literally it means a laying bare, which we can take to mean holding nothing back, showing everything. In this case, it is a book of revealing.

To most people, the title would appear somewhat of a non sequitur, puzzling in that the Book of Revelation appears to be one of the most confusing in all the Biblical record especially as our modern day connotation of the word apocalypse, rather than a revealing, is one of worldwide catastrophe, doomsday, the great tribulation that has yet to occur. However, the word *apokalypsis*, or the verb form, *apokalypto* is used in nearly half of the New Testament's 27 books.

Verse one also states, "… to show his servants things which must *shortly* come to pass…." This too can be a bit confusing as most people probably think of the Book of Revelation as something relating only to the future cataclysmic ending of the world. The word shortly in Greek is *tachos*, and does not refer to a popular fast food item. It does refer to something that happens with quickness or with speed however.

There are two sides to this coin. Some things in the Book of Revelation began occurring very soon in the first century, and continue to this day. Others, such as the Lords day, or day of the Lords [See the chapter *Guess Who's Coming to Supper?*] will happen with suddenness, as a thief in the night, when we don't expect it, hence with quickness.

Yet all these events are threads connected by one story. Some occur at the beginning and others at the end.

For example, the first five seals in chapter six began occurring shortly after Christ's resurrection. The first seal opened by Christ reads, "And I saw and beheld a white horse: and he that sat on him had a bow; and a crown was given to him: and he went forth conquering and to conquer." This is a reference to the appearance of false prophets who were responsible for the division that Christ spoke of in Luke 12.

Christ warned the apostles, saying "And many false prophets shall rise and deceive many." This was during his ministry. And by the 60's CE, the apostle Peter was writing that this was a fact. "But there were false prophets also among the people, even as there shall be false teachers among you...." [2 Pet. 2:1]. By the time the apostle John wrote 1 John, likely the early 90's CE, he is saying, "... because many false prophets are gone out into the world."

As we can see from the apostles themselves, false prophets were revealed in the first century. Seals two, three, and four, war, famine, and pestilence were opened as well.

The fifth seal in Revelation six, "And when he had opened the fifth seal, I saw under the altar, the souls of them that were slain for the word of God and for the testimony which they held." Christian martyrdom began with Stephen [See Acts 7:59] when the apostle Paul was still known as Saul and was instrumental in the killing of Christians before his conversion. Paul, himself, was martyred in 68 CE or thereabouts. Peter was martyred not long after Paul.

The Prophecies
Apokalypsis

As we can readily see, the first five seals of Apokalypsis chapter six were opened in the first century.

Also mentioned in the Book of Apokalypsis, there are seven churches beginning in chapter one when John saw seven golden candlesticks. These represent seven eras of the *ekklesia* or church from the first century up to the advent of the kingdom of God, Laodicea being the last church era before the return of Christ.

Thus, the apokalypsis, or revealing, took place right away, beginning in the first century. What we think of as being the Apocalypse or the "end of the world," actually occurs much later, time-wise. It occurs with the opening of the sixth seal in chapter six revealing the sixth empire of 666. This has yet to occur. It is discussed in detail in chapter five of *The Hijacked Elephant*.

In total, there are seven church eras, seven seals, and seven last plagues before Christ establishes the kingdom of God on Earth. It is during the seventh church era that the sixth and seventh seals will be opened, followed by the seven last plagues, all of which is what we commonly think of as "The Apocalypse." "And to you who are troubled rest with us, when the Lord Jesus shall be *revealed* from heaven with his mighty angels, in flaming fire taking vengeance on them that know not God, and that obey not the gospel of our Lord Jesus Christ." [2 Ths. 1:6, 7]. The word revealed here is *apokalypsis.* And the gospel, or good news of our Lord Jesus Christ is that he came to redeem those who sat in darkness, the lost sheep of the House of Israel. [Mat. 15:24; see the chapter *What Exactly Is The Gospel?*].

We should keep in mind when reading the Book of Revelation that the key players and events mentioned here originated in the Book of Genesis. Genesis is defined as an origin or beginning. Thus, apokalypsis is a revealing of what was intended from the beginning. It is the time period from Genesis 1:1 "In the beginning, God created the heaven and the earth" until it comes around full circle in Revelation 21:1, "And I saw a new heaven and a new earth: for the first heaven and the first earth were passed away: and there was no more sea."

To fully understand the Book of Revelation, we need to fully understand that the Biblical record is one story from Genesis to Revelation. It is written to the same people. When we step back, the big picture is revealed and then we come to understand how the pieces of the puzzle aptly fit together.

Christ Against Christians?

According to the most common Christian perception of "The Apocalypse," it is a general reference to the end of the world as a judgment upon evildoers while saving those who belong to Christ. Christians, most especially those who consider themselves to be of the conservative, evangelical variety, believe they will be the ones saved or raptured from "The Apocalypse." Of course, in the Book of Revelation it clearly states only 144,000 will be redeemed from the Earth. If the world has a population of about seven billion people, our chance is about .000002 to make the cut.

And on top of this, all 144,000 are from the nations of Israel. "... and *no one* could learn that song [the *song of Moses[1], see endnote; Rev. 15:3, Deu. 31:30*] except the hundred and forty-four thousand who were redeemed from the earth." [Rev. 14:3]. In addition, 12,000 of the 144,000 are Jews! [Rev. 7:5]. So if Christians are "gentiles of the world," and not the House of Israel, then it looks like we all are out of luck according to the Biblical record.

The book of Revelation, or *Apokalypsis* in Greek, primarily covers the time period of Christ from the first century until his return. This period of time prophetically is what the Biblical record calls the last days. It is the time period, spiritually speaking, of the summer harvest, which is marked beginning with Pentecost and ending with the Day of Trumpets. It was the day of Pentecost in the first century when our Father sent, in the name of his son Christ, the Spirit of God. A blowing of seven trumpets as described in chapter eight of Revelation heralds Christ's return. [For details, see chapter five, *Christ's Return, Trumpets*... in *The Hijacked Elephant* book].

What Christians don't realize is that, according to the Biblical record, the Apocalypse is, foremost, *Christ chastising Christians*. And if you've read any of the preceding chapters herein, you realize that Christians are the House of Israel. However, until Christianity wakes up to this reality, it's unlikely any intelligent changes will be made to the wide and broad path we currently traverse.

Let's take a look at both the Old [OT] and the New [NT] Testaments.

OT Prophesy in Isa. 63:7, 8 Edom, Israel's non-identical twin, is speaking:

"I will mention the loving kindnesses of the LORD, and the praises of the LORD, according to all that the LORD has bestowed on us, and the great goodness toward the **House of Israel**, which he has bestowed on them according to his mercies, and according to the multitude of his loving kindnesses. For he [*Christ*] said, Surely they are my people, children that will not lie: so **He was their Savior**."

NT The apostle Paul writing to Timothy:

But is now made manifest by the appearing of our **Savior Jesus Christ**, who has abolished death, and has brought life and immortality to light through the gospel..." [2 Tim. 1:10; see the chapter *What Exactly Is The Gospel?*].

In the gospel of Matthew:

"But he [*Christ*] answered and said, I am not sent but unto the lost sheep of the **House of Israel**." [Mat. 15:24].

OT Prophesy in Isa. 63:9:

"In all their [*House of Israel's*] affliction he was afflicted, and the angel of his presence saved them: in his love and in his pity **he redeemed them**."

"...and all flesh shall know that I the LORD am your **Savior** and your **Redeemer**, the **mighty One of Jacob** [*all Israel*]." [Isa. 49:26].

NT In the gospel of Luke:

Blessed be **the Lord God of Israel**; for he has visited and **redeemed his people**." [Luke 1:68].

Paul in Galatians:

"**Christ has redeemed us** from the curse of the law, being made a curse for us: for it is written, Cursed is every one that hangs on a tree...." [Gal. 3:13].

NT Book of Acts:

"Therefore let all the **House of Israel** know assuredly, that God has made that same Jesus, whom you have crucified, both Lord and Christ... Then Peter said unto them, Repent, and be baptized every one of you **in the name of Jesus Christ** for the remission of sins, and you shall receive the gift of **the Holy Spirit**." [Acts 2:36-38].

OT Prophesy in Isa. 63:10a:

"But they [*House of Israel*] **rebelled**, and **vexed his Holy Spirit**..."

OT Prophesy in Isa. 63:10b:

"...therefore **he** [*Christ*] **was turned to be their [*the House of Israel's*] enemy, and he fought against them**." How angry must we have made Christ that he would turn to fight us *as an enemy*? And how fierce will be his anger turned against us? It will be the worst time in human history.

Prophecy in Jer. 30:7, 15 made by the Lord concerning Israel and Judah:

"Alas! For **that day is great, So that none is like it**; And it is the **time of Jacob's** [all Israel's] **trouble**, But he [*144,000*] shall be saved out of it... *Why do you cry about your affliction? Your sorrow is incurable. Because of the multitude of your iniquities, your sins have increased,* **I have done these things to you**."

Prophesy in Jer. 10:1, 10:

"Hear you the word which the LORD speaks unto you, **O House of Israel**... But the LORD is the true God, he is the living God, and an everlasting king: **at his wrath the earth shall tremble**, and *the nations [of the House of Israel] shall not be able to abide his indignation*."

NT Prophesy in Rev. 6:12-14, 16:

"And I beheld when he had opened the sixth seal, and, lo, there was **a great earthquake**; and the sun became black as sackcloth of hair, and the moon became as blood. And the stars of heaven fell unto the earth, even as a fig tree casts her untimely figs, when she is shaken of a mighty wind. And the heaven departed as a scroll when it is rolled together; and every mountain and island were moved out of their places... And said to the mountains and rocks, Fall on us, and hide us from the face of him that sits on the throne, and from **the wrath of the Lamb**: For **the great day of his wrath is come**; and *who shall be able to stand*?"

Both testaments agree on this one point, "The Apocalypse" is directed towards Jacob, or all Israel meaning the House of Judah, and the House of Israel, i.e., Christians, by Christ. Part of the reason for this predicament is that Christians don't even know they are of the House of Israel. In our ignorance, we have "vexed his Holy Spirit," forsaking our true heritage. We've gone from "children who will not lie," to those who embrace the lies, who venerate the lies, walking after false gods, thereby causing our Redeemer to fight against us. [See the chapter *A Christmas Message*]. But are we really concerned? The resounding answer is, "No!"

The last church era in Revelation leading up to "The Apocalypse" is Laodicea. Let's read its description in chapter three. "... because you are lukewarm, and neither cold nor hot, **I will spit you out of my mouth**. Because you say, 'I am rich, have become wealthy, and have need of nothing' [*our perspective*]--and do not know that you are wretched, miserable, poor, blind, and naked [*God's perspective*]...."

This is not exactly the expected outcome of the prosperity gospel preached in mega-churches today. It is a subtle and clever stratagem that the wealth of this world is obtained by seeking God. God does not say, "Blessed are the rich...."

When the heart's intent [See Jer. 17:9] is appeasing God to gain the wealth of this world, the scheme fails in the eyes of God. The paths leading to the wealth of this world and to God's kingdom are divergent, and never the two shall meet. They are intrinsically in opposition to each other. Anxiety about the material things of this world "... and the *deceitfulness of riches*, choke the word [*of God*], and he [*or she*] become unfruitful." [Mat. 13:22; see the chapter *Brown Paint: Quantum Potentialities*].

What advice does Christ give to Christians in our age? "I counsel you to buy from me gold refined in the fire [*spiritually purified*], that you may be rich; and white garments, that you may be clothed, that the shame of your nakedness may not be revealed; and anoint your eyes with eye salve, that you may see. As many as I love, I rebuke and chasten. Therefore be *zealous* and *repent*." [Rev. 3:14-22].

We are counseled to be consistently zealous. Zealous, the Greek *zeloo,* means to burn with zeal. In other words, we best get really serious about living our life with the correct priorities. Repent means to change one's mind *and* behavior.

The game is afoot as Sherlock Holmes would say. The evidence of future events surrounds us when we know for what we are looking. Therefore, we need to get back to the teachings Christ gave us in the first century. And we should realize exactly who we are and begin making changes without delay. But it appears only a very few will do so. Everyone else will continue walking through the wide gate with the rest of the herd.

If it is riches we seek, it should be the riches of the word of God. We should heed the lesson of the sixth empire of Revelation, Babylon the Great, whose immense earthly wealth will quickly come to naught. "For in one hour such great riches came to nothing." [Rev.18:17]. And as to the riches of this world some people hold so dearly, "Behold, the day of the LORD is coming, And your spoil will be divided in your midst." [Zec. 14:1]. Of what value, then, are individual riches of this world by comparison to the royal power and authority of God? Read James 5:1-12. "Come now, you rich, weep and howl for your miseries that are coming upon you!" And while we may excuse ourselves here, not being rich in terms of earthly possessions, we need to be rich in the truth of God, children who will not accept lies.

No matter what we think is important in this world, it is all vanity and vexation. [Ecc.1:14]. If all the wealth and existence of this mighty world empire in Revelation will be brought to nothing in one hour, of what lasting value to us is earthly wealth? What profit do we gain seeking these same things? We may as well store away as treasure the wind we grab with our hands.

When Matthew wrote in chapter six, "... seek first the kingdom of God," it is not a reference to seeking a kingdom as in a place to go or to be. The word kingdom in Greek is *basileia*, which means royal power, kingship, and dominion. In other words, Babylon the Great, which represents the power and wealth of this world, will be brought to nothing by the power and authority of God. Therefore, which kingdom or which power and authority do we want to grab hold of in life? It can't be both. Is it the one in front of our faces on television everyday that hypnotizes us with celebrity and false riches that leads to death, or the one in the Biblical record that is discerned by faith through works that leads to life?

Those of this world cannot understand the sovereign power and might of God, the Creator. Instead we are made fools by the illusionary power of earthly wealth, sheep to the slaughter and therefore will be fooled by the power of the sixth empire in Revelation. This is why we need to understand the world we live in. What we think is real is an illusion. And what man thinks is the illusion, is the reality. And what is not an illusion, but is reality is that Christians are of the House of Israel.

We need to open our eyes to our true identity and our true heritage. As advised, we need to be *zealous* and make these changes. Otherwise, we will experience, in the most dreadful way, the full power and might of our Savior and Redeemer whom we, in our utter ignorance and rebelliousness, have made our enemy who is fighting against us. Unless we change our ways, we are in a no win situation because it is Christ doing these things to us.

"I, Jesus, have sent my messenger to testify to you these things *in the churches*. I am the root and the offspring of David, the bright and morning star. And the Spirit and the bride say, 'Come!' And let him who hears say, 'Come!' And let him who thirsts come. Whoever desires, let him take the water of life freely." [Rev. 22:16, 17].

---

[1] Moses was not a Jew, but a Levite. The Levitical priesthood was in service to God for all Israel. They were not considered

to be either of the House of Judah or the House of Israel. Thus, the song of Moses is a song for all the nations of Israel and therefore is not a "Jewish" song. The song of Moses is thought to be similar to modern day national anthems, the song of a country played, for example, at the gold medal ceremony during the Olympics. Thus, it could only be learned, or have relevant meaning to the citizens of that nation. The implication here in Revelation, therefore, is that of the approximately 1-2 billion descendants of Israel on the Earth today, only 144,000 of them will live through the Apocalypse to learn this song.

Revelation 17

This chapter's format is a bit of a departure from the others in that it is somewhat of a commentary. Reading this chapter is best served by first reading chapters five and six in *The Blind Man's Elephant* as these chapters provide in depth context as well as a 4000 year long introduction to the events in Revelation, chapter 17. Many of the statements made here have their supporting details in these chapters. Nevertheless, you can still follow along and grasp the big picture. You will need to go to the above chapters in the book to fill in the specifics however.

Many devout people assert that Revelation 17 is the most difficult chapter in the Book of Revelation to understand. Yet, like so many things, it is easier to understand when we let the Biblical record interpret itself. Rather than use contemporary events as a prism through which we attempt clarity, we need the correct context. This context is the entirety of the Biblical record, which is one book written to the same people. Grasping this vital principle, our task is made that much simpler.

There are characters mentioned in this chapter of Revelation that are key to understanding epochal events in our future. These same characters also are in the book of Genesis. Going full circle, Genesis and Revelation are bookends to the story of the Biblical record. Yet, if we are not aware of these characters shared Biblical history, then we cannot completely understand what is being prophesied here. If we don't know our identity in Biblical history, then we cannot know our place in Biblical prophecy as it relates to events in this chapter. For a glimpse here, see the chapter,

Abraham's Seed and Heirs. To begin with, we'll list these characters and mention who they are. Then as we read through the verses in chapter seventeen, we'll expand the Biblical context to give us a greater awareness.

The **SEVEN HEADS** first description is found in the Book of Daniel with the first five being described in detail as "the great image" by Daniel to Nebuchadnezzar, king of ancient Babylon.

The sixth head is the **GREAT HARLOT** or Edom, aka Babylon the Great, the "one is" empire in this prophecy. [See 2 Ths. 2:7-10].

The **WATERS** are the multitude of nations and peoples over which this sixth empire will rule.

During their now historical existence, the spiritual force behind the first five empires, or heads, was Satan. The **BEAST** is a reference to the "Antichristian world power, [*that*] returns worse than ever, with satanic powers from hell." [A.R. Fausset, *Jamieson, Fausset and Brown Commentary*, Revelation 17]. The sixth head or empire, Edom will be the reincarnation of the beast, the next in line from previous five heads, all of whom derived their power from Satan.

And at the zenith of their power these first five of seven empires ruled over the **WOMAN**, which is the city of Jerusalem. The same will be true for the sixth empire.

The **TEN HORNS** are the ten nations of Israel in the last days [See Gen. 49], the Christian nations of the world and those of the House of Judah that will unite themselves with the beast according to God's will, until such time as the ten nations of Israel turn on their earthly persecutors, Edom, the sixth manifestation of the beast and will destroy her with fire. *Edom and Israel are brothers*. [See Gen. 25:25, 26]. The key characters in Genesis are all here in Revelation. The Bible is one book written for the same people, all the nations of Israel.

Chapter seventeen is an inset chapter, which means it is not in the chronological flow of Revelation's chapters. It provides a summary of events. "Then I heard a loud voice from the temple saying to the seven angels, "Go and pour out the bowls of *the wrath of God* on the Earth." [Rev. 16:1]. Chapter seventeen is the description given in vision to the apostle John concerning the wrath of God by one of the angels holding a bowl.

GREAT HARLOT Edom

Verse 1: **Then one of the seven angels who had the seven bowls came and talked with me, saying to me, "Come, I will show you the judgment of the great harlot** [Greek, *porne*,] **who sits on many waters…**

This summary chapter in Revelation primarily concerns itself with the judgment of Edom, which as we see ends in desolation and destruction by fire. The reason why this empire is referred to as the great harlot is that Esau, before his name was changed to Edom, sold his birthright inheritance. The Genesis birthright was given by promise of God to Abraham. Yet for a morsel of food, Edom sold it to his brother Jacob, aka Israel. "And Esau [*Edom*] said to Jacob [*Israel*], 'Please feed me with that same red

[Heb. adjective, *adam*] stew, for I am weary.' Therefore his name was called Edom [Heb. noun, *red*]... Then Jacob said, 'Swear to me as of this day.' So he [*Edom*] swore to him, and *sold his birthright to Jacob*." [Gen. 25:30, 33]. The Genesis birthright belongs to all the nations of Israel through the sons of Joseph, Ephraim and Manasseh.

As the apostle Paul stated it in the first century, "... lest there be any fornicator or profane [*ungodly*] person like Esau, who for one morsel of food *sold his birthright*." [Heb. 12:16]. The word fornicator used by Paul is the Greek, *pornos*. Thus, Edom's incarnation as the sixth head of the beast here in chapter seventeen is portrayed as the great whore or harlot because he sold the greatest inheritance in the history of the world.

It is difficult to imagine the full magnitude of what the birthright inheritance encompasses as we have but a faint glimpse of what it ultimately entails. It goes far beyond life on this Earth. But imagine selling off ownership of all the material wealth of the US and Europe for a bowl of stew. Multiply that by a factor of a million or more, and we get a tiny idea of what Edom sold. Too late, Edom has sought for millennia to get back that birthright inheritance from his brother Israel. The sixth empire is the culmination of those efforts.

The point of this chapter is that Edom did not respect that which was his by birth. Essentially, it was an insult to God. And now in this chapter, it is coming back full circle on Edom by God, but not before exactly a terrible toll on the rebellious Christian nations.

The great harlot, the Edomite Empire, is said to sit on many waters. These waters are peoples, multitudes, nations, and tongues over which this sixth empire will have dominion, which primarily are the Christian nations of the world as well as the nation-state of Israel, which is of the House of Judah. This is where we chiefly find Edom today. [Gen. 27:28, 29 and compare to 27:37-40 especially verse 28 with 39].

v.2 ... with whom the kings of the earth committed fornication, and the inhabitants of the earth were made drunk with the wine of her fornication.

This is the effect of Edom's sixth empire on the world in terms of worldly wealth, both with governments, in terms of financial and military power, and with the people. It's all the "goodies" provided by this empire, which daily divert our attention from the kingdom of God. All we need to do is objectively watch television commercials, look at the programming offered, page through magazines to see what this emerging empire is offering. It's the proverbial sex, pharmaceuticals and rock 'n roll of the "good life." It's the "candy is dandy, but liquor is quicker" approach to deceiving the nations of Israel, the Christian nations of the world as well as those descended from Judah in order to get back the birthright Edom seeks.

In other words, Edom will succeed in getting the nations, especially the Christian nations of his brother, to forsake the truth of God's word and to indulge in the orgy of chasing after the material wealth of this world while consistently lowering their levels of morality. For those of a religious bent, there will be miracles and the false doctrines of "goodness and light," not unlike the charlatans

Christmas and the Babylonian inspired Easter we have blindly accepted because we have lost track of our Biblical identity [See chapter two, *The Hijacked Elephant*; also the chapters *Merry Christmas?* and *Funny Bunny*].

The WOMAN Jerusalem

v.3 **So he carried me away in the Spirit into the wilderness. And I saw a woman sitting on a scarlet beast, which was full of names of blasphemy, having seven heads and ten horns.**

The apostle John, who is writing this, was carried away into a desolate or uninhabited place where he saw the woman sitting on a scarlet beast. The woman is the city of Jerusalem, which in verse eighteen is the city that has sovereign power over the kings of the Earth.

In terms of context, there are two cities of importance in the Biblical record, Jerusalem and Babylon. Rome is not among them. The city of Babylon represents the seat of authority of Satan while Jerusalem is the city of God. It is important to note that from the time of the first Babylonian captivity [about 600 BCE] forward, the Ark of the Covenant, the earthly seat of power of God, never again was found in Jerusalem where it had been in the temple since it was built by Solomon. "Then the priests brought in the Ark of the Covenant of the LORD to its place, into the inner sanctuary of the temple, to the Most Holy Place, under the wings of the cherubim." [1 Kng. 8:6]. The Babylonians laid waste to the temple of Solomon along with Jerusalem.

But the Ark vanished, never to be seen until John mentions it in his vision of apokalypsis. "Then the temple of God was opened in heaven, and the Ark of His Covenant was seen in His temple. And there were lightnings, noises, thunderings, an earthquake, and great hail." [Rev. 11:19].

Interestingly, the second temple in Jerusalem was known as the temple built by Herod, who was a descendant of Edom. The Romans, the fourth of the seven heads or empires mentioned in this verse, totally destroyed this second temple and completely laid waste to Jerusalem in 70 CE, which never had the Ark of the Covenant in residence. [See the chapter, *The Tale of Two Covenants* for the relevance of the covenants]. Regarding the Edomite Herod's temple, "Then Jesus went out and departed from the temple, and his disciples came up to show him the buildings of the temple. And Jesus said to them, 'Do you not see all these things? Assuredly, I say to you, not one stone shall be left here upon another, that shall not be thrown down.'" [Mat. 24:1, 2].

The scarlet beast here is a reference to the anti-Israel, anti-Christian, power of these empires embodied by their kings or leaders. And the word scarlet is a reference to the blood of the nations of Israel shed by the seven heads here in this chapter.

The beast was full of names of blasphemy. As we read in Revelation chapter thirteen regarding the sixth empire, the great harlot, "Then I stood on the sand of the sea. And I saw a beast rising up out of the sea, having seven heads and ten horns, and on his horns ten crowns, and on his heads a blasphemous name... Then he opened his mouth in blasphemy against God, to blaspheme His name,

His tabernacle, and those who dwell in heaven." [Rev. 13:1, 6]. Of course, the instigator of this blasphemy is Satan "And another sign appeared in heaven: behold, a great, fiery red dragon having seven heads and ten horns, and seven diadems on his heads." [Rev. 12:3] "Now the beast which I saw was like a leopard, his feet were like the feet of a bear, and his mouth like the mouth of a lion. The dragon gave him his power, his throne, and great authority." [Rev. 13:2].

The seven heads are seven empires: *Babylonian, Persian, Greek, Roman, Ottoman, Edomite [Babylon the Great] and Gog-Magog.* The first five heads are explained by Daniel to Nebuchadnezzar, king of Babylon, who literally lived as a beast for seven years. "Let his heart be changed from that of a man, let him be given the heart of a beast, and let seven times pass over him." [Dan. 4:16].

The reason for this is apropos to chapter 17 and is applicable to our understanding of the events contained herein. "The decision is announced by messengers, the holy ones declare the verdict, so that the living may know that *the Most High is sovereign over the kingdoms of men and gives them to anyone he wishes and sets over them the lowliest of men.*" [Dan. 4:17, NIV; read Jer. 27:6-11 regarding ancient Babylon and it's implications for Babylon the Great].

The ten horns are the ten nations of Israel in last days. [See the chapter *Ten Horns, Ten Nations*]. The reason the dragon has the ten nations of Israel is that he has deceived all Israel and has dominion over them through the beast, of which the sixth head is Edom. In Genesis 49, they are *Reuben, Judah, Zebulon, Issachar, Dan, Gad, Asher,*

Naphtali, Joseph, and Benjamin. These ten horns are *national* entities today, but this list differs from the listing in Revelation seven. However, that's another story for a different book.

v.4 The woman was arrayed in purple and scarlet, and adorned with gold and precious stones and pearls, having in her hand a golden cup full of abominations and the filthiness of her fornication.

The city of Jerusalem will be the seat of power and wealth for the beast of this sixth empire. Purple and scarlet were two of the colors used in the veil or curtain at the entrance to the holiest place within the temple in Jerusalem wherein the Ark of the Covenant was located. The beast "shall plant the tents of his palace between the seas and the glorious holy mountain." [Dan. 11:45]. Thus Jerusalem will become the royal center of this sixth empire whose ruler will not only compare himself to God, but will glorify himself above God. This comes from the author of these thoughts. "For you [*Satan*] have said in your heart, 'I will ascend into heaven, I will exalt my throne above the stars of God; I will also sit on the mount of the congregation, on the farthest sides of the north; I will ascend above the heights of the clouds, I will be like the Most High.'" [Isa. 14:13, 14].

"Then the king [*the beast of the sixth empire*] shall do according to his own will: he shall exalt and magnify himself above every god, shall speak blasphemies against the God of gods, and shall prosper till the wrath [*of God upon Israel, Rev. 6:12-18; see v. 17 below and upon Edom as well*] has been accomplished; for what has been determined shall be done." This is why Jerusalem is important to the sixth beast. He is exalting by sitting over the city of God, home to three of the world's major Abrahamic religions.

"He shall regard neither the God of his fathers [*Edom's fathers were Abraham and Isaac*] nor the desire of women, nor regard any god; for he shall exalt himself above them all. But in their place he shall honor a god of fortresses [*specifically military bases, by extension all things military*] and a god, which his fathers did not know, he shall honor with *gold and silver, with precious stones and pleasant things*. 'Thus he shall act against the strongest fortresses with a foreign god, which he shall acknowledge, and advance its glory; and he shall cause them to rule over many, and divide the land for gain.'" [Dan. 11:36-39].

This is not surprising because when Isaac passed along the birthright to Israel, Isaac also told Edom, "You shall live by the sword [*profiting from wars and the buying and selling of military arms*], and you shall serve your brother [*the nations of Israel*]; and it shall come to pass <u>when you have dominion</u> [*including, but not limited to controlling the world's largest military with its worldwide network of military bases?*], <u>you will break his yoke from off your neck.</u>" [Gen. 27:40].

By way of perspective, and understanding where Edom is prophesied to be in the last days, it should be considered that the US is the world's largest arms exporter according to the Stockholm International Peace Research Institute. Also, the annual US military budget is *greater than the rest of the world's combined*. The US has approximately 800 military bases [fortresses] worldwide, including US billion dollar heavily armed fortresses referred to as "enduring presence posts," the size of small cities courtesy of the US taxpayer. This doesn't include US naval forces worldwide.

The Pentagon [*the five-sided pentagram is a symbol used in Satan worship*] has divided most of the world's landmass into command centers with names such as Centcom [short for Central Command]. This is the Middle East. It's worthy of note that the Pentagon, who oversees all these military bases, has designated the land area, which includes both Jerusalem and Babylon, the two cities of importance in this chapter of Revelation, as the *central* command with its HQ temporarily located in Florida.

Even though the Pentagon is located near the US capital in Washington, D.C., rather than designate the US as Centcom, the US and Canada are Northcom [North America]. Additionally, there is Eucom, which is HQ'd in Germany as is Africom, Paccom, Southcom, etc. all of whose cultural, social, economic and geo-politically diversity [the **Waters**] are presided over by generals and admirals on behalf of the Pentagon. These pay grade 07 and higher officers exercise authority like "kings" controlling military bases, as well as such things as nuclear weapons, arms sales, special ops, military satellites and cyberspace based weapons, when CYBERCOM became operational.

Yet, this appears not to be enough as a recent Secretary of Defense wanted a substantial increase in the military budget which, according to organizations that keep track of these things, already is a nation breaking 50-55% of the total US federal budget when all direct, indirect and "black op" expenditures are included based on the Government Accounting Office's US Budget Fiscal Year 2009.

The nations of Israel are buying rope from those who will ultimately put it around our necks due to our ignorance of the truth. For a startling look at the compelling force behind US military fortresses around the globe, read *The Sorrows of Empire,* by Chalmers Johnson.

Thus, the city of Jerusalem will be polluted and defiled by the great whore, Babylon the Great.

v.5 And upon her forehead was a name written, MYSTERY, BABYLON THE GREAT, THE MOTHER OF HARLOTS AND ABOMINATIONS OF THE EARTH.

Jerusalem as the woman here is portrayed having a name on her forehead. While the city of Jerusalem should be pure as the city of God, the capital of the nations of Israel, during the times of occupation for more than 2500 years, running from the time of the first Babylonian empire until the end of the fifth head, the Ottomans in 1918, it was the under the authority of the beast in one form or another. Daniel refers to it as the great image. [Dan. 2:31].

It's moniker will be as written above during the time of the sixth empire, the Edomite empire, hence, "... he exercises all the authority of the first beast in his presence, and causes the Earth and those who dwell in it to worship the first beast [*the first head*] whose deadly wound was healed." Babylon's deadly wound was healed because of God's judgment on the first Babylon. "And Babylon, the glory of kingdoms, the beauty of the Chaldees excellency, shall be as when God overthrew Sodom and Gomorrah. It shall never be inhabited, neither shall it be dwelt in from generation to generation...." [Isa. 13:19, 20].

While God caused the original Babylon to lie desolate, the new Babylon shall rule over Jerusalem. The occupation of Jerusalem, as the seat of power of the sixth head, distinguishes it from the first Babylonian head of the beast. As Daniel noted, the first Babylonian empire, the head of gold was magnificent, however, Babylon *the Great* shall exceed it.

The mother of harlots again is a reference to Edom selling the birthright and causing others to follow in her idolatrous path most especially the Christian nations who merrily celebrate holidays changed from God's. [See *The Hijacked Elephant*]. The abominations of the earth refers to the idol or false god this sixth head will cause to be worshipped.

v.6 **I saw the woman, drunk with the blood of the saints and with the blood of the martyrs of Jesus. And when I saw her, I marveled with great amazement.**

Jerusalem, drunk with the blood of the saints and the martyrs of Jesus is both a historical reference as we know from the first century [See the chapter *Peace on Earth?*], and a current situation from John's perspective. Jerusalem as the seat of power of the sixth empire and the beast to which, "It was granted to him to make war with the saints and to overcome them. And authority was given him over every kindreds, tongue, and nation." [Rev. 13:7]. *This will include authority over Christians, Jews and Muslims, three sons of Abraham who have strong religious roots in Jerusalem. Edom's religious roots are in Babylon.*

Primarily in this chapter, however, this pertains to the nations of Israel. Edom, having sold his birthright to his brother, while keeping it a secret from his father, was very angry when the Genesis birthright was passed to Israel, rather than to him by Isaac. Edom spoke a prophesy that will be fulfilled by the sixth empire. "So Esau [*Edom*] hated Jacob [*Israel*] because of the blessing with which his father blessed him, and Esau said in his heart, 'The days of mourning for my father are at hand; then I will kill my brother Jacob.'" [Gen. 27:41]. The fulfillment of this prophecy began with the Edomite ruler Herod and with the crucifixion of Christ. Again, you'll have to read chapter six in *The Blind Man's Elephant* for details.

We see more of this in the prophesy concerning all Israel in Isaiah 63, "Who is this who comes from Edom, with dyed garments from Bozrah [*Edom's historical capital city*], this one who is glorious in his apparel, *traveling* in the greatness of his [*military*] strength?- 'I who speak in righteousness, mighty to save.' [*It's not a coincidence this sounds a lot like US foreign policy. Even though US "fighting" forces have left Iraq, home of ancient Babylon, there remain several city size "enduring" military bases housing more than 50,000 troops*]. Why is your apparel red, and your garments like one who treads in the winepress? [*i.e., drunk with the blood of the saints and martyrs of Christ*]. I have trodden the winepress alone, and from the peoples no one was with me. For I have trodden them [*Israel*] in my anger, and trampled them in my fury; their blood is sprinkled upon my garments, and I have stained all my robes." [Isa. 63:1-3].

And when John saw the woman, Jerusalem in this condition, drunk on the blood of Christians, he was truly astounded. By the time he penned the Book of Revelation, the Jerusalem he remembered had been reduced to a barren land, a wilderness as Christ said. John had walked the streets of Jerusalem in the first century, then saw it destroyed by the Roman legions and now in prophecy, he saw it again in a completely different state. Later, he saw in vision, the new Jerusalem coming down from God out of the sky as described in chapter 21. This truly would have been an incredulous thing to witness.

The WOMAN Jerusalem and The BEAST sixth empire

v.7 But the angel said to me, "Why did you marvel? I will tell you the mystery of the woman and of the beast that carries her, which has the seven heads.

Obviously John would have been astonished to see such a vision. And no doubt he was mystified by what he saw. The woman we know is Jerusalem and the beast are the seven heads or empires to which Satan has given power and authority.

v.8 The beast that you saw was, and is not, and will ascend out of the bottomless pit and go to perdition. And those who dwell on the earth will marvel, whose names are not written in the Book of Life from the foundation of the world, when they see the beast that was, and is not, and yet is.

The beast that John saw here was the first five of the heads. These are the Babylonian, Persian, Greek, Roman and Ottoman empires. The time period from the end of the Ottoman Empire in 1918 until the emergence of the sixth empire of Edom, is the period described here as "and is not." This time period is described by Daniel. "Then the iron [*Roman*], the clay [*Ottoman*], the bronze [*Greek*], the silver

[*Persian*], and the gold [*Babylon*] were broken in pieces together, and became like chaff from the summer threshing floors; the wind carried them away so that no trace of them was found. And the stone that struck the image became a great mountain and filled the whole earth." [Dan. 2:35].

The beast that ascends out of the bottomless pit is a reference to that in chapter thirteen, "Then I stood on the sand of the sea. And I saw a beast rising up out of the sea, having seven heads and ten horns, and on his horns ten crowns, and on his heads a blasphemous name." [Rev. 13:1].

The "yet is" refers to the emergence of the sixth head after it seemed the first five had long vanished, "... so that no trace of them was found." Of course, the reason for this is that there is no apparent connection between these empires past and the one to emerge.

Perdition means destroying or destruction. This could have a double edge meaning in that this empire, Edom will be devastating to Israel, the Christian nations and those descended from Judah. But in the end, this empire too is destroyed at the second coming of Christ, as this chapter is a judgment upon the great harlot, Edom.

Those who are not written in the Book of Life will marvel when they see these events take place. And as a result, "All who dwell on the earth will worship him, whose names have not been written in the Book of Life of the Lamb slain from the foundation of the world [*kosmos*]." [Rev. 13:8]. This is opposed to "Just as He chose us in Him before the foundation of the world [*kosmos*], that we should be holy and without blame before Him in love." [Eph. 1:4].

v.9 Here is the mind, which has wisdom: The seven heads are seven mountains on which the woman sits.

The seven heads are seven mountains or seven kingdoms on which Jerusalem sits. Many have thought this to be a reference to Rome as Rome is built upon seven hills. But this is not the case. Rome was the capital of the Roman empire for little more than a few hundred years. The capital of the Roman Empire was moved by the emperor Constantine from Rome to Constantinople in 330 CE. It remained the capital of the Roman [Byzantine] empire for more than a 1000 years, from the early fourth century until it gave way to the fifth empire, the Ottomans in the mid-fifteenth century, 1453 to be exact. The last emperor being Constantine XI.

As the woman here is Jerusalem, this is a reference to the fact that at the zenith of their power, the first five heads of this great image ruled over Jerusalem, which is historically true. We are being told the sixth empire of Edom will also rule over Jerusalem as we saw above in verse 4. However, Edom differs from the previous five in that Jerusalem will be the official seat of power for this empire, ruling over his brother Israel's capital city.

v.10 There are also seven kings. Five have fallen, one is, and the other has not yet come. And when he comes, he must continue a short time.

Of course, the seven empires will have kings or leaders over each one. History has shown us that the first king was Nebuchadnezzar of Babylon. The Persian empire had Cyrus and Darius. Alexander was the head of the Greek empire initially. Rome had its Caesars and the Ottoman empire its sultans.

Five are fallen is a reference to the first five empires that vanished. The reign of this great image lasted exactly 2520 years as Daniel's prophecies indicated from 602 BCE beginning with Nebuchadnezzar's reign until the defeat of the Ottoman empire in 1918. Daniel's prophecy says this great image was put to an end by a stone.

"You saw until a stone was cut out without hands, which struck the image upon his feet that were of iron and clay [*the Ottomans*], and broke them to pieces." [Dan. 2:34]. This is a description of the fifth head in Daniel. The stone mentioned here is Great Britain and, to a lesser extent, the United States at the end of WW1. [Gen. 49:24]. The Ottoman territory containing both Jerusalem and Babylon, its ancient site, became known as British Palestine. For a further discussion, read the chapter, *Is The US In End-times Bible Prophecy?*].

The "one is" is a reference to that of Edom, forming, but not yet emerged, but was the one John saw in his vision. The other that has not yet come, the seventh head or empire, refers to Gog-Magog, which occurs after the millennium or thousand years of peace following Christ's second coming.

v.11 The beast that was, and is not, is himself also the eighth, and is of the seven, and is going to perdition.

The beast is the power and authority given to this image of seven heads. The image here, the beast that was, refers to the first five fallen empires and up to the time prior to the emergence of the sixth empire, hence the "and is not." Of course, the power and authority for all seven heads of the beast is that of Satan, which is why it says here "is himself also the eighth." "So the great dragon was cast out, that serpent of old, called the Devil and Satan, who deceives the whole world; he was cast to the Earth, and his angels were cast out with him." [Rev. 12:9]. In other words, all seven of these worldly empires are of the empire of Satan who was, is and will be their driving force.

The phrase, "is going to perdition" here also has a double edge to it. While Satan, the Destroyer, seeks to destroy God's people, he too shall be destroyed. "Then I heard a loud voice saying in heaven, 'Now salvation, and strength, and the kingdom of our God, and the power of His Christ have come, for the accuser of our brethren, who accused them before our God day and night, has been cast down.'" [Rev. 12:10].

At this point, the second coming of Christ, "He laid hold of the dragon, that serpent of old, who is the Devil and Satan, and bound him for a thousand years...." [Rev. 20:2].

After the millennium, Satan is loosed, and the seventh head emerges for a short time. After which "The devil, who deceived them, was cast into the lake of fire and brimstone where the beast and the false prophet are." [Rev. 21:10].

TEN HORNS

v.12 The ten horns which you saw are ten kings who have received no kingdom as yet, but they receive authority for one hour as kings with the beast.

Ten horns are the nations of Israel in the last days as we read in Genesis 49, here represented by their leadership or kings, which refers to the government rather than the people. The kings have received no kingdom, which indicates they may be leaders of the people, but have no formal authority to rule. In a sense, they are puppets or a government in absentia.

However, they get authorization from the beast to have the power to rule with the beast that lasts for one hour. One hour is the Greek *mia hora*. It is a one-twelfth portion of the natural daytime, which we take to mean sixty minutes.

v. 13 **These are of one mind, and they will give their power and authority to the beast.**

While the ten rulers over the nations of Israel have no formal authority under the rule of the beast, they unanimously agree to give their support, their influence over the nations of Israel, to the sixth empire and apparently in return receive an hour of power. In Micah 2:12 the children of Israel, Jacob, gathered by God are referred to as "… the sheep of Bozrah [*Edom*], as the flock in the midst of their fold: they shall make great noise by reason of the multitude of men." The timing of the ten kings is just a tad bad.

v. 14 **These will make war with the Lamb, and the Lamb will overcome them, for He is Lord of lords and King of kings; and those who are with Him are called, chosen, and faithful.**

During their one-hour of power, these ten kings of Israel will be united in one purpose with Edom, to wage war on Christ. "And I saw the beast, the kings of the earth, and their armies, gathered together to make war against Him who sat on the horse and against His army." [Rev. 19:19;

Jer. 27:8]. Remember, too, only 144,000, out of a possible 1.5 billion or so of the now anti-Christian nations of Israel [Rev. 7] shall survive this war against Christ. [See the chapter *Christ Against Christians?*] Remember, Satan has deceived the whole world by this time.

But Christ will overcome these ten rulers of the nations of Israel and in the process overcome the beast and the seat of his authority, Jerusalem. "And the beast was taken, and with him the false prophet that wrought miracles before him, with which he deceived them that had received the mark of the beast, and them that worshipped his image." [Rev. 19:20].

And it is at this time that the sixth empire, whose seat of power is in Jerusalem, comes to an end. "Alas, alas, that great city Babylon, that mighty city! for in *one hour* is your judgment come." [Rev. 18:10]. Read chapters 18 and 19 for the course of events.

v.15 **Then he said to me, The waters which you saw, where the harlot sits, are peoples, multitudes, nations, and tongues.**

This indicates that the Edomite empire, the sixth head, will have an encompassing empire headquartered in Jerusalem putting into subjection much if not all the world. It will include the nations of Israel in the last days, who are Edom's brother, the Christian nations of the world and those descended from Judah.

v.16 **And the ten horns which you saw on the beast, these will hate the harlot, make her desolate and naked, eat her flesh and burn her with fire.**

At this point, after the one-hour of judgment is come on the sixth head, the tide turns on the remainder of Edom. Whoever remains of the ten nations of Israel, formerly of one mind, which sided against Christ with the beast with seven heads, now of one mind again, turns on the sixth head, the empire of Edom, the harlot, and what's left of Babylon the Great. [See Jer. 49:7-22].

"Thus says the Lord GOD concerning Edom; We have heard a rumor from the LORD, and an ambassador is sent among the nations [*of Israel*], Arise you, and let us rise up against her [*Edom*] in battle. Shall I not in that day, says the LORD, even destroy the wise men out of Edom, and understanding out of the mount of Esau? And your mighty men, O Teman [*son of Esau*], shall be dismayed, to the end that every one of the mount of Esau may be cut off by slaughter. For your violence against your brother Jacob [*all Israel*] shame shall cover you, and you shall be cut off forever.

"For the day of the LORD is near upon all the nations [*of Israel*]: as you have done, it shall be done to you: your reward shall return upon your own head. But upon mount Zion [*in Jerusalem*] shall be deliverance, and there shall be holiness; and the house of Jacob [*all Israel*] shall possess their possessions. And the house of Jacob [*including the House of Judah*] shall be a fire, and the house of Joseph [*the House of Israel*] a flame, and the house of Esau for stubble, and they shall kindle in them, and devour them; and there shall not be any remaining of the house of Esau; for the LORD has spoken." [Obadiah: 1, 8-10, 15, 18]. "As it is written, Jacob have I loved, but Esau have I hated." [Rom. 9:13].

The Prophecies
Revelation 17

From the time of the selling of the birthright by Edom, Babylon the Great, the great harlot, to his brother Israel in the Book of Genesis, the struggle for the Genesis birthright comes full circle between the brothers in the Book of Revelation.

"Then I saw an angel standing in the sun; and he cried with a loud voice, saying to all the birds that fly in the midst of heaven, 'Come and gather together for the supper of the great God that you may eat the flesh of kings, the flesh of captains, the flesh of mighty men, the flesh of horses and of those who sit on them, and the flesh of all people, free and slave, both small and great." [Rev. 19:17, 18].

v. 17 **For God has put it into their hearts to fulfill His purpose, to be of one mind, and to give their kingdom to the beast, until the words of God are fulfilled.**

The ten nations of Israel and their rulers will have one mind to give their power and authority to the beast according to God's purpose, until all that which is written in Revelation and the prophets are fulfilled. Remember Christ said he came to fulfill the Law *and* the Prophets. [Mat. 5:17]. The Law and the Prophets were for all Israel.

"And then the lawless one will be revealed, whom the Lord will consume with the breath of his mouth and destroy with the brightness of his coming. The coming of the lawless one is according to the working of Satan, with all power, signs, and lying wonders. For the mystery of lawlessness is already at work; only until he who now withholds is taken out of the way. And with all unrighteous deception among those who perish, because *they did not take the love of the truth in hand*, that they might be saved. And *for this reason God will send them strong delusion, that they should believe the lie, that they all may be condemned who do not believe the truth, but had pleasure in unrighteousness."* [2 Ths. 2:7-12].

God gave Israel over to one mind to give their kingdom over to Edom and to fight against him as a punishment upon all Israel for their ungodliness and love of the lie. "Alas! For that day is great, so that none is like it; And it is the time of Jacob's [*Israel's*] trouble [*most commonly referred to by Christians as the Apocalypse*]... Why do you cry about your affliction? Your sorrow is incurable. Because of the multitude of your iniquities, because your sins have increased, I [*Jesus Christ*] have done these things to you." [Jer. 30:7, 15]. But once their punishment was sufficient, then again of one mind, they put an end to all of Edom so that the words of God will be fulfilled.

v.18 And the woman whom you saw is that great city which reigns over the kings of the Earth.

The woman is Jerusalem. Christ will have established the kingdom of God on Earth, beginning the thousand years, the millennium, of peace during the interval between the sixth head of Edom and the seventh of Gog-Magog. This is the day portrayed in the Law as the feast of Tabernacles and spoken of by the prophets. "And it shall come to pass, that every one that is left of all the nations which came against Jerusalem shall even go up from year to year to worship the King, the LORD of hosts, and to keep the feast of tabernacles [*or the thousand years of peace*]." [Zec. 14:17]. See chapters 5, 6 and 7 in *The Hijacked Elephant* for details concerning these events.

The Prophecies
Revelation 17

No doubt, you probably will have some questions after reading this. If you haven't read chapters five and six in *The Blind Man's Elephant*, please do so as this will answer many of your questions.

The Holidays

Peace On Earth?

The holiday time of the year is filled with greeting cards that people send to family and friends. Typically, they have tranquil scenes, often with some snow on the front cover or will have a Nativity scene showing the wise men with their gifts as well as some shepherds at the manger. Very often the cards will say, "Peace on Earth," as did the one I got in the mail. Inside it said something about glad tidings, joy and peace on Earth at Christmas.

As a president of the Southern Baptist Leadership Conference proclaimed, "Christmas is about peace on Earth and goodwill towards men." But did Christ come to bring "Peace on Earth" as these greeting cards and Christian leaders joyously proclaim? Well, seeing as how this sentiment is attributed to Christ, let's read what he said. In Luke 12, we read, "Do you suppose that I came to give *peace on earth*? I tell you, *not at all*, but rather *division*." Then in Matthew 10, Christ said, *"Do not think that I came to bring peace on earth. I did not come to bring peace, but a sword."* Three times in two verses Christ said he didn't come to bring peace on earth. And both verses are references to his first coming.

It's starkly apparent, Christ and Christians have two very different perspectives about his first century purposes. Christmas cards and Christian leaders say peace on earth. Christ says no peace. Who are we going to believe? Of course, all we need do is watch the news or read the headlines to see, that indeed, we don't have, and haven't had peace on earth, particularly in the Middle East. Just maybe Christ knew what he was talking about?

Christ brought division amongst the Jewish establishment as John relates in his chapters seven through ten. Today the House of Judah and the House of Israel remain divided as Paul explains in Romans eleven and as is prophesied in Zechariah chapter eleven. And regarding Luke's account about division, Christ said, "Father will be divided against son and son against father, mother against daughter and daughter against mother, mother-in-law against her daughter-in-law and daughter-in-law against her mother-in-law."

So not only was Christ being truthful about his bringing division, he gave specific examples. All we need do is ask ourselves, "Has the Christian religion caused division and strife in families?" You bet. And as a result of these divisions, today there are more than 30,000 recognized Christian denominations according to the various sources who track these things. One message delivered by Christ in the first century has fractured into more than 30,000 different interpretations. I believe this qualifies as division just as Christ said.

But what about Christ saying he came not to bring peace, but a sword? Let's take a look at Revelation 6. "Now I saw when the Lamb opened one of the seals; and I heard one of the four living creatures saying with a voice like thunder... When He opened the second seal, I heard the second living creature saying, "Come and see. Another horse, fiery red, went out. And it was granted to the one who sat on it to *take peace from the earth*, and that *people should kill one another*; and there was given to him *a great sword*."

Wow. Christ was right again. The Lamb here in Revelation 6 is Christ. "And looking at Jesus as He walked, he said,

The Holidays
Peace On Earth?

'Behold the Lamb of God!' [John 1:36]. Christ took peace away from the Earth that people should kill one another. This is not the Christ of Christmas cards. This is not the image we have of "baby Jesus." But he is the first century Christ he said he would be. And what Christ said is extremely relevant to our lives today in the 21st century as it has been for Christians from the first century forward. It's just that we aren't listening.

The opening of the second seal, as with all of the first five seals in Revelation 6, is not a future reference to his second coming as many mistakenly assume. In the book of Mark, Christ was on the mount of Olives talking with Peter, James, John and Andrew telling them they shall hear of *wars and rumor of wars*, but not to be troubled, for such things must be, but *this is not the end*, but *the beginnings of sorrows.* The word for sorrows here is *odin* in Greek and refers to the pain of childbirth. The implication being that mankind will travail in pain and sorrow until the kingdom of God is established on Earth. The time between Christ's first coming and his return is the period commonly referred to as "the last days" of our age, or the age of mankind.

Killing in the name of religion, Christianity in particular, began in the first century almost immediately after Christ's death. And if you scan through the history books, this has been an ongoing theme, which continues daily as we can read in the headlines, including seemingly failed shoe and underwear bombers. Wars in the name of religion have killed more people than just about any other cause throughout history. And it will continue up to the establishment of the kingdom of God by Christ, just as he said, all of which is quite relevant to us in the 21st century with the wars in the Middle East.

Christ said what he meant and meant what he said. We have no peace on Earth.

Merry Christmas?

By the way, Christ wasn't born in December either. What!? Of course, whether or not he was born in December, is irrelevant to many folks. Some will say, we can't know his date of birth, so one day is as good or bad as another. This being the case, then we should drop the pretense that Christmas is about celebrating the birth of Christ. It's not. It's all about buying and selling if we're honest with ourselves.

For the purists to say Christ was born in December and the wise men showed up with presents at the manger in Bethlehem, well, it's a legend or myth. And the Biblical record clearly contradicts the myth. Luke 2 tells us, "Now there were *in the same country shepherds living out in the fields*, keeping watch over their flock by night… So it was, when the angels had gone away from them into heaven, that the shepherds said to one another, Let us now go to Bethlehem and see this thing that has come to pass, which the Lord has made known to us. And they came with haste and found Mary and Joseph, and *the baby* lying in a manger… And all those who heard it marveled at those things which were told them by the shepherds."

Two things should be carefully noted. One, there is no mention of wise men with gifts when Christ was born. Two, only shepherds who were living out in the fields, showed up, and they showed up without gifts. As to Christ being born in December, shepherds are not out living in the fields with their flocks, especially at night in the area of Bethlehem in December. It's too cold for one with freezing rain and snow a real possibility. And there's nothing for the sheep to graze on. The very latest shepherds would be out in the fields would be late October. So for shepherds to show up at Christ's birth, he would have been born months earlier than late December.

The December date was chosen in the 4th century by the Roman emperor Constantine because of religious unrest in the empire. He chose what was the winter solstice then, or December 25th the first day of winter not only for Christians, but for Egyptians and Romans in their religious celebrations. Had he been picking a date out today, it would be the 21st of December.

In fact, there is no consensus among scholars and historians even as to the year Christ was born. The dates generally range from 1 to 6 BCE or earlier. Dating the death of Herod, which the Jewish historian Josephus puts about 4 BCE, then Christ could have been born as early as 5-7 BCE, which seems to be the most commonly accepted timeframe. This still puts the actual date in the realm of "best guess." What we know then is that Christ was not born on December 25th, and it is very unlikely the year was 1 CE. Even more importantly, the actual day and date of his physical birth is not essential to the Christianity we find in the Biblical record. None of the apostles mention it nor is there any mention of its celebration. There are other more significant matters for Christians to be concerned with today.

But what about the gift giving, as all this buying and selling is attributed to the wise men at the birth of Christ. In fact, how come there is no mention of them with the shepherds? Well, the wise men weren't there with the shepherds. The wise men most likely didn't show up for close to two years.

The Holidays
Merry Christmas?

And when they did, they visited Christ who was a young child living in a house.

Let's see what Matthew 2 actually says. "And when they [*the wise men from the east*] had come into the house, they saw the young child with Mary His mother, and fell down and worshiped Him. And when they had opened their treasures, they presented gifts to Him: gold, frankincense, and myrrh." The Greek word for *young child*, as in a house, is *paidion*. The Greek for *baby*, as in a manger, is *brephos*.

"Then Herod, when he saw that he was deceived by the wise men, was exceedingly angry; and he sent forth and put to death all the male children who were in Bethlehem and in all its districts, *from two years old and under*, according to the time which he had determined from the wise men." Christ was probably about two years old or a little younger when the wise men with their gifts visited him in a house.

So Christ wasn't born in December. And he didn't get birthday presents from the wise men either. But, what about the Christmas tree? Well, the evergreen tree was used by heathens in their winter solstice festivals. They believed the Sun was dying as was everything else except the evergreen trees, hence, these trees must have special powers. So they cut them out of the forests each year. The prophet Jeremiah said, "They decorate it with silver and gold; they fasten it with nails and hammers so that it will not topple." You can see these trees with little wooden stands hammered to the base of the trees, so they won't fall over, every December in lots everywhere. As did the heathens of old, so-called Christians decorate their trees with gold and silver colored things.

What are we told about observing this practice of evergreen trees in the prophecy of Jeremiah? "Thus says the Lord [*Christ*]: *"Do not learn the way of the heathens*; Do not be dismayed at the signs of heaven, For the heathens are dismayed at them." The signs of heaven is a reference to the winter solstice. And what do Christians do? We celebrate the wrong date, for the wrong reasons, wrongly learning the way of the heathens. For Christians, breaking this habit is the first step on the way to having a love for the truth.

What we discover then is that Christ only had shepherds show up when he was a baby in a manger. It wasn't in December. They had no gifts. The wise men, who did brings gifts, showed up maybe a couple years later when Christ was a child living in a house. We have no idea exactly what time of the year this was either. The gifts they brought were for Christ the king, not the birthday boy. And the evergreen tree is a heathen symbol used in pagan observances. As to Santa and Rudolph, why do we, who claim to be Christians, teach our children fairy tales or myths in place of the truth? [See the chapter *A Christmas Message*].

For those of you who may care about such things, ultimately, our celebration of this thing called Christmas will result in the opening of the sixth seal according to the prophecies in Jeremiah and Revelation. It is the seal associated with what is commonly referred to as the Apocalypse. For a detailed explanation, see chapter five, *The Hijacked Elephant*.

Funny Bunny

While we're on the subject of holidays not occurring when we think they did, what about Easter? Was Christ resurrected on a Sunday morning? What do the eyewitnesses from the first century say in the Biblical record? When we examine the account closely, we find a very surprising answer. If you truly have a holy curiosity, as Einstein phrased it, then continue reading.

Of course, the whole point of the "Easter" resurrection is moot. Christianity inanely celebrates Easter, which is rooted in the festival of the Babylonian [see the chapter *Revelation 17*] prostitute goddess of fertility, sex and war, Ishtar, including the rising of the spring Sun in the east, which explains all the fertility symbols, the colored eggs and chocolate bunny rabbits. None of this, obviously, has anything to do with Jesus Christ according to our accounts from the first century especially as Christ was not resurrected on a Sunday morning. Peter, John and the other apostles had nary a brightly decorated egg between them at Christ's sepulcher when they showed up that Sunday morning when the big egg, the Sun, was about to rise in the east. And, just where exactly, according to the Biblical record from the first century, was the Easter Bunny that morning?

On a more profound note, let's take a look at the question of Christ's resurrection. In Mark's chapter 16 account, he says Mary Magdalene arrived at Christ's sepulcher at the rising of the Sun. Luke's account in chapter 24 says it was early dawn. John's account in chapter 20 says that when it was yet dark, Mary arrived at the tomb. Taken together, it appears that while it was still dark, just before the initial light of dawn, Mary Magdalene arrived at the tomb. She saw that it was empty. Christ was gone. He had risen by then. She ran back to tell Peter and the others that Christ was not there. Mary then ran back with Peter and John this time to see for themselves. All this running back and forth would indicate that the apostles and others were fairly close by, perhaps just outside the area of the tombs.

This course of events began, most likely, when it was still dark and by the time that Mary arrived back with the apostles, the Sun was rising. In either case, Christ was not resurrected at sunrise on a Sunday morning. The idea of a Sunday morning resurrection comes from a verse in Mark's account.

Mark 16:9 says, "Now when [*Jesus*] was risen early the first day of the week he appeared first to Mary Magdalene out of whom he cast seven devils." How this verse is interpreted is due to how it is punctuated in relation to its context. There are two possibilities.

If we put a comma after risen, and after the word week, it would read that Christ was risen on the first day of the week, or Sunday morning before sunrise.

However, if we put the comma only after the word risen, it would read that Christ appeared *first* to Mary, before seeing anyone else, and that this was early on Sunday morning. This would not reference the timing of his resurrection, but rather that Mary was the first one he appeared to after the resurrection. The latter appears to be the case, because we know for certain, according to the context of events, that Mary was the first person he appeared to, and it was early

Sunday morning. Thus, the one verse in Mark's account is not a reference to the timing of Christ's resurrection. Rather context shows us it is about seeing Mary first after his resurrection.

Perhaps most startling to 21st century Christians, is that all the gospel accounts are in agreement that when Mary and the others went to Christ's tomb, *none of them* were expecting that Christ was resurrected. "For as yet they knew not the scripture, that he must rise again from the dead." [John 20:9; see also Psa. 16:10]. Even after Mary saw and talked to Christ, well after his resurrection, and she told the apostles, they still didn't believe her. [See Mark 16:11]. They didn't know for certain that Christ was risen until later in the day when he appeared to them. This would hardly support the fact that Mark's wording in verse nine in this chapter was about the timing of the resurrection.

When the apostles saw the empty tomb, their concern was that perhaps someone had stolen Christ's body and taken it someplace else, allegedly to prevent them from doing the same thing and falsely proclaiming Christ's resurrection. [See Mat. 27:64-66]. Disheartened no doubt, they left for their homes. Their vigil by the tomb site apparently was for naught.

However, Mary Magdalene stayed behind at the tomb. A voice asked Mary where was Christ? Weeping, Mary answered, "… they have taken away my Lord, and I don't know where they have taken him." It is perfectly clear, at this point in time, that Mary and the apostles, upon discovering the empty tomb, did not know Christ was risen from the dead. This point is reinforced, because Christ asked Mary this question.

It's obvious then, that the first time Mary was at the tomb, Christ had already risen. Mark's account prior to verse nine, in 16:5, 6, says, "And entering the tomb, they saw a young man sitting on the right side in a white robe; and they were amazed. And he said to them, Be not amazed: you seek Jesus the Nazarene which has been crucified: he is risen; he is not here."

Even when Mary Magdalene and Mary the mother of James were told he was risen, "... they went out quickly, and fled from the sepulcher; for they trembled and were amazed: neither said they anything to anyone; for they were afraid." [Mark 16:8]. This is why Mary ran to get the apostles so they could see for themselves. Their conclusion was Christ's body had been taken away. [See John 20:2] Even upon being told he was risen, Christ's resurrection did not enter either Mary's minds.

The question remains, can we determine when the resurrection took place? Yes we can. It just takes a little common sense, understanding the Passover and its relationship to the Days of Unleavened Bread, some elementary deductive sleuthing, and we can find the surprising answer in the very pages of the gospels merely by taking Christ at his word.

First, how long was Christ to be in the grave? Christ tells us, in answering some of the scribes and Pharisees who were looking for a sign, when he said, "An evil and adulterous generation seeks after a sign; and there shall be no sign given to it, but the sign of the prophet Jonah: for as Jonah was three days and three nights in the great fish's belly, so shall the Son of man be three days and three nights in the heart of the earth."

The definition of the word three in Jonah, *shalowsh*, actually means three. It does not mean portions of three.

Okay, Christ seems clear about the three days and three nights. Now some folks today take it upon themselves to say that Christ didn't really mean three days and three nights, but just parts of three days. Yes, no doubt Christ was totally confused about his death and resurrection. Some folks make this claim because they are ignorant of the fact that Christ wasn't put into the tomb before a weekly sabbath. If we go back and look at the account of Jonah in the Old Testament, the Hebrew word used there for "days," is *yowm*. Yowm refers to 24-hour days, and not portions of days. So three days and nights, repeated twice for emphasis by Christ, would certainly mean a 72-hour period.

Now the Greek words used in John for three days is *treis hemera*. Treis means three, not parts of three. Hemera can refer to a civil day, which like yowm refers to a 24-hour day. Or it can refer to the natural day meaning sunrise to sunset. Thus, Christ would be either in the grave for a 72-hour period and/or he would be resurrected during the natural day meaning sometime between the third sunrise and sunset. This would exclude a sunset to sunrise timing for the resurrection as is commonly believed today.

In fact, after Christ was laid in his tomb, Pilate was reminded by the Pharisees that Christ had told them [not his disciples], "After three days [*treis hemera*], I will rise again," so he instructed the guards to secure the tomb of Christ "until the third day…." [See Mat. 27:59-66]. Thus, Pilate was clearly referring either to the third 24-hour day or the third day between sunrise and sunset.

It gets more intriguing. When was Christ put into the grave? Was it a Friday afternoon? If so, the resurrection took place on a Monday afternoon. But Monday is not the first day of the week. This would seem to preclude Friday afternoon as the time when Christ was placed in the grave. Let's read the account. We are told Joseph of Arimathaea "... took the body of Jesus... Now in the place where he was crucified, there was a garden: and in the garden a sepulcher never used. There they laid Jesus because of the Jews' preparation day...." [John 19:42].

A preparation day is the day before a sabbath day [Mark 15:42], in which all work was completed, including cooking, etc., so the sabbath could be a day of rest. But a Friday afternoon before sunset doesn't mesh with 72 hours, three days and three nights according to the account. Is it possible there is some other explanation? Yes, very much so. But let's let the gospels tell us their answer rather than making up our own stories that Christ meant parts of three days and nights to get the account to fit from a Friday evening to an alleged Sunday morning resurrection.

John tells us, "The Jews therefore, because it was a preparation day, that the bodies should not remain on the cross on the sabbath day, (for that sabbath was a high *holy* day)...." [John 19:31].

John is telling us this was not a normal weekly preparation day when Christ was put into the grave, but a preparation day for an annual high holy day. A high holy day is one of the seven days of observance given to the children of Israel through Moses. The day before each of these seven annual high holy days is a preparation day too. The nations of Israel began days at sunset. Thus, a high holy day would start at sunset. Now Christ was our sacrificial Passover lamb. The Passover is a preparation day because the day after Passover is a high holy day being the first Day of Unleavened Bread.[1] Thus, Christ was put into the grave before the start of the annual high holy Day of Unleavened Bread at sunset. It was not a weekly sabbath preparation day. [See the book *The Hijacked Elephant* for relevant details on all the high holy days].

We can eliminate Friday before sunset as this is a normal preparation day for the weekly, not an annual sabbath. This is where we use a little deductive reasoning. Christ was in the grave for 72 hours or three days and three nights. And he was placed there **before a sunset**. Therefore, *he would be resurrected before a sunset.* We also know Mary showed up on a Sunday morning, initially when still dark, and he was gone. When was the first sunset prior to early Sunday morning when it was still dark? That's easy. It's Saturday's sunset, which marks the end of the weekly sabbath day. Therefore, Christ was resurrected on the weekly sabbath before sunset.

Three days and nights before this puts Christ into the grave Wednesday before sunset, near the end of the Passover and preparation day for the first high holy day of the year. Using the Greek treis hemera as the words for the three days and three nights, not only was Christ in the grave a full 72 hours in terms of civil days, but accordingly, he was resurrected during the third natural day between sunrise and sunset fulfilling both uses of the word exactly as he said.

[1] The Days of Unleavened Bread, of which the first and seventh days are high holy days, pictured the removing of sin, leaven, out of our lives. [See Exd. 12:19; Lev. 6:17]. Sin results in death. [See Rom. 5:21]. Christ as our Passover sacrifice took us out from under the penalty of sin, death. Christ's death broke the law covenant that Passover day [See Zec. 11:10, 11] whereby sin is imputed. [See Rom. 5:13]. Therefore, that Day of Unleavened Bread after this Passover marked the first day the law covenant was broken and sin was no longer imputed to the children of Israel. Good news indeed. The apostle Paul told us, Christians, "Therefore purge out the old leaven, that you may be a new lump, since *you truly are unleavened*. For indeed Christ, our Passover, was sacrificed for us." [1 Cor. 5:7; also see Heb. 10:1-10]. For a detailed understanding of the significance of Passover and the Days of Unleavened Bread for Christians, see chapter three, *The Hijacked Elephant*. It should be noted that the KJV's use of the word Easter in Acts 12:4 is the mistranslation of the word, *pascha*, or passover.

Guess Who's Coming To Supper?

Christ ate the "Last Supper," with his apostles the night of the Passover. It has become an epochal event in Christianity perhaps best known by Leonardo Da Vinci's popular painting, "The Last Supper." The painting itself has become the focus of many intriguing stories. However, it is best to keep in mind, Leonardo did not make the painting in the first century. He was fifteen centuries too late for that. The painting is absolute fiction, Leonardo's interpretation. Nothing more.

Some other people go so far as to claim Christ did not eat the Passover meal. Yet Christ said to his disciples, "Go into the city to a certain man, and say to him, 'the Master says, 'My time is at hand; I will keep the Passover at your house with my disciples.'" [Mat. 26:18]. "And He sent Peter and John, saying, "Go and prepare the Passover for us, that we may eat." [Luke 22:8]. The last meal with the apostles was a Passover according to Christ. However, the "Last Supper" portion of this evening took place *after the Passover meal was eaten*. It was a separate event meant only for the apostles in attendance.

Much confusion arises because the difference between the Passover and the Days of Unleavened Bread is not clearly understood by many reading the New Testament. The Passover was not a holy day, but a preparation day as we read above. It was the day preceding the first Day of Unleavened Bread, which was a high, or annual, holy day. The Passover meal was eaten beginning at sunset the day before. [See Leviticus 23:5, 6].

For example, if the Days of Unleavened Bread began at sunset on a Wednesday, then Tuesday at sunset would begin Passover. While the Passover is not a holy day, it came to be included with the Days of Unleavened Bread in common usage. As we read in Luke 22, "Now the Feast of Unleavened Bread drew near, which is called Passover." However, in Mark 14, we see the distinction of the two days. "After two days it was the Passover and the Feast of Unleavened Bread." The Feast of Unleavened Bread lasted for seven days, with the first and last days being high holy days or annual sabbaths.

Christ eating this Passover meal with the apostles also has come to be commonly known as the "Lord's Supper." However, these were two separate events with the "Lord's Supper" taking place after the Passover meal. It was a tipping point. The old covenant was about to be broken and the new covenant was shortly to be instituted.

But is the "Lord's Supper" of today a scripture sanctioned practice of the first century event? As Paul wrote to the Corinthians, "Therefore when you come together in one place, it is not to eat the Lord's Supper." Or as the scholarly commentary of Jamieson, Fausset and Brown states, "... there is no such thing as eating the Lord's Supper." This appears to be the more accurate translation.

Isn't it odd, then, that Paul would tell the Christians in the Corinthian church in the first century, "... there is no such thing as eating the Lord's Supper" when churches all over Christianity today practice communion, or eating the "Lord's Supper?" With many denominations, communion or eating of the "Lord's Supper" is a point of doctrine. Was the apostle Paul wrong? Did Christ institute a Christian practice that Passover night?

Christianity's practice comes about from the example in Matthew 26, "And as they were eating, Jesus took bread, blessed and broke it, and gave it to the disciples and said, 'Take, eat; this is my body.' Then He took the cup, and gave thanks, and gave it to them, saying, 'Drink from it, all of you. For this is my blood of the new covenant, which is shed for many for the remission of sins.'" Christians usually take this to mean they should do this too until Christ's second coming.

The key to understanding what Paul meant by "there is no such thing as eating the Lord's Supper" is the word Lord's in Greek. Lord's, in the King James English translation, is a possessive noun. It has an apostrophe "s" at the end of the word. This would infer it is Christ's supper. But that's not what Paul meant. He didn't use a possessive noun.

It appears that the King James translators or scribes made a mistake. The word Paul used in 1 Corinthians is the Greek word, *kyriakos*. Kyriakos is an adjective. It is not the noun, *kyrios*. Thus, Paul was describing the type of supper, not whose supper it was. It was a supper attended by lords, plural. The only other use of this word in the Biblical record is Revelation 1:10. Correctly, it reads, "I was in the Spirit on the Lords Day [*or day of the lords, which in context of Revelation is correct, see 1:6 "… made us kings…" or in Greek, basilieus, leaders of the people, lords*], "and I heard behind me a loud voice, as of a trumpet…."

It's the same use as with the House of Lords in England. This doesn't refer to a house belonging to a lord as in the Lord's house. It is a House comprised of lords. Paul was saying the same thing. The portion of the evening in question, after the Passover meal, was comprised of lords. Christ told the apostles, "... that you may eat and drink at my table in my kingdom, and sit on thrones judging the twelve tribes of Israel." Christ made them lords of Israel. They got promoted from apostles to lords. [See Mat. 19:28].

Therefore, the only ones present at that meal were lords, Christ being the Lord of lords. This is why Paul said, "... there is no such thing as eating the Lords supper," because it was a one time event in the early part of the first century, and it was meant only for those lords in attendance. We can't travel back in time to join them. And we weren't invited.

Yet Christians generally believe they should take communion or eat and drink of the body and blood of Christ. But as we just learned, the Lords supper was for a specific group of lords who ate with Christ that night. It was not the Lord's supper implying it is a commandment for every Christian to observe. Who of us will presumptuously step forward to tell Christ he or she qualifies to sit on the thrones of Israel judging them along with the other lords? Anyone? If we partake of "communion," that's exactly what our actions are saying.

We should heed the words of Paul. "What! Do you not have houses to eat and drink in? Or do you *despise* the church of God and *shame* those who have nothing? What shall I say to you? Shall I praise you in this? *I do not praise you...* Therefore whoever eats this bread or drinks this cup of the Lord in an unworthy manner *will be guilty of the body and blood of the Lord."* [1 Cor. 11:27]. Unless we're one of those worthy apostles reincarnated, we might want to reevaluate partaking of the "Lord's Supper."

Another reason Paul said, "… there is no such thing as eating the Lords supper" is that there was a *timing element* to it that Christ gave the lords. It wasn't a forever commandment. Remember, Christ ate the Passover meal the night before his crucifixion. And as he said to the scribes and Pharisees, he would be in the grave three days and three nights. With this in mind, Paul tells us, "In the same manner He also took the cup *after supper,* saying, This cup is the new covenant in my blood. Do this <u>*as often*</u> *as you drink*, in remembrance of me. For <u>*as often*</u> as you eat this bread and drink this cup [*wine*], you make known *the Lord's* [*kyrios*, the possessive noun] *death till He come.*" [1 Cor. 11:26].

It should be noted that the day after Passover began the first holy feast of the sacred year, the Days of Unleavened Bread. The bread the apostles would be eating often until Christ returned from the dead was without leavening or flat bread. It was not a normal leavened loaf of bread that we use to make sandwiches.

The new covenant only came into effect after Christ's death and resurrection from the dead. Thus, this Passover was still under the authority of the Old Covenant. And the *you* Paul references Christ directing his remarks to are the lords in attendance after the Passover meal with Christ, not Christians millennia later. Unless, of course, we believe Christ hasn't been resurrected and is still dead. And then we'd need to do this <u>*as often*</u> as we eat bread and drink wine, not just on Sundays.

In essence, Christ's command was a homework assignment for the apostles, the lords. Christ did this to keep the lords in remembrance of him. While in hindsight, we take his resurrection for granted, this would be the first time in years that the apostles would be without Christ in their daily lives. He realized their faith would be put to the test. So Christ gave them a simple repetitive task to help keep them in remembrance. As often as they ate bread and/or drank wine, from the Passover meal *until he came back from the dead*, the lords were to do just that. This was necessary for them to do because the apostles did not know Christ would be resurrected in three days and three nights. As John noted, when the apostles first showed up at Christ's tomb, they saw it was open. "For as yet they knew not the scripture, that he must rise again from the dead." What was their assumption? Christ's body had been stolen and moved someplace else, not that he was resurrected. [See John 20:9-19].

After the Passover meal, Christ gave the lords, a repetitive task to perform in his absence or until he returned from the dead, to keep them in remembrance of him. Repetitive reinforcement is a technique used by companies and individuals in business and education. And in case you were wondering, it's the same technique employed today in informercials.

How long did the lords have to do this? Given that Christ was 72 hours in the grave, and that their Passover meal likely finished by midnight, the lords did this for about three and a half days. When they saw Christ again after the resurrection, *till He comes back from the dead,* the lords once again ate a meal with Christ. They no longer needed to be in remembrance of Christ's death, for he was now resurrected from the dead and stood before them.

However, they still had to wait to drink wine with Christ again. "But I say to you, I will not drink of this fruit of the vine from now on until that day when I drink it new with you in my Father's kingdom." If the "Lords supper," including the drinking of wine, was a forever commandment for all Christians, then why is Christ himself waiting to drink it new again with the lords in his Father's kingdom? If anything could be gotten from this, it is that Christians should abstain from drinking wine until Christ's second coming. But this is not necessary either. Christ's remarks were to his lords only.

So who was commanded to eat and drink in remembrance of Christ, to make known the Lord's death? The apostles, the lords. And how long were they to do this? Until he returned from the dead. And when did Christ return from the dead? It was about three and half days after the Passover meal. So how long were the lords to eat bread and drink wine in remembrance of Christ? About three and a half days. Is it now possible for any of us to partake of the Lords supper? Nope. "For there is no such thing as eating the Lords supper."

When we look at the "Last Supper," the supper of lords, we should view it in its proper context, respect it for what it was, and focus on those things Christ said Christians should be doing lest we be guilty of the body and blood of our Lord.

A Christmas Message

The Love of the Truth

In love, there is truth. In greed and lust, there is deceit.

We want our government leaders to champion our traditional democratic values and culture, the liberty and way of life that strikes a resounding cord within us. Yet if we were told what *we, the people,* needed to do to attain this state of wellness, we'd balk at doing so. Why?... because we've become indifferent. No longer feeling empowered to shape our lives in any meaningful way, we resign ourselves, tolerating lies and fables in place of the truth, most notably at airports, during election years and each year regarding the ever expanding Christmas tradition, which has become so deeply rooted in our society on so many levels.

We even have an official national Christmas tree. Being politically correct, it is surrounded by 56 little Christmas trees, representing 50 states, five territories and one for the District of Columbia. This annual three week long tradition, begun in 1923, is the Pageant of Peace despite the ongoing undeclared wars in which the US is engaged. Are we Christians even aware Christ said, "Do not think that I came to bring peace on Earth. *I did not come to bring peace* but *a sword.*" [Mat. 10:34]. Perhaps this event should be renamed the Pageant of the Sword. At least this would be in keeping with what Christ actually said and what we do.

Our society today is a direct result of what we've allowed it to become and continue to willingly embrace.

It's blowback, the negative consequence of cause and effect. Evangelicals, at the Third Lausanne Congress on World Evangelization in October 2010, were frantic, warning that people are abandoning the traditional churches and atheism is becoming the new religion. No wonder.

Our Christian actions, in terms of time and money, confirm we already prefer the mythical god Santa Claus, still embraced and celebrated with their children by these very same evangelicals, over Christ, in large part due to the irrelevancy of what is passed off by mainstream Christianity as the "gospel." [See the chapter *What Exactly is the Gospel?*]. If these same evangelicals genuinely claim to speak and live the truth, it would seem logical that they would denounce Santa Claus and the entire Christmas myth. Yet, they wonder why people are turning away from the hypocrisy and futility they see daily in corporate religion. This is not to say individuals are not sincere. But sincerely believing a fable does not make it the truth.

However, we would do well to be introspective rather than look to politicians who spin deceit into the appearance of truth to get elected, or to "Christian" leaders who have become ignorant. As Jeremiah put it, "For the shepherds have become brutish [*stupid*], and Jehovah they have not sought. Therefore, they have not acted wisely, and all their flock is scattered." [Jer. 10:21, YNG].

A straightforward case in point, a multitude of churches still display a nativity scene showing wise men at the manger. Yet it is so clear in the second chapter of the New Testament, Matthew two, that they didn't show up until upwards of two years later when *Christ was a young child living in a house!* While this may seem like a trivial point of fact, it is huge in principle. We either love the truth or we don't. [Gal. 5:9]. For those who are judicious regarding these matters, this season consider giving yourself, your children, and if you have them, your grandchildren the gift of the love of the truth.

There is a square one in all this if we choose to extricate ourselves from the escalating and pervasive holiday morass and make a clean start. Our daily lives can have relevancy, provided we have the resolve to make a change, no longer settling for the status quo. And it begins with simply knowing the truth of who we Christians are in the Biblical record. It is contained in Christ's very direct and simple statement. "I am not sent *except to* the lost sheep of the House of Israel." [Mat. 15:24]. In fact, Christ specifically instructed the twelve apostles, when he sent them out, not to go to the Gentiles, but "go rather to the lost sheep of the House of Israel." [Mat. 10:5, 6].

At first blush, this is completely foreign to our historical perspective of Christianity, which just goes to show how far off the path we've wandered from our first century roots. Our children know more about the imaginary Santa Claus and his reindeer than they truthfully know about Christ and his apostles. Yet, are we to believe Christ was ignorant of what he was saying or worse, lying when he made this statement about the House of Israel?

Secondly, according to the New Testament, it is the God of the living, *our Father*, who is the Savior of all men or mankind [Greek, *anthropos*, 1 Tim. 4:10], and not his Son Christ. [See Mat. 16:16; see the chapter *What About Everyone Else?*].

And does not Christ himself instruct us that when we pray, it is to our Father? And whose "kingdom come..." whose "will be done on earth as it is in heaven?" Was Christ wrong here too? Contrary to the specious nature of what we've come to believe, our Father sent Christ for a very specific purpose to a specific group of people, you and me... the House of Israel.

It's probable that few today have even heard of the House of Israel, not to be confused with the nation-state of Israel, or the Jews, who Biblically, are the House of Judah. They are two entirely different Biblical entities. Theologically, it's as if the House of Israel was made of the element gallium and somewhere between the last page of the Old Testament and the first page of the New Testament, it was dipped into a cup of warm water, vanishing before our very eyes. [See the book *The Disappearing Spoon*, p.54, Sam Kean, 2010].

Knowing our true Biblical identity puts us back on the right path of insight and relevancy in life. It makes new the entire Biblical record, providing us with the understanding of the two thousand year old original message lost along the way since it was delivered to our ancestors of the House of Israel in the first century. Yet, instead of Christians taking Christ at his word [now there's a concept for you], many take the ubiquitous John 3:16 out of context and run with it assuming it means something it does not. It's highly probable that it is the most misused verse in the New Testament. "For God so loved *the world* that He gave His only begotten Son, that whoever believes in Him should not perish but have everlasting life." [See the chapter *Mirror, Mirror On The Wall*]. Not knowing our true Biblical identity has erroneously taken us down a far and wide path to Santa's snowy doorstep. [Mat. 7:13, 14].

The Holidays
A Christmas Message

So, lo and behold, here we are in a very large, complicated mess, with the past decade costing us trillions in war related expenditures, not to mention the deleterious wars, both foreign and domestic, that affect society in general and families and friends in particular. With state governments bankrupt, very high unemployment rates, coupled with trillions of dollars in lost housing values the past few years, plus the millions of people in the US who've lost their homes, with all those chimneys for Santa to slide down, and others who are close to it, so that as the Christmas season grows longer year by year, our situation seems to grow corresponding worse. Collectively, we've managed to garner a sock full of coal. I wonder why.

By the way, the correct context of John 3:16 is contained within the entirety of the Biblical record, which is rooted in the promises made back in the book of Genesis and addressed in the New Testament. Before we address John 3:16, answer this question, "Is Christ or the Antichrist a liar?" Now answer this too, "Do Christians believe Christ was sent only to the lost sheep of the House of Israel as he made bluntly clear to a **gentile** woman?" If we believe the Antichrist to be the liar, and we don't believe Christ was being completely truthful when he said he was sent only to the lost sheep of the House of Israel, who, exactly, is it we believe? By default, it looks likes Santa Claus again.

The "yes, buts" with their disingenuous understanding will hurriedly run down the path to John 3:16, to show that Christ came to save the whole world. Of course, if you've read many of the preceding chapters in *The Curious Elephant* and the preceding two *Elephant* books, you will realize the Greek word world here is not *anthropos*, meaning mankind, nor *oikoumene*, the inhabited Earth, but it is the word *kosmos* which refers, correctly in context of the Biblical record, to a harmonious arrangement, order or covenant rather than a world full of people. In its greatest manifestation, the kosmos is the totality of *God's plan*.

As we read in John 3:19, "And this is the *condemnation* that light [*the truth through Christ, which leads to life*] is come into the world [*kosmos*], and men [*anthropos*] loved darkness [*lies and deceit, John 8:44, that lead to death*] rather than light because their *deeds* were evil." This is not only applicable with theological issues, but it is rather apparent in secular issues, as recent events have shown.

In the context of John 3, we see that kosmos, translated as world, and men, or mankind, are not one in the same. God's plan, in context, was corrupted by evilness, which is authored by Satan and is why the House of Israel was divorced to begin with. Adam and Eve had the same problem. God's plan for us is corrupted by lies and deceit when we stray from his truth. Satan is the destroyer. His plan, or world, is the corruption of that which God has put in place. Christ brought victory, ultimately bringing God's plan to fruition in the establishment of the kingdom of God on Earth. "And the great dragon was cast out, that old serpent called the Devil and Satan, which deceives the whole *world*...." [Rev. 12:9; also 1 Cor. 15:57; Isa. 25:6-9]. The word world here is *oikoumene* meaning the inhabited earth.

As part of God's plan, his harmonious arrangement, the kosmos, the House of Israel has a unique relationship with Christ based on the promises of our ancestral covenant. And of course, if we understood this in the context of the Biblical record, and followed its history, rather than Santa on his annual trek across the winter solstice skies [Tts. 1:13, 14], we would realize this. And we would realize that Christ gave us the law *covenant* and the Abrahamic *covenant*. And we would realize that the Abrahamic covenant was made, as we can read in the book of Genesis, with Abraham and his Seed, Christ, as the apostle Paul so clearly pointed out. [See Gal. 3:16-19]. Properly understood, it is this part of the kosmos or harmonious arrangement with Abraham, the Abrahamic covenant, which is referenced in John 3:16. It returns us, the formerly divorced House of Israel, to our deliberate place in God's plan. This is the good news or gospel.

When we realize, for purposes of the covenant made with Abraham and his heirs, [See the chapter *Abraham's Seed and Heirs*] that Abraham's grandson was Israel, and not the entire gentile population of Earth, a little bit of logic goes a long way in helping us understand that Christ was being truthful when he said our Father sent him only to the lost sheep of the House of Israel, nations with national identities today according to the Biblical record. [See Gen. 49]. This bit of relevant information in today's world, lost in large part due to our misreading John 3:16, has disappeared from the collective consciousness of Christian churches as well.

However, we should not be lulled into the false comfort that Christianity, to borrow a recent phrase, is too big to fail. Not only is Christianity today on track to fail, but is on track to fail spectacularly. Bluntly, what we know as Christianity today is on a collision course with its own destruction. This event is commonly referred to as the Apocalypse. And who is it that will visit upon Christianity the horrible events of the Apocalypse? It's none other than Christ himself. [Isa. 63:10]. Poignantly, the Third Lausanne Congress chairman Doug Birdsall said, "We are not here to relive the glory days of previous years but to say 'God do something fresh *in our times*.'" Perhaps we should be careful what we ask for.

"I Myself [*Christ*] will fight against you with an outstretched hand and with a strong arm, even *in anger* and *fury* and *great wrath*." [Jer. 21:5] "All your lovers have forgotten you; They do not seek you; For *I have wounded you* with the wound of an enemy, with the chastisement of a cruel one, for the multitude of your iniquities, your sins have increased." "Alas! For that day is great, So that none is like it; And it is the time of Jacob's [*all Israel's*] trouble...." [Jer. 30:14, 7]. Seems like the Pageant of the Sword is not only doable, but a given.

Notice this is not referred to as the time of the Gentile's trouble for the simple reason that the harmonious arrangement or covenant referenced by John was made with Abraham and Christ. [See Mat. 1:1]. And the reason why the Book of Apocalypse or Revelation is so difficult for Christians to understand is that we don't understand our place in Biblical history. If we did, then we would understand our place in Biblical prophecy. Discerning our place in Biblical prophecy, we would hasten with all haste to ditch Santa and all the Christmas folderol. Alas, all this falls on deaf ears because we Christians refuse to take Christ at his word. Instead, our deeds show we prefer the familiar and comfortable mendacity of Santa and our decorated pine trees. [Read the chapter *Christ Against Christians?*].

To put this into perspective as to why it is so important that we follow the truth as set out in the Biblical record, rather than our personal opinions, it goes to the heart and core of why Christ became our, the House of Israel's Savior, as opposed to all the people in the world. Rather than put forth our own reasons why we think he did or didn't do this, let see what the Biblical record, which is one book written for the same people, says.

As we find written in the prophecy of Isaiah, "... the great goodness toward the **House of Israel**, which he [*Christ*] has bestowed on them according to his mercies, and according to the multitude of his loving kindnesses. For he said, Surely they [*the House of Israel*] are my people, **children that will not lie**: so **He was their Savior**." [Isa. 63:7, 8].

First, we see in the Biblical record that our Lord, Christ, has bestowed great goodness and mercies according to the multitude of, not just kindness towards the House of Israel, but also his loving kindnesses. And it was Christ who pointed out that "Greater love [Greek, *agape*] has no one than this, than to lay down one's life for his friends [Greek, *philos*]." [John 15:13].

Christ also made the indisputable point in the Old Testament that the House of Israel *are **my** people*, which together with the plain statement by Christ in the New Testament, "I am not sent *except to* the lost sheep of the House of Israel," should give us a big clue as to whom Christ was truly sent.

Why are we of the House of Israel Christ's people? Because Christ said, they are children that *will not lie*, or deal falsely as the Hebrew verb *shaqar* means. And because the children of the House of Israel will not lie or deal falsely, Christ did what? He was our, the House of Israel's, Savior, which takes us back to square one.

Theologically, then, the House of Israel has moved from being children who will not lie to our situation today in which we don't even know we are the House of Israel much less what is the truth. Instead, we lie to our children about Santa Claus and the gifts he allegedly brings them. The true gifts of Santa are our ignorance, lack of prudence and love of the lie. Therefore, we shouldn't be too surprised that many young adults are taking the atheist route. If our elders lied to us about Santa Claus and the gifts he supposedly brought us as young children, how can we be sure they aren't lying to us now about Christ and the gift of the Holy Spirit? [Pro. 22:6]. Unwittingly, we have trained our children well.

The core question we need answered is why, specifically, did the House of Israel need Christ to be our savior and not the whole world? It's because the House of Israel, and the House of Israel *only*, was divorced from God, excluded from the covenant promises, which are part of God's plan. Excepting the House of Judah, no other people on Earth were included in the law covenant, or are the beneficiaries of the covenant promises made with Abraham. And, it was because of Solomon's less than exemplary reign as king of all Israel, that all Israel was split into two houses, the House of Judah, the Jews, and the House of Israel, who are all the other sons of Israel excepting the Levites who were priests for both houses.

The Holidays
A Christmas Message

A couple centuries or so after this split, we read in Jeremiah, "Then I saw that for all the causes for which backsliding [*House of*] Israel had committed adultery, I had put her away and given her a certificate of divorce; yet her treacherous sister [*House of*] Judah did not fear, but went and played the harlot also." [Jer. 3:8].

The House of Israel was divorced. Our ancestors, being divorced, were the only people outside the covenant agreement made with Abraham and all Israel. The only way to restore the harmonious arrangement or agreement and covenant promises for us beginning with our ancestors in the first century, the House of Israel, was to get us from under the penalty of death of the Mosaic covenant. And the only way to get us from under this covenant to the Abrahamic covenant [the *kosmos*, John 3:16] was to fulfill the terms of the law covenant on our behalf. And there is only one way the new covenant could come into effect for us.

"And for this reason He [*Christ*] is the Mediator of the new [*Abrahamic*] covenant, by means of death, *for the redemption of the transgressions under the first covenant*, that those who are called may receive the promise of the eternal inheritance." The apostle Paul makes it very clear here. Christ gave his life to redeem those who transgressed the first covenant. Who was under the first or law covenant, all the gentiles of the world or all twelve nations of Israel? [See the chapters *The Tale of Two Covenants* and *Galilee of the Gentiles*].

The apostle Paul continues, "For where there is a testament, there must also of necessity be the death of the testator. For a testament is in force after men are dead, since it has no power at all while the testator lives. Therefore not even the first [*law*] covenant was dedicated without blood. For when Moses had spoken every precept to all the people according to the law, he took the blood of calves and goats, with water, scarlet wool, and hyssop, and sprinkled both the book itself and all the people, saying, 'This is the blood of the covenant which God has commanded you.'" [Heb. 9:15-20].

And this was the covenant, according to the Biblical record, under which the House of Israel, and the House of Israel *only*, was put away or divorced from God. No other nations or peoples in "the world" qualify here.

"For Christ has not entered the holy places made with hands, which are copies of the true, but into heaven itself, now to appear in the presence of God for us; not that He should offer Himself often, as the high priest enters the Most Holy Place every year with blood of another-... so Christ was offered once to bear the sins of many. [*Sin being the transgression of the law covenant made only with Israel, 1 John 3:4; many*, Greek, *polus*, meaning many, and not all as in all the world]. To those who eagerly wait for Him, He will appear a second time, apart from sin, for salvation." [Heb. 9:24, 25, 28].

Thus Christ, who was sent only to the lost sheep of the House of Israel, many people to be sure, but not all people, was telling the truth. There was a testament or covenant, which in this case was the law covenant, under which only the House of Israel was divorced. Christ broke that law covenant as we can read in the Old Testament prophecy of Zechariah.

"And I took my staff, Beauty, and cut it in two, that I might break the [*law*] covenant which I had made with the people

[Hebrew, '*am, kinsmen of Israel, Exd. 24:3-8*]. And the LORD said to me, 'Throw it to the potter, that princely price they set on me.' So I took the thirty pieces of silver and threw them into the house of the LORD for the potter. Then I cut in two my other staff, Bonds, that I might break the brotherhood between Judah and Israel." [Zec. 11:12-14].

"And [*Judas*] said [*to the chief priests*], 'What will you give me, and I will deliver him [*Christ*] unto you? And they covenanted with him for thirty pieces of silver.'" [Mat. 26:15]. It is interesting that Christ was betrayed by Judah, as it reads in Greek, as the bonds of brotherhood that were broken were between the House of Judah and the House of Israel exactly as Christ said. But it was not the descendants of Judah who put Christ to death. Read chapter six, *The Blind Man's Elephant*, for details very relevant for us today.

While Israel was divorced, the children of Judah, the Jews, did not suffer this lot but were taken captive about a century and a half later by the Babylonians. "Solomon's" temple was destroyed and the Ark of the Covenant never returned to an earthly temple.

Thus, the House of Israel was divorced from God, cast outside the promises of the Abrahamic covenant, the harmonious arrangement, the kosmos that God so loves. In a word, they were lost. They sat in darkness, children without light until Christ ransomed them with his life fulfilling the law covenant on behalf of the House of Israel, and first granting to our ancestors the Holy Spirit according to the terms of the Abrahamic covenant, which is of faith and not of the works of the law.

And on the *very first day of Christianity*, we read in the New Testament, which by now should not be surprising, "Therefore let **all the House of Israel** know assuredly that God [*who sent Christ to begin with*] has made this Jesus, whom you crucified, both Lord and Christ [*Savior*]... Then Peter said to them [*House of Israel*], Repent, and let every one of you be baptized in the name of Jesus Christ for the remission of sins; and *you shall receive* the gift of the Holy Spirit." [Acts 2:36, 38]. This was the first time in history that the gift of the Holy Spirit was made available, and it was available to the House of Israel, exactly to whom Christ said he was sent. [See John 15:26].

It's appropriate then that we should consider here that the House of Israel is even warned about staying away from Christmas trees. "Hear the word which the LORD speaks to you, *House of Israel*. Do not learn the way of the heathens; Do not be dismayed at the signs of heaven [*winter solstice, December 25, the date chosen by the Roman emperor Constantine in the 4th century*], For the heathens are dismayed at them. For the customs of the heathen are futile; For one cuts a tree from the forest, The work of the hands of the workman, with the ax. They decorate it with silver and gold; They fasten it with nails and hammers so that it will not topple." [Jer. 10:1-3]. This is why those supermarket parking lot trees don't fall over. In case you were wondering, the US national Christmas tree, a Colorado Blue Spruce, was transplanted from Pennsylvania. [However, it was destroyed in a storm Saturday, 19 February 2011].

Where are we today, then, in light of this? First, the House of Israel is told by our Lord not to learn the way of the heathen, cutting trees out of the forest, decorating them with ornaments at the winter solstice. Then Christ emphatically said he didn't come to bring peace on Earth, but a sword. So what does Christianity do? We learn the way of the heathen, we decorate our trees with gold and silver colored ornaments, and then during the winter solstice period, our national leaders institute a three week long event, with a national tree surrounded by 56 other little ones, supposedly honoring Christ, and then we name it the Pageant of Peace!

Irrationally, we don't believe Christ was sent only to the lost sheep of the House of Israel as he said. Instead, we not only have learned the ways of the heathen, but we have far exceeded anything they would have imagined, again contrary to what we are told by our Lord and Savior. We've become anti-Christ Christians. Hence, we find ourselves in our current predicament. And why is this?

Isaiah the prophet has our answer. "But they [*House of Israel*] rebelled, and **vexed his Holy Spirit**, therefore *he* [Christ] *was turned to be their enemy*, and *he fought against them*." [Isa. 63:10].

Not only has current day Christianity rebelled by dealing falsely with our heritage, we have lost sight of it and the truth. We don't believe Christ. We don't take him at his word. No wonder our children are becoming atheists. And if we don't follow Christ, who is it we follow? Again, it looks like the mythical Santa Claus.

And because we don't take Christ at his word, we have come to embrace the deceits and lies. Thus, we are a people who once would not lie, to become people who deal falsely with the truth. While we embrace Santa Claus, we have turned our backs to Christ despite the superficial lip service we give. And for the most part, we really don't care. [Rev. 3:15-19]. Because of this, our Savior has told us he has become our enemy. And as long as we continue on this path, we are destined to pay an increasingly heavy price for our willful ignorance.

The reason for our date with the apocalypse is simple. "... because they did not receive **the love of the truth**, that they might be saved. And for this reason God will send them strong delusion, that they should believe the lie, that *they all may be condemned who did not believe the truth* but *had pleasure in unrighteousness*." [2 Ths. 2:10-12].

I would be remiss if I didn't bring this to you especially at this time of the year. After all, the apostle Paul admonished us, "Lie not to one another, seeing that you have put off the old man with his deeds; and have put on the new [*baptism and receiving of the Holy Spirit as Peter told the House of Israel on that first day of Christianity*], which is *renewed in knowledge after the image of him that created him*." [Col. 3:9, 10].

What will we, the redeemed House of Israel, do this Christmas season? Receive the love of the truth or, continue placing our faith in fables and lies, "vexing His Holy Spirit" with its very real consequences?

Merry Christmas? Don't count on it.

P.S. Biblical ID in 3-D

I am continually amazed that professed Christians don't believe Christ when he makes plain statements. Rather than trust Christ explicitly, we boorishly assume we are right, and proceed to use other verses, evidently out of context, to show that Christ obviously didn't know what he was talking about or was just plain wrong. Else how do we explain our disbelief of Matthew 15:24?

Therefore, we need to ask ourselves, why is it so important for Christians to believe Christ when he said I am sent [by God the Father] only to the lost sheep of the House of Israel?

Imagine attempting to watch a 3-D movie with just our own eyes. Everything on the screen would be a jumbled blur. It would be so frustrating to continue, that we'd probably get up and leave. But what happens when we pop on a pair of those special 3-D glasses? Suddenly, everything on the screen becomes acutely clear. The action jumps out at us putting us right in the middle of these events. The movie has much more relevance for us as active participants rather than merely being confused observers.

Understanding that Christians are the descendants of the House of Israel, and that Christ was telling us the truth about being sent only to the House of Israel is like putting on a pair of Biblical 3-D glasses.

Suddenly, the Biblical record comes into focus with alarming clarity; the big picture jumps out at us, helping us see that we are vital participants in the events written about and for us.

We can actually read our own history in astonishment, for the first time making sense of historical events as well as those warnings for us in Biblical prophecy.

We need to be well read in the truth, not in the lies. Our erudite shepherds would be astounded to know how deep our ignorance runs and how much understanding and insight we are missing. [Heb. 5:12-14]. The events of the past 2000 years have a completely new meaning and relevance when seen in the light of the love of the truth. How stupid we are to cling to the lies and deceits of the Santa Claus season. It's perfectly reasonable why Christ has turned against us in great anger and fury. No longer children who will not lie, we pleasure in the desecration of his sacrifice for us.

Refusing this knowledge, we've become disinterested observers of Christianity, left only to dimly guess at our own prophetic future until, too late, these events come crashing down on our bewildered heads. However, with this insight, we manifestly see the path we should be traveling, which is exactly the one Christ told us of from the beginning in the first century.

Yes, Virginia, there is a square one. It's time we go back.

The Blind Man's Elephant

Atheistic Phone Apps And Yellow Pencils

The debate over whether or not God exists has been around for a long time. Now there are phone apps for those who wish to engage in the debate, which usually centers on the idea put forward by atheists that "You can't prove God exists." This in turn usually gets a professed Christian's dander all riled up. The sparks fly from this point forward leading to strife and contention while each participant attempts to prove they are right. It's a bit like debating the outcome of the immovable object versus the irresistible force.

Other times the debate takes a less obvious approach involving the validity of the Biblical record. Their point is that it is written by men, and has flaws. Most often, this is put forth by someone, usually second or third hand, supposedly offering up what appears to be a contradiction, and then in total faith jumps to the conclusion that if they can't explain it, it has to be an error. But as Sherlock Holmes said, "It is a capital mistake to theorize in advance of the facts."

It never ceases to amaze me how proclaimed atheists take a quote or quotes out of context from the Biblical record, draw a false conclusion, and then move on with great haste to proclaim they have found an error in the Biblical record. Therefore, they say, as there are falsehoods in this record, nothing can be believed. Of course, if this is a display of their deductive abilities, then no wonder they are atheists.

I bring this up because recently a phone app for atheists was released apparently in response to Christian apps used to rebut atheistic claims. Debating and arguing the existence or non-existence of God is, in my opinion, an exercise worthy of pre-school. I've never known these debates to end in conversion of one party or the other. And I'm not sure which party is more insecure about their beliefs in these arguments. Note to Christians: chill out. God doesn't need us to defend him. [2 Sam. 6:6, 7; Rev. 6:15, 16]. And God doesn't need anyone to believe he exists for him to exist.

In a New York Times article, the author of this atheistic phone app is quoted as saying, "If Jacob saw the face of God (in Genesis 32:30), and God said, "No man shall see me and live" (in Exodus 33:20), then 'which one is the liar?' he asks. His conclusion: If we know the Bible has content that is false, how can we believe any of it?"

From my perspective with decades of study and research as a theologian, this appears to be an embarrassing display of ignorance. It is even more so for Christians if they don't know the answer. First, the NYT article states the author's credentials as being a musician and real estate investor. No disrespect, everyone is entitled to his or her personal opinions, but I do not consider this to be a credible theological source, as personal opinion is not fact. Too many Christians, however, suffer from this same malady as well albeit on the other side of the coin. [See the chapter *What Exactly Is The Gospel?*].

Next, taking statements out of context is always dangerous and usually erroneous, which is the case here. The normal mistake made by those not familiar with the English text of the Biblical record is that many different words in the Hebrew or Greek manuscripts are translated as one word in English or one word in the Hebrew or Greek is translated into many English words.

For example, the Greek word *ethnos* in the New Testament is translated into English as heathen, gentiles, nations or people. Taking any one of these translated words out of context and then unequivocally declaring that we know something is the boldness of ignorance.

In the case of the example cited in the Times article, the word God in the Genesis 32:30 verse is the Hebrew word *elohiym.* Elohiym is a plural noun very much like the word family. In this case, we could say the family name is God. And as in all our families, it consists of more than one person. We can have a father, a mother, a son or a daughter, an uncle, an aunt, a grandfather or niece or nephew. It would be a huge mistake to assume all these family members are the same person even though they may share the same family name.

In the Exodus 33:20 example, however, the Hebrew word here for God is not *elohiym*, rather it is *Yehovah*. So if we merely look at the two verses, even out of context, with these two words in place, "Jacob saw the face of elohiym" versus "Yehovah said, No man shall see me and live," then the correct logical conclusion would be that possibly there are two different entities involved, and therefore no contradiction.

The problem with these verses is in the eye of the beholder not in the text itself. Thus, a conclusion declaring that these two verses, when contrasted in English, constitute a lie, and saying we *know* the Bible has content that is false is a wildly reckless and erroneous deduction. And then jumping to the conclusion that the entire Biblical record is in doubt based on this faulty information and reasoning, well, this is truly deficient logic to say the least. The prospect that Christians would feel threatened by this argument is even scarier.

The next point is that the verse in Exodus is taken out of context. Prior to the quoted verse, Moses, who had conversed with Yehovah up to this point, wanted Yehovah to show himself in all his *glory*, the Hebrew word *kabowd*. "And he [*Moses*] said, I beseech you, show me your glory." Yehovah's response was that if he were to reveal himself to Moses in his full spiritual power and majesty, Moses, as a physical being, would not survive.

I don't claim to know the physics or dynamics involved, but when we consider the existing power and energy in the created physical universe, even in one small black hole, or with gamma ray bursts associated with neutron stars, as relayed to us by credible scientists, this is well within the realm of scientific possibility. After all, we feeble mortals can't even climb Mt. Everest without protective gear and expect to survive. [See Heb. 12:20, 21].

However, the statement in Exodus says nothing about Yehovah revealing himself to man in a form other than his full majesty, which we know from other examples in the Biblical text is perfectly survivable. [See Gen. 17:1; also the chapter *The Tie That Binds*]. Our author of the atheistic phone app misses this point entirely. It goes to show that any verse in the Biblical record can be taken out of context and turned into something it was not intended to be. To answer the question posed, however, the liar is the one who misrepresents the facts.

While these two verses may superficially appear to make the point intended by the phone app creator, the inaccurate assumptions are not based on fact. As we noted above, "It is a capital mistake to theorize in advance of the facts." And this is a prime example of why Mr. Holmes' axiom is spot on.

As to the arguments over whether or not God exists, merely because one cannot prove the existence of God does not mean he doesn't exist. To conclude such is faulty logic. For example, let's say we have an "apencilist," that is a blind person who doesn't believe yellow pencils exist much less believe that people miraculously can communicate using them without speaking. If you have a yellow pencil, you cannot prove to this blind person that, indeed, you have a yellow pencil in your hand. No matter what you say, you can't do it. If you could, then all one needs to do is substitute the word God for yellow pencil in your argument, and voila, God exists. No more philosophical discussions required.

But you can't prove the yellow pencil exists to a blind person. In referring to our classical state of existence, not its quantum state, does this mean the yellow pencil in your hand doesn't exist? No. It merely means the person is blind and can't see it. Would you seriously consider debating a blind person if he or she said they didn't believe your yellow pencil existed? So it is with the existence of God. Some people are blind in the flesh, others are blind in the Spirit. [Rom. 8:5] And if we were discussing the colors of a sunset as opposed to the colors of pencils, what benefit is there to either party in debating the beauty of a sunset?

As the apostle Paul pointed out, "And even as they did not like to retain God in their knowledge [*atheists*], God gave them over to a debased mind, to do those things which are not fitting; being filled with all unrighteousness, fornication, wickedness, covetousness, maliciousness; full of envy, murder, **debate**..." [Rom. 1:28, 29].

Rather than vainly debate the existence of God, stirring up strife and contention, the better course of action is to show our faith in our daily lives by the way we live life. And then when someone truthfully inquires about why we do what we do, be prepared with answers from the Biblical record. Everyone has to walk his or her own path in life whether it is as a non-believer or a believer. And, as we all know, actions speak louder than words.

Paul's advice to Timothy was, "Let no one despise your youth, but *be an example to the believers* in word [Greek, *logos* meaning his speech], in conduct, in love, in spirit, in faith, in purity." [1 Tim. 4:12].

This is good advice for all Christians today.

P.S. Freedom of Religion Versus Worship

Whether or not the participants realize it, the debate between atheists and Christians is a function of the principle of the freedom of religion, or the freedom to believe or not. It is choice and the freedom to make choices for one's self. In the US, this is guaranteed in the Constitution, "Congress shall make no law respecting the establishment of religion, or prohibiting the free exercise thereof; or abridging the freedom of speech, or of the press; or the right of the people to peaceably assemble, and to petition the Government for the redress of grievances."

Of course, this just limits the Congress. It says nothing about the Supreme Court nor the Executive branch. Recently, it has been noted in Christian media that the US President and Secretary of State have been using the term "freedom of worship," rather than freedom of religion. The PATRIOT Act has already abridged some of the Bill of Rights. So where might this not so subtle change lead?

First, freedom of religion is about choosing one's beliefs and being able to follow them. We could say it is pro-choice. The act of worshipping and the freedom to choose who we worship are two different beasts. In North Korea, the people have the freedom to worship; it's just that they have to worship the current dictator or his deceased father. Otherwise, they face death or imprisonment. For the time being, we enjoy the freedom to choose whether to be an atheist, a Christian, a Buddhist or anything else for that matter under the protection of the Constitution.

However, the secular definition of worship can be defined as the honoring of a deity or an idol. When someone tells us who we can worship, we no longer have the freedom of religion, but we have freedom of worship. It would not be surprising that in the future, the US Supreme Court interprets the first amendment establishment of religion as the right to worship.

"He was granted power to give breath to the image of the beast, that the image of the beast should both speak and *cause as many as would not **worship*** the image of the beast to be killed." [Rev. 13:5]. Presumably, this includes atheists as well as Christians, who at this point no longer enjoy freedom of religion. [See the chapter *Christ Against Christians?*].

It might be wise to monitor the use of the term "freedom of worship" on the part of government leaders and others. For a look at where this all came from and where it is headed, read chapter six, *The Blind Man's Elephant*. Also see the chapter *Revelation 17*.

Is Genesis 1 A Jolly Good Myth?

There are those who, while believing in a Creator, have a problematic time believing that the account of creation in Genesis 1 is nothing more than a myth; one of the many creation myths found in various cultures. If asked, most often the various reasons put forth usually are not based on any specific criteria or evidence. Most people probably have never really taken the time to carefully look at the specifics of Genesis 1.

This approach may not be too different than what many people in Spain about 1492 assumed: a round Earth was a myth. Columbus was certainly asking for trouble. A round or spherical Earth couldn't be comprehended. A round Earth would mean things would just fly off willy-nilly. Once a ship sailed past a certain point, it would have to fall off. It made no sense. But as ships never fall off the planet, provided they didn't sail too close to the edge and not return from a voyage, then the world must be flat. And on top of this, it even looks flat, provided you don't look too closely at the horizon.

All this was before Newton's scientific discovery of gravity by 1666 [according to various sources, it's a myth that Sir Isaac discovered gravity by watching an apple fall from a tree] as well as centripetal force by 1679, which we know now allows those ships to sail all over the planet without falling off. Genesis 1's account of creation must be much the same for people. It isn't until science catches up with the Biblical record that some people will believe it. So let's take a look at Genesis 1 and see what we can discover in the way of evidence. I believe we'll find enough evidence at this point to give the Genesis account the credit it deserves.

As we'll also find out, science has very recently caught up with another intriguing aspect of Genesis 1's veracity.

But first, let's turn our view to the Earth and the moon. Again, it was only rather recently, historically speaking, that scientists have been able to discover the ages of the Earth, and the moon. However, our concern here for the moment is not the absolute age of the Earth, which is estimated to be about 4.55 billion current Earth years, but rather the age of the Earth relative to that of the moon.

According to rock samples from NASA's Apollo missions, the oldest rocks from the moon are about 4.4 billion years old. This has led scientists to believe that the moon as we know it solidified about 4.4 billion years ago. Thus, the moon is a bit younger than the oldest rocks on Earth by at least 150 million years or more, which is a fair bit of Earth time.

In examining Genesis 1, we discover that on day three, [See chapter four, *The Blind Man's Elephant,* for a discussion of these days], the Earth was formed including the seas and the dry land. [Gen. 1:9-13]. The moon, however, was created on day four of the Genesis account. [Gen. 1:14-19]. The order of creation discovered by scientists is exactly the same order as the account in Genesis 1, although the author who penned the account did it without going to the moon to gather up some rock samples and using sophisticated equipment and tests in order to know the Earth was created before the moon.

Thus, it appears that the creation of the Earth on Genesis day three before the lesser and greater lights on Genesis day four is supported, once again, by scientific evidence.

How is it possible that without the benefit of NASA moon rocks for comparison, the author of Genesis was able to make this determination? Maybe Genesis 1 isn't myth.

Another interesting aspect of the Genesis 1 account of creation are days five and six. This concerns the order in which complex life appeared on Earth. According to an article by Corey Binns in *LiveScience*, 14 August 2007, he wrote, "Ancient four-limbed fish crawled out of the sea. Dinosaurs, insects and mammals took to the air. Our closest relatives straightened their backs and began walking upright on two legs." This is the generally accepted progression of evolution as discovered by scientists. Fish first, flying creatures and then land animals.

But what does Genesis 1 say about this order? In Genesis 1, verse 20 we read about day five, "And God said, Let the waters bring forth abundantly the moving creature that have life, and fowl that may fly above the earth in the open firmament of heaven."

On day six, verse 24 states, "And God said, Let the earth bring forth the living creature after his kind, cattle, and creeping thing, and beast of the earth after his kind: and it was so."

Scientists have discovered that life progressed in exactly the same order as it occurs in Genesis 1. As science supports the Genesis 1 account, it hardly can be considered myth.

What may be the most amazing verification of Genesis 1 by science concerns the first four verses. Let's start in verse one. "In the beginning God created the heaven and the earth. And the earth was without form, and void; and darkness was upon the face of the deep. And the Spirit of God moved upon the face of the waters. And God said, 'Let there be light:' and there was light. And God saw the light, that it was good: and God divided the light from the darkness." [Gen. 1:1-4].

What's interesting is that these verses in the Biblical record, concerning the Genesis account of creation, begin with a fundamental event, separating light from the darkness. This is an important point. Light [matter and energy] was separated from the darkness [dark matter and energy] not the other way around. In other words, first there was the dark, then light was divided or separated, providing the impression that light could possibly be re-absorbed by darkness once again. As light is real and not a scientific myth, then so too the dark matter and energy from which it originated must be real as well.

Now a casual reading of this account in Genesis, perhaps originally written on clay tablets or papyrus thousands of years ago, even before the advent of the ancient technology of manual typewriters, it doesn't seem all that remarkable or significant except when you add in the relatively recent discoveries of high tech science. Namely, it's the suggestion that 70-90% of our universe is made of dark matter, yet we can't even see it. This is not too surprising as everyone knows, when it's really dark, you can't see a thing. Like gravity, which we can't see either, the reason scientists know this dark matter exists is that certain measurements taken in the universe tells us that what they are measuring can't be accounted for, in this case, solely by "light matter."

In a *Discovery News* article by Larry O'Hanlon on 21 August 2006, he says, "The astrophysicists know the visible stars still have the dark matter with them because they weighed the mass in the starry patches by measuring how those patches bend the light from far more distant objects. The more a starry region bends light, the more massive it is."

"In this case, the starry areas in the colliding clusters have far more mass than can be accounted for by visible stars or by interstellar gases - since the stars left the gases behind. The only thing left to explain it is dark matter."

As Astrophysicist Maxim Markevitch of the Harvard-Smithsonian Center for Astrophysics concluded, "This proves in a direct and simple way that dark matter exists."

Thus, science proved that dark matter existed by 2006. In the first few verses of Genesis 1, we knew that dark matter was part of the universe as much as light matter, although for scientists, it may have been a case of "out of sight, out of mind" the past fourteen billion or so years. But let's move on to what is the most intriguing aspect of darkness in relation to "light matter."

In another *Discovery News* article about dark matter by Nicole Gugliucci, 9 May, 2010, she writes, "… most of the evidence points to an undiscovered particle [*WIMP, Weakly Interacting Massive Particle*] that does not interact with "normal" matter or light in any obvious way." [Emphasis added].

This is an intriguing aspect of dark matter that it *does not interact* with "light matter" [normal matter plus light].

It's as if there is a barrier between the two keeping "light matter" particles from getting pulled back into dark matter. Perhaps this is why nothing travels faster than the speed of light in our universe. As we read, "God divided the light *from* the darkness" in Genesis 1.

Of particular interest here is that the English word *divided* in Genesis 1:4 is not one, but is two words in Hebrew. The first Hebrew word is *badal*. Badal means to divide. But the key to the dividing the light from the darkness is the second Hebrew word, *beyn*. It holds the key to the mystery of separating light from the darkness. Beyn is used as a preposition referencing an interval or a space between. In other words, God not only separated light from darkness, but God put an interval or *a space between the light and the dark* to keep them apart. It's not much different than using the space bar on our keyboards to keep wordsapart, or words apart. As we read above, "... the evidence points to an undiscovered particle that does not interact with "normal" matter or light in any obvious way."

As there is an interval or space between darkness and light, then we would not expect the two to interact with each other would we? By definition, a direct interaction between the two would mean they no longer have a space between them. And if that space between dark matter and "light matter" disappeared, "light matter" would no longer be divided from dark matter. All would be darkness once more, and it would signal the end of the universe as we know it. Again, science has discovered what God has created.

The alleged "myth" of Genesis 1 seems to be as follows. Scientists have discovered that the Earth is older than the moon. Days three and four in Genesis 1 says the Earth was created before the moon. No myth.

Anthropologists and evolutionists have discovered life began in the seas, moved to the air and then to land creatures. Days five and six in Genesis 1 have the same order of events taking place. No myth.

Scientists have not only recently discovered dark matter, but that it "does not interact with normal matter or light in any obvious way." We learned that God on day one placed a space, dark energy perhaps, between the darkness and the light to keep them apart. Again no myth.

The major events in Genesis 1 are supported by scientific evidence. Therefore, in answer to our original question, "Is Genesis 1 a jolly good myth?" our answer has to be no. Genesis 1 is not a mythical account of the creation of our universe and life on Earth. It is supported by scientific fact just like gravity and centripetal force support the fact that the Earth need not be flat.

While at first blush, some folks may dismiss the Genesis 1 account as nothing more than another creation myth, science has proven otherwise once again. As Sherlock Holmes said, "When you eliminate the impossible, whatever remains, however improbable, must be the truth."

P.S. "Adam and Eve were Jewish."

A discussion between Stephen Prothero, a Boston University religion scholar, and Stephen Colbert on his televised

"Colbert Nation," concerning the superiority of Christianity versus the world's other religions, Mr. Colbert quipped, "Adam and Eve were Jewish. Check under the fig leaf, my friend."

It may come as a shock to Mr. Colbert, whose theological credentials according to Mr. Prothero's article include teaching Sunday school at his local parish, but Sunday school is not exactly a critical hotbed of theological thought. First, Adam and Eve were not Jewish. It's not even close. Second, checking under the fig leaf would not have revealed a circumcised male organ. Both Mr. Colbert's statements qualify as myth.

Question: Abraham, Israel, and Moses were Jewish. True or false? Answer: false, at least according to the Biblical record. The first time the word Jews is mentioned in the Old Testament or Jewish Bible, the Jews were at war with Israel and Syria [2 Kng. 16:5, 6] about the eighth century BCE.

The term Jew or Jews has come to be applied to just about everyone in the Old Testament. But this is a gross misunderstanding that has lead to lots of confusion by Christians and Catholics. The term Jew comes from just one the twelve sons of Israel, Judah. *Only the descendants of Judah* Biblically can be accurately called Jews.

Adam and Eve preceded Judah by millennia. You'd have to go from Adam and Eve through all the generations to Noah; then through all the generations of Noah to Abraham. Abraham had Isaac who begat Israel who, with his wife Leah, begat Judah. Abraham was Judah's great-grandfather. Israel, Judah's father, as well had eleven other sons with three other wives. So none of the above are Judah's descendants or Jews. Rather they are all his progenitors.

As for Moses being Jewish, well that's not correct either. Moses was a descendant of one of Judah's other eleven brothers, Levi, making Moses a Levite, not a Jew. Thus, the Ten Commandments were not delivered by a Jew, but by a Levite to all twelve sons of Israel including Judah. [See *The Hijacked Elephant*, Appendix One, Most Old Testament Authors Were Not Jewish].

As to what was under Adam's fig leaf, it wasn't circumcised. Circumcision was prescribed only as a covenant condition, first mentioned in the Biblical record in Genesis 17 with Abraham, long after Adam's death. Later, with Moses the law covenant prescribed circumcision as a condition of the law covenant between God and all twelve sons of Israel and their descendants including the one son Judah. Adam would not have been circumcised as the progenitor of all mankind.

While Mr. Colbert's retort was witty, it was fiction. Thus, it would qualify as Genesis myth.

Three Creations: Neanderthal to Adam to Christ

In May 2010, scientists came forward proclaiming that some of us are walking around with varying amounts, one to four percent, of Neanderthal DNA. While this may explain what many of us have long suspected about some of our co-workers, this appears to pose a dilemma for Christians who say that Adam was the first man.

Neanderthals are said to have disappeared about 28,000 years ago, which is quite a bit before the commonly accepted Christian date for Adam's creation about 6000 years ago. Thus, how can Adam be the first man if Neanderthals pre-dated Adam and adamkind has some Neanderthal DNA today? And if we have this DNA in us today, how did it possibly get there, making it through Noah's flood, especially as Adam was created in the image and likeness of God, and Neanderthals definitely weren't? And would this negate the creation story of Adam in Genesis?

Christian media sources have been silent to date about this discovery that modern man has some Neanderthal DNA. This discovery means, obviously, that some Neanderthal DNA is compatible with human DNA, though filtered through intermediary species, which made its way into the modern day human genome. This unsettling news disrupts the commonly believed timeline for creationists and the uniqueness of the creation of man.

How close to human DNA would a hominid have to be to be able to produce viable offspring? Chimps are about 99.6% like humans, but genetically that's too far. Today, modern man's DNA is about 99.9% alike according to geneticists. How close is close enough... 99.8%, 99.7%?

Chromosomes probably would have to be identical in number to produce children that are not sterile. Horses with 64 diploid chromosomes, and donkeys with 62 chromosomes produce sterile mules. Humans have 46 diploid chromosomes, 23 from each parent. Chimps have 48 diploid chromosomes while orangutans have 44 and monkeys have 42.

In the second chapter of *The Blind Man's Elephant,* it clearly shows that when Cain left Adam and Eve and crossed the river leaving Eden, *there is **no Biblical record** of his taking any female, much less a sister with him*. None. It's just not there. Yet, the Biblical record plainly states Cain had offspring.

Religious reasoning basically says Cain had to have left with his sister because if it is any other way, it conflicts with our traditional beliefs about creation. This is another example of mankind projecting onto God our human shortcomings and lack of understanding. It is in the same vein of reasoning that gave us the flat Earth and geo-centric theories of creation.

The Biblical record says Cain had offspring with a female, Hebrew *ishshah*, who likely was a female hominid, and definitely not his sister. The Biblical record shows that Cain's offspring were fertile [Gen. 4:17, 18]. Obviously then, *adamkind* DNA was compatible with *hominid* DNA 6000 years ago. For the creationists reading this, relax, it's better than you think. It's also different than what you think.

All the above concerns, however, place the sole emphasis on our physical container, *the natural body.* But to do so is to completely miss the importance of Adam's creation. This apparent conundrum is discussed in detail in the first chapter of *The Blind Man's Elephant*, "Three Creations Of Life: A Bridge To Understanding."

The significance of Adam's creation is not of the flesh, but rather the significance is of the spirit. When life on land was created on day six according to the account in Genesis, [See chapter four in *The Blind Man's Elephant* for a discussion about the six days of creation], it is stated, *"And God said, Let the earth bring forth the living creature after his kind, cattle, and creeping thing, and beast of the earth after his kind: and it was so."*

Yet with Adam, it is stated, *"And God said, Let us make man in our image, after our likeness...."* Thus, the significance of Adam's creation, what made him the first man, is that he was the first to be made in the image and likeness of God. And as God is not of the dust of the Earth or natural, but is of the spirit, the key is that mankind, as opposed to creaturekind, has a difference that gives life to mortal bodies. That difference is the *spirit of man* as opposed to the spirit of creatures. [See Zec. 12:1].

This noteworthy difference between creaturekind and mankind is apparent at death as Solomon said, "Who knows the spirit of man that goes upward, and the spirit of the beast that goes downward to the earth?" [See Ecc. 3:21; 12:7]. Both the *natural bodies* of animals and mankind, however, return to the dust of the Earth. *Life similarities are of the flesh. Life differences are of the spirit.*

While some people may believe it is our physical appearance that separates us from creatures and makes us "like God," our natural bodies have no preeminence over animals in this regard. "For that which befalls the sons of men befalls beasts; even one thing befalls them: as the one dies, so dies the other; yes, they have all *one breath*; so that a man has no preeminence above a beast: for all is vanity." [Ecc. 3:19; also see Job 34:15]. Our natural bodies and the bodies of animals are the same before God. We all come from the earth and the natural bodies return to the earth.

Even if it was discovered that Neanderthals or some other hominid and modern man had identical DNA, this is only a mortal similarity. Our natural bodies are just vehicles through which our spirit interacts with this "reality" we call life. [See the chapter *Brown Paint: Quantum Potentialities*]. What sets man apart from creatures is of the spirit, the spirit of man.

For mankind, then, life is about choice. Do we choose to follow the way of the flesh, which leads to death or do we choose the way of the Spirit, to elevate our lives following the "narrow way, which leads to life"...? This duality of life is unique to mankind, which provides us a portal to immortality with Christ as the mediator.

The separation of Adam from hominids didn't stop with the spirit of man. There is the third creation of life, a step above the spirit of man that was made manifest in the first century by Christ, the last Adam. [See 1 Cor. 15:45]. This portal is not available to any creature.

"But if the Spirit of him that raised up Jesus from the dead dwell in you, he that raised up Christ from the dead shall *also make alive your mortal bodies by his Spirit* that dwells in you." [Rom. 8:11]. The third spirit that gives life to mortal flesh, the natural body, is the Spirit of God. The apostle Paul's words to the Christians in Rome here are not a reference to being resurrected back into a mortal body. [See 1 Cor. 15:50-54].

The DNA closeness of our modern day natural container with hominids past is spiritually irrelevant. The significance of Adam's creation was the spirit of man. And the significance of a Christian's re-birth, made available by the last Adam, is the Spirit of God. Thus, there are three levels of spiritual consciousness in living creatures. This is where the consequence of life's distinctions is manifested.

When we read or listen to the polarized discussions sure to appear regarding this subject, it would be wise to bear in mind what the apostle Paul said, "For they that are after the flesh do mind the things of the flesh; but they that are after the Spirit the things of the Spirit." [Rom. 8:5].

For a detailed discussion of this subject, read chapters one and two in *The Blind Man's Elephant*.

Life In The 'hood

The latest strategy by those who believe life begins at conception is the drive to create a status designated as "personhood" for embryos. Personhood Kansas was quoted as stating, "As a movement, we know what our goal is: *to have all children in the womb protected by love and law.* It is important that we learn the lessons of history and rely on the moral clarity of our God-given moral law to guide our efforts not on demoralizing legal and moral subterfuge."

While their motives are likely well meaning and good intentioned, and this criticism may initially come across as harsh, their actions appear to be a bit hypocritical, even misdirected, and their theology off center as to when life begins, if using the Biblical record as their source text.

It is a bit hypocritical because their stated goal, "… to have *all children in the womb protected…"* is geared only towards the abortion issue, which from their point of view, is all about not killing those children in the womb. This seems to imply that once we're out, we're on our own when it comes to moral law guiding their efforts. Morally speaking, it seems they do not take into account that the US has the largest military budget in the history of planet Earth, more than all the other countries of the world combined.

This answers the question why a country that is 5% of the world's population outspends the other 95% on its military and doesn't have universal health care to protect all those children in the womb. Those of a conservative political bent who favor "pro-life" are the same ones who mostly favor militarism as a form of foreign policy. Yet, the connection between these two polarities escapes them. Unless of course, the end game is producing more cannon fodder for future wars.

Robert Gates, the former Secretary of Defense, wanted a "substantial increase in the military budget" according to the Fall 2010 issue of *Foreign Policy* magazine, despite the fact the US can't afford to spend money at the current budget levels for weapons to kill people outside the womb *and* take care of its "persons" inside the womb. The "personhood" initiative folks apparently are unmindful of this contradiction, and that each of these same people in Kansas regularly contributes hefty financial sums through federal taxes [apparently more so than billion dollar profit making weapons companies, legally aka individuals, such as GE] for bombs and weapons delivery systems that are known to kill pregnant mothers with "children in the womb." So much for moral clarity.

In fact, the cost incurred for killing those still in or who've exited the womb, including current direct military budget items, ever increasing interest payments on past, cumulatively multi-trillion dollar military expenditures, add-on requests to fund on-going wars, now expanded into Pakistan, post-war medical costs, the more than 260 new intelligence agencies created since 9/11 that have more information about US citizens than ever before, and hidden CIA, NSA et al expenditures, is estimated by organizations who track these things, based on the "Budget of the US Government, FY 2009," that upwards of a nation-killing 50-55% of federal taxes, directly or indirectly, go to feed the world's largest socialized institution, the US military beast.

This tidy sum amounts to multiple thousands of dollars every year, for every person in the US including, presumably, "all the children in the womb." *No nation has ever sustained these socialized levels of military spending and continued to survive. Substantially increasing the level of military spending is a formula for the ultimate failure of the US nation-state as we know it.* The apocalyptic prophecies of Revelation also show us this is the case. [See the chapter *Revelation 17*]. Noting this, then, it's possible that the urgency and priority of the "personhood" for embryos folks may be misdirected too.

If this "personhood" push becomes reality, it raises lots of new questions. Do these embryos get social security numbers with "personhood" like any other person? What about passports? What photo gets put on it? And what name? Will doctors start charging for two person visits when a woman is pregnant? Will medical insurance companies, in this case, double their rates for coverage of two persons rather than one? When a woman gives birth to a stillborn "personhood" child, will she be tried for first or second-degree murder or just manslaughter? Can we qualify for social security and Medicare benefits nine months sooner if "personhood" is adopted? What about driver's licenses and legal drinking age? These conditions should change if someone accused of killing a pregnant woman is charged with two crimes. This "personhood" thing can cause some big social and financial waves in society.

What each person in Kansas ponies up every year for military weapons to kill people post-utero is a whole lot more than what they spend on the "personhood" initiatives to save all those children in the womb. If all this seems a bit contradictory, that's because it is.

These conundrums all come about for one reason primarily. And that is the belief that physical life, "personhood," begins at conception. This misguided belief, according to the "personhood" people, comes from the pages of the Biblical record. But does it? And while there are a few sets of verses they use to show life exists in the womb, let's focus on one set in particular that is a favorite of personhood advocates. This is the Old Testament account in Psalm 139 written by King David of Israel.

As a side note, the Jewish religion does not take these verses to mean life begins at conception. In fact, it isn't *until 30 days after birth* that they consider a newborn to have full "personhood" status. While there is a very definitive verse, Genesis 2:7 regarding the beginning of life for mankind, which the Jewish religion acknowledges, and which we'll look at below, this gets shunted aside by those seeking "personhood" for embryos in favor of verses that were never meant to delineate the beginning of life.

Now a psalm is simply lyrics or a poem set to music. And for most people, using song lyrics or lines from a poem as proof to verify fact is a bit dicey. After all, if a song lyric says, "She broke my heart," who of us would use this as proof positive that she breached a guy's chest, and literally ripped apart his heart? And would we deduce from this that she must be on trial for murder? Hardly. The lyric is allegorical not literal. It simply means the guy was hurt emotionally.

The Blind Man's Elephant
Life In The 'hood

Psalm 139 is a song. In fact, the first line of the psalm says, "To the chief Musician. A Psalm of David." David wrote the lyrics of this song. Now when we examine the words of this psalm, used as definitive proof that we have life in the womb by those seeking "personhood," one can understand why they would want to take this to mean David had life in the womb. But it is a song. Songs are meant to be allegorical just like "She broke my heart."

We need to make a very strong point here, which is vital to our understanding of what David was saying. *The consensus among Old Testament scholars is that the context of David's poem-song is not the beginning of life, but God's omnipresence and omniscience, which are manifestations of His pure consciousness.* We can't hide from God. He knows all things about us, where we are, past and present and future, whenever in our classical state of consciousness that may be as David points out. [See Luke 12:7]. However, *David also is expressing a quantum point of understanding concerning the nature of God.* [See the chapter *Brown Paint: Quantum Potentialities*].

Interestingly, in his book, *The Quantum Doctor,* physicist Amit Goswami makes the point that quantum physics has much in common with poetry. To understand what David is saying, we can't use a classical, literal frame of reference. We have to understand it in more fundamental terms. This may be why David chose to use poetry set to music to convey an understanding of these particular aspects of the nature of God.

One can certainly make the argument that David was king of the psalmists with Psalm 139 being regarded as his quintessential work by scholars. But stating that these verses literally mean life begins at conception or that David had "personhood" in the womb totally misses the point of what David is expressing. It's much, much bigger and far more profound than this. It's a bit akin to claiming that the sole significance of $E = mc^2$ is that it contains letters of the alphabet on both sides of the equal sign.

So, let's read the verses allegedly used to show "personhood" in the womb using the Jewish Publication Society's Bible. Verses 13-16 are the ones in question.

We read beginning in verse 13: "For you [*God*] have made my reins [*literally kidneys; seat of emotion and affection*]; you have knit me together in my mother's womb. [*Tiny, tiny nano-knitting needles?*]

Verse 14: I will give thanks to you, for I am fearfully and wonderfully made; wonderful are your works; and that my soul knows right well.

Verse 15: My frame was not hidden from you, when I was made in secret, and curiously wrought in the lowest parts of the earth.

Verse 16: Your eyes saw my unformed substance, and in your book, they were all written, even the days that were fashioned, when as yet there was none of them." *Italics* and [ ] added.

In a literal sense, we can hardly consider David's reference to an embryo as an "unformed substance" to mean a high state of order, a fully formed human who is a person.

David isn't conveying that he had life as an unformed substance. *He is talking about the power and nature of God.* When he speaks of "days that were yet fashioned, when as yet there were none of them," David is making the point that God knows the potential us in the future, when there were no days for us as an unformed substance, because we were yet without life in the flesh. Remember, this psalm is about God's omnipresence and omniscience, not about the beginning of life.

At the quantum level, the past, present and future are all one [a singularity] as David's son Solomon pointed out in the book of *Ecclesiastes* 3:15. While we can't know the future because of the construct of the universe, God is not impaired in this regard. This simply means that before we are manifested in the flesh as a human being in our universe, the space-time continuum, God already knows our future. God knows when we will be born, how long we'll live, when we'll die. Therefore, God can look into the future and see us as an unformed substance, when the days that we will live are not yet in existence.

David also mentions that if he were in hell [v.8], meaning the grave, God knows him there too. Does this mean our bodies are still alive after we are dead or that we bury people alive? No. David is alluding to our spirit, the spirit of man. And at death of the body, this spirit returns to God who gave it. "Then shall the dust [*our body*] return to the earth as it was; and the spirit shall return to God who gave it." [Ecc. 12:7].

And when Christ said in Mark 12, referencing the resurrection, that God is the God of the living and not the dead, the word living is *zao,* meaning *to breathe*, to live. The Greek word for dead is *nekros,* meaning one who *breathed his last*. Throughout the Biblical record, the beginning of physical life is tied to our first breath at birth and death to our last breath. As Solomon pointed out, there is "a time to be born, and a time to die." He said nothing about a time to be conceived.

David Brown, in the Jamieson, Fausset and Brown Commentary states in his remarks on Mark 12, when Christ is explaining the resurrection to the Sadducees, who didn't believe there was a resurrection, "It is true, indeed, that to God no human being is dead or ever will be, but all mankind sustain an abiding conscious relation to Him." And in the flesh, that means having zao, or breath.

At the death of the body, the spirit of man, our spiritual consciousness, disengages from that which we experienced in the natural body and completely re-enters the spiritual domain of consciousness from which the spirit of man came. Our consciousness leaves the physical body and returns to God who gave it. [See the chapter *Heaven Can Wait*]. After all, each of us is a spiritual consciousness experiencing "Big Bangland," the physical or natural universe, not vice versa. Mankind has this spiritual/physical duality that no other creature has. As Paul states in the New Testament, Christ is the mediator between mankind and God. [1 Tim. 2:5]. There is no mediator for animals.

Some folks also use Jeremiah 1:5 to show that we have life, "personhood" in the womb. "... before you came forth out of the womb, I sanctified you; I ordained you a prophet to the nations." This they say proves Jeremiah had "personhood," or life in the womb because God sanctified and ordained Jeremiah before birth! Rather, it is a facet of God's omniscience.

However, taken together, if Jeremiah was sanctified in the womb before birth, and God knew David in the womb, knit him together there, it must mean life begins at conception! If so, we now have a real dilemma on our hands. Using this very same logic progression, we find life begins *before conception!!*

Let's go back to Jeremiah 1:5, it also says, *"Before I formed you in the womb, I knew you...."* Conundrums of conundrums, Conceptionists, we now have life before conception!!!

And, this doesn't even begin to address what Paul wrote to the church in Ephesus. "According as he has chosen us in him *before the foundation of the world...."* [Eph. 1:4]. We had life before the universe and Earth were even formed?!

Does this mean that Monty Python was right all along!? Every sperm, and egg too, is sacred? The pope insists life begins at conception. However, life has to begin before conception using "personhood" people's Biblical logic. If life begins before conception, that means only one sperm and one egg is sacred, only one of each is destined to be "us." Which one? How do we know? How do we know some future pope or president hasn't disappeared in a wet dream? What person is doomed each month when a woman has her period!? Imagine the photos the Pre-Conceptionists will show us!

My apologies if this seems a tad gross, but this entire line of reasoning that Psalm 139, and Jeremiah 1 are definitive when it comes to conception as the origin of life, just leads to the absurd. We might as well discuss the number of angels dancing on a potential particle.

If "personhood" people wish to use Psalm 139 in a literal sense, one can make the case for David having life in the womb. By the same token, however, Jeremiah had life, "personhood," before he was conceived. So when does life begin? At conception? Before conception? How is it God can know us before conception, and in the womb, while alive and after we are in the grave? And if God knows us in any or all of these potential states, does this mean we have physical life in all of them? Or does it mean something else?

It simply means David was providing examples of God's omnipresence and omniscience. David was not intending to address the issue of the beginning of physical life. That was made clear with the creation of the first man in Genesis 2. David is pointing out that the effects of the Big Bang, space and time, are not binding factors on the Creator in terms of man's potentialities.

"Now a mediator does not mediate for one only, but God is one," as the apostle Paul wrote to the Galatians. And as we noted above, Christ is the mediator between God and mankind as he explained. Thus, man, and man alone has a duality of life as it were. While we have a consciousness in the flesh, the spirit of man is made manifest at first breath. When our flesh dies, after its last breath as James writes [Jam. 2:26], man's spiritual consciousness returns to the "other side" of the Big Bang to God who gave it. David is stating that man's relationship to God, therefore, is unique compared to all other life.

The spirit of man is separate from all that which was created in the Big Bang. The spirit of creatures is of the Big Bang. It is inherent in the nature of the Big Bang's creation, "Let the earth bring forth kind after kind" as opposed to "Let us [the plural, *elohiym*; also see Job 38:4-7] make man in our image, and in our likeness, and let them have dominion...." Regarding man's duality, Solomon pointed out, "Who knows the spirit of the sons of men, which goes upward, and the spirit of the animal, which goes down to the earth?" [Ecc. 3:21].

Man's unique spiritual consciousness enters our physical body at first breath and exits at last breath. Our physical bodies are vehicles, interfaces, for our extra-Big Bang spiritual consciousness in this manifested illusion we call reality, or life even though we may not fully understand how it is mediated. [See chapter one in *The Blind Man's Elephant* regarding the three creations of life].

Solomon also pointed out, "Then I beheld all the work of God, that a man cannot find out the work that is done under the sun: because though a man labor to seek it out, yet he shall not find it; even further, though a wise man think to know it, yet shall he not be able to find it." This is an apt description of the quandary we face when contemplating the mysteries of life presented to us when we venture into the realm of quantum physics. Remember, this is from the guy who wrote of time's singularity at the quantum level and the space-time continuum 3000 years before Einstein.

Everything of the universe "this side" of the Big Bang, the space-time continuum, has one consciousness or quantumness. It is the construct of the natural universe. The "other side" starts at the point called *owlam* in Hebrew.

Owlam is defined as "concealed or hidden, the vanishing point; generally, time out of mind past or future." Prior to the Big Bang, and what's ahead of the cosmological arrow of time, is kept from us. Only the theological arrow of time lets us know future events, and this is from God on the other side of owlam.

We read in Ecclesiastes, "He has made every thing beautiful in his time: also he has set the world [*owlam*] in their heart [*mind*], so that no man can find out the work that God makes from the beginning to the end." [Ecc. 3:11]. We can explore everything this side of the Big Bang. But what's on the other side is a door we can't open. One aspect of our consciousness is of this side of the Big Bang, and the other is of the other side. Man's spiritual duality sets us apart from all other creatures. Consciousness's similarities are of the Big Bang. Consciousness's differences are of the spirit of man and the Spirit of God.

To keep it simple, concerning the beginning of life of the physical body for the very first man in the Biblical record, made in the image and likeness of God, let's look at Genesis 2:7. God makes it extremely clear and direct. It's not a song or a poem. There are no allegorical meanings here. It doesn't get any plainer than this although "personhood" people completely dismiss it.

"And the LORD God formed man of the dust of the ground, and breathed into his nostrils the breath of life; and man became a living being."

What's happening here? The first man, Adam is being made. And who is the one forming man? The LORD God.

This is a credible source for "personhood" people. And what did the LORD God do? He formed man of the dust of the ground. This seems clear enough. Then what did the LORD God do? He breathed into the man's nostrils that he formed. Okay, this seems clear too. And what exactly did the LORD God breathe into man's nostrils? The BREATH of LIFE. The breath of what? *LIFE!* You mean as in when does *LIFE* begin? Yup. Same one.

Okay, then what happened as a result of the LORD God breathing the *BREATH of LIFE* into man's nostrils? Man *became* a living being. Nowhere else in the Biblical record is there such a clear statement of plain fact concerning the beginning of physical life.

So why is this overlooked in place of Biblical verses that do not address the beginning of life? I can't speak for the "personhood" people, but it appears they really don't like abortion. And it appears, the only way they believe they can convince others to forsake abortion is to find a Biblical basis for life beginning at conception rather than at birth or first breath. Thus, abortion becomes murder. And as murder is illegal and immoral, so too should abortion.

Apparently, not only is it sufficient to say life begins at conception, but a legal status of "personhood" needs to be conferred on embryos as the verses in Psalm 139 and Jeremiah allegedly show for both David and Jeremiah. Rather what these verses show is a quantum aspect of the nature of God and his all-knowingness as well as our spiritual nature. It does not prove life in the flesh begins at conception or before. The Biblical record clearly shows that our physical life begins at first breath, which is the breath of life.

Merely because physical life begins at first breath, it does not imply a pro-abortion mindset or automatically means abortion is something society should take frivolously. A balanced and thoughtful approach should guide society's standards. But neither can "personhood" people claim it is murder according to the Biblical record when we "rely on the moral clarity of our God-given moral law to guide our efforts...."

Speaking of moral clarity guiding efforts, rather than wage a battle about conferring "personhood" on an embryo, perhaps the combined energy of those efforts should scrutinize the short and long term implications of the US military's huge socialized financial millstone, and its consequences on the lives, not only those in the womb, but of every person in every country outside of it. It is eviscerating the US from the inside as sure as any abortion procedure. If it is important to learn the lessons of history, then we should learn that military extravagances have proved to be the leading cause of death among empires past. Therefore, what profit is there if personhood is gained and a nation is aborted?

Brown Paint: Quantum Potentialities

When we peer under the foundational plancks[1] of the space-time continuum, we find the consciousness that is God.

What we observe to be the world, our life or our physical reality is an illusion. As Einstein said, "Reality is merely an illusion, albeit a very persistent one." This comment is based on the way our universe is constructed at the quantum level as it manifests itself in our everyday, 4-D "real" world. Our four dimensional physical universe, three dimensions of space, and only one of time, is fundamentally much different than what we perceive it to be.

Contrarily, that which is of the eternal life force, the Spirit of God, which originates outside our 4-D world, is the true reality. It's somewhat of an ironic juxtaposition, which is perhaps why the meaning of life is so elusive. As integrated observers, we experience and, in fact, affect our everyday 4-D illusion, but it is of no consequential value for us. But the one we can't observe, the one accessed by faith, has eternal value.

This is what Christ is telling us when he says, "Do not lay up for yourselves treasures on Earth, where moth and rust destroy and where thieves break in and steal; but lay up for yourselves treasures in heaven, where neither moth nor rust destroys and where thieves do not break in and steal." [Mat. 6:19, 20]. In the aftermath of the recent Wall Street and international banking fiasco, one would be hard pressed to find greater financial motivation for following this advice.

Rather than heed this wise counsel, however, most of us are so steeped in the acquisition of material goods or ego driven in pursuit of the power and wealth of our 4-D Earth, living the deceptive illusion of the "good life" rather than seeking the spiritual sovereign power of God, we fail to grasp that our chosen "reality" path is a lifelong fruitless pursuit of a mirage. It's literally a dead-end. [Mat. 6:21-24].

Solomon, a king that had incomparable power and riches while experiencing this illusion, asked the question, "What does man gain by all the toil at which he toils under the Sun?" His conclusion, "I have seen all the works that are done under the Sun; and indeed, all is vanity and chasing after the wind." [Ecc. 1:3, 14] How valuable, then, are the power and riches of this illusion we call reality if they vanish in a breath? And why do we vainly spend so much effort in their pursuit? Despite their monumental efforts, the pharaohs didn't manage to take either wealth or power with them. Even their mummified bodies are still here. They left with nothing more than that with which they arrived. This aptly qualifies as chasing the wind.

In our classical state of existence, "reallusion" is made up of quantum potentialities, particles observed at the collapse of the wave function. By way of analogy, think of a summer stock theater stage. You arrive to see a play one evening. When the actors appear on stage, you observe a forest behind them, though you know this is not a "real" forest. It is an illusion made to represent a forest. The forest is comprised of trees painted on paper attached to a lightweight wooden frame that can be easily hauled onto or off the stage by stagehands.

If the next scene takes place in the king's treasure room of his castle, the forest props are quickly removed, replaced by others depicting a castle with a room full of treasure chests. Would we consider this stage king's treasure as real? No, but we perceive it as such for the sake of theater.

The next scene is in a meadow with horses grazing in the background. Are these "real" horses? No. They are painted onto the prop's background.

Now we know that the trees in the forest, the treasure chests in the castle, and the horses in the meadow are not "real." They actually are painted props. And in our case they are all brown. So we know that in the workshop, the prop makers built the props and consciously set out to paint trees, treasure chests, and horses using brown paint.

Before the props become trees or treasure chests or horses ready to be observed on stage, they exist backstage in their quantum wave function state as brown paint. Brown paint in the can is a quantum universe of potentialities be they horses or treasure chests or trees or dirt roads or plowed fields or just about any other potential we choose them to be for the sake of theater.

Speaking of theater, the apostle Paul wrote of our "reality," "For I think that God has set forth us apostles last, as it were appointed to death; for we are made theater [Greek, *theatron*] to the world [*kosmos*], to the angels and to men." [1 Cor. 4:9]. The brown paint that we perceive in the theater of life to be a "real" tree or a horse or treasure on our Earthly stage, is the brown paint of quantum potentialities formed, or perhaps vibrated up the sub-atomic scale into observed particles, making the amino acids that in toto are perceived to be a "real" horse or tree. The reality is that both theater stages are comprised of nothing more than illusions, one of no more meaningful value than the other just as Einstein pointed out.

From God's perspective outside the 4-D universe, what we observe to be our reality, this Earth that we inhabit, is nothing more than a temporary summer stock theater stage, which will be taken down at the conclusion of the production. [See Rev. 21:1]. We are its actors. But as its actors, we are observers who are integrated into the illusion through our costumes, our natural bodies. What we observe to be "real" trees or horses or treasure or any other aspects of our daily lives are merely observations of the wave function collapse, potentialities made up of those, according to string theory, tiny quantum vibrations or waviness that is our brown paint in the can.

What we know as conscious human life is the spirit of man interfacing with quantum potentials, the brown paint becoming you or me or whatever else. It's just a matter of which potential. What was the brown paint used to make?

The quantum state bottom line is that our universe, metaphorically speaking, is all brown paint. That which exists at the quantum level in turn only becomes "real" trees, treasure and horses in our classical state of existence *when we observe them*. Upon exiting our human bodies at death, we are no longer integrated conscious observers of what we commonly call our 4-D space-time reality. We've exited our Earthly stage just like the pharaohs. From this perspective, the illusion, our life and all the riches and power we accumulated as observers on Earth, vanishes. It all ceases to exist for us. Thus, it is not "us" who cease to exist at the death of the natural body, but our status as conscious observers of the illusion we called life. [See 1 Ths. 4:14; also the chapter *Heaven Can Wait*].

In this sense, we are avatars. The Hindu word avatar, which has entered into mainstream awareness largely due to the movie of the same name, is the manifestation of a spiritual consciousness in a physical body form on Earth. Our physical bodies are 3-D representations that our spiritual selves occupy during the time we play out the game of life in the space-time continuum. The Biblical record is our "player's manual."

So man's physical body, too, is of the brown paint. But, we have that avatar quality that differentiates us from horses or trees. Our spiritual consciousness, the spirit of man, returns to God who gave it [See Ecc. 12:7] because its existence originates off-stage, as it were, on the other side of potential space-time states that were created as the result of the Big Bang. This aspect of mankind is not of the brown paint. It is of the spirit God gave to mankind that sets us apart from creatures and everything else in the universe. [See Gen. 1:27; also chapter one in *The Blind Man's Elephant*].

What is this life all about? It's about not getting sucked into believing the illusion in and of itself has tangible, meaningful value for our ultimate purpose in experiencing this consciousness. [See Luke 17:33]. It goes back to that ironic juxtaposition. There is a real treasure hidden in the illusion. It takes grasping the idea that what appears as the real treasure we see everyday in front of our faces, on television, on the Internet or in magazines and ads is spurious. And what is not seen and intangible in our 4-D life is the real thing. It boils down to this, are we spiritually savvy enough, being bound in a physical body that is of the illusion, to get it?

Christ gave us lots of hints as to which we should pursue including, "Again, the kingdom [*Greek, basileia, not a place but the sovereign power and authority of God*] of heaven is like treasure hidden in a field, which a man found and hid; and for joy over it he goes and sells all that he has and buys that field." [Mat. 13:44].

All that we see and observe around us is just an illusion as Einstein said. Access to the true power and riches lie outside the space-time continuum and are accessible through faith. As the apostle Paul so accurately pointed out, "Now faith is the substance [Greek, *hypostasis,* foundation] of things hoped for, the *evidence of things not seen*." [Heb. 11:1]. In quantum terms, we can state that faith is the conviction of things not observed, or not of this space-time illusion.

And faith, [Greek *pistis*, a conviction of the truth], translates to a love for the truth, not for the illusion. [See chapter *A Christmas Message*]. Therefore, it's how we live this life, not what we accumulate in terms of fortune and fame that is of any lasting value. The one who dies with the most toys has been the least wise of all. Their time here well wasted.

When we examine all the works that are done under the Sun, Solomon was right to conclude that all is vanity and a chasing after the wind. Our world that we consider to be reality is just the temporary illusion of nothing more than brown paint originating from its quantum state. Consequently, the power and riches of this world that we hold in such high esteem and after which we so diligently chase are nothing more than the persistent illusion of brown paint on the props of life. [Read the entire book of Ecclesiastes].

What is real is the eternal life force of the Spirit of God. This is what is of true and ultimate worth for each of us, which is accessible by faith. This is why Christ told us very plainly, "You cannot serve God and mammon." [Mat. 6:24]. The point is if we chase after the power and riches of this persistent illusion, by definition we walk away from the sovereign power and authority that is the kingdom of God. The two are polar opposites and mutually exclusive. We have to choose which one we believe in. Do we have the conviction of this truth to follow the words of Christ or do we fall prey to the temporary illusion? Which power and wealth do we choose to pursue?

If we are truly wise and trust the word of Christ through our actions, then we will reap the rewards. "Therefore I say to you, do not worry about your life, what you will eat or what you will drink; nor about your body, what you will put on. Is not life more than food and the body more than clothing? … But seek first the kingdom of God [*God's royal power and sovereign authority*] and His righteousness, and all these things shall be added to you." [Mat. 6:25, 33].

Therefore, "Listen, my beloved brethren, has not God chosen the poor of this world, *rich in faith [the conviction of truth]*, and heirs of the kingdom [*the sovereign power and authority of God*], which he has promised to them that love him?" [Jam. 2:5]. The answer is yes.

The power and riches of this illusion are nothing more than vanity that disappears in a breath. It's all brown paint, a chasing of the wind. Being rich in faith, the conviction of the truth, we will inherit the eternal royal power and sovereign authority of God. Understanding this, we stand to gain the true reward with the passing away of this illusion. [See Rev. 21:1]. "... [*Christ*] has made us kings and priests to His God and Father, to Him be glory and dominion forever and ever." [Rev. 1:6; 5:10].

---

[1] Planck Length and Time are the results of calculations made by physicist Max Planck. Planck length is the smallest mathematical measurement of length that has any validity. And Planck time is the time it would take a photon traveling at the speed of light to cross that distance making it the smallest amount of time that has any validity. It is at these points that our classical reference of space-time and gravity break down and quantum physics takes over.

The Hijacked Elephant

The Three Dualities In God's Plan

Ironically, while Christianity is ignorant of these dualities and, consequently, gives no credence to them, they are more important for Christians than ever before. The primary reason for this ignorance is that we don't know our Biblical identity, as Christ made clear to us in the first century. [Mat. 15:24]. And even though we are ignorant of the duality that Christ has and is fulfilling on our behalf, our continuing refusal to acknowledge our heritage means we will have to "pass through the fire," aka the Apocalypse, for the remnant to reach the fulfillment of the third duality as is made clear in the Biblical prophecies.

The three dualities in God's plan, our Biblical record storyline, begin in the Old Testament. All three have a physical-spiritual duality to them. That is, they were part of ordinances given to our ancestors to observe. At Christ's first coming, our contractual obligations to physically observe them ended completely. [See Zec. 11:10 ff]. Christ began spiritually fulfilling them on our behalf beginning with his death and resurrection. Taken together, we see God's plan for us unfolding today.

Let's start at the beginning so we can comprehend Christ's fulfillment. "Three times you shall keep a feast unto me in the year" is first mentioned in Exodus chapter twenty-three. The first of the three times of the year was in the spring beginning with the Passover and the Days of Unleavened Bread, followed by Pentecost or the summer harvest, and then thirdly, the Feast of Tabernacles which begins with the Day of Trumpets in the autumn. The Day of Trumpets represents the return of Christ.

The Passover marked the night when the angel of death passed over all the children of Israel and killed the firstborn sons of the Egyptians. Upon leaving Egypt in haste, the children of Israel had no time to prepare bread normally, as in a leavened loaf, but instead only took with them unleavened, or flat, bread.

Israel was freed from bondage to the Egyptians. This is the actual occurrence in the history of Israel. This event was to be commemorated annually by all Israel as a remembrance of their deliverance from bondage when Christ took them by the hand to lead them out of Egypt, much like a parent would take his child by the hand to safely cross the street.

As the apostle Paul plainly made it clear in the first century to the Christians in Corinth, which is fully applicable to Christians today, "Moreover, brethren, I do not want you to be unaware that *all* our fathers were under the cloud, *all* passed through the sea, *all* were baptized into Moses in the cloud and in the sea, *all* ate the same spiritual food, and *all* drank the same spiritual drink. For they drank of that spiritual Rock that followed them, and *that Rock was Christ.*" [See *the chapter The Tie That Binds*].

The physical observance of the Passover/Days of Unleavened Bread was to continue throughout their generations for *all twelve sons of Israel*, not just with the one son Judah, the Jews. Let's fast forward to the first coming of Christ.

Both in the Old Testament and the New [Deu. 18; Acts 3:12ff], we read, "For Moses truly said unto the fathers, A prophet shall the Lord your God raise up unto you of your brethren, *like unto me*; him shall you hear in all things whatsoever he shall say unto you." This was Christ. Moses presented the law covenant to Israel. Christ is fulfilling the law covenant for *Israel*. What we don't get is that this means *Christians are the lost sheep of the House of Israel*.

Christ clearly stated, "Think not that I came to destroy the Law and the Prophets; I have not come to destroy, but *to fulfill*." The Law and the Prophets, the first two divisions of the Old Testament, were given to *all Israel*. They were not given to the gentiles of the world. Just as a road map represents a real world road, so, too, *the three times of the feasts in the law covenant served as a physical map of real future events to be fulfilled on a spiritual basis by Christ, the Seed of Abraham*. This is the duality of the three feast times. And it was intended this way from the beginning as Moses said. While Christians need to know and understand this, we remain as blind sheep, "the wool pulled over our eyes."

The biggest roadblock for Christianity, who mistakenly believes we are just a bunch of gentiles, is in thinking that the significance of these High Holy Day feasts stopped on the last page of the Old Testament. They didn't. Only their physical observance did. In fact, their significance greatly increased for all Israel when Christ began their *spiritual fulfillment* on our behalf with his death and resurrection. It was now a matter of grace and faith with the Abrahamic covenant, and no longer a matter of keeping physical ordinances of the law covenant given by Moses. We live in a new age.

So, from the very beginning these high holy days, physically observed during three times of the year, would point to a higher fulfilling of the three feast times by Christ on a spiritual level, currently on behalf of Christians in our age. This is the message of the Biblical record when considered holistically. It's *all* one story for *all Israel*, not just the descendants of one of Israel's sons, Judah, the Jews, as is the common Christian misconception.

As Paul explains in the New Testament, "And for this cause, he [*Christ*] is the mediator of the new testament, that by means of death, for the redemption of the transgressions that were under the first testament, they which are called might receive the promise of eternal inheritance." This plainly says that Christ, the Redeemer, died for the sins of those who were under the first testament. Who was under the first testament... Israel or the gentiles of the world? It is exactly as Christ plainly said. "I am only sent to the lost sheep of the House of Israel." Ultimately, his death and resurrection will apply to the House of Judah as well.

The fulfilling of the Passover and Days of Unleavened Bread by Christ occurred *under the terms of the Old Covenant*. The Old Covenant was still in force. All our sins were covered by Christ's death once, and for *all Israel*. The daily sacrifices of bulls and goats were passed over. We were out of bondage to sin, the transgression of the law covenant given by Moses.

It was Christ's death and resurrection that opened the door for the Abrahamic covenant by fulfilling the terms of the law covenant. A testament only comes into effect upon the death of the testator. The next two feast times of the year, spiritually speaking, were to take place under the new covenant, not written upon stone, but upon our hearts by the Spirit of God. The age we now live in is the second of these three times; the time between Christ's first and his second coming or the last days as it is referred to prophetically.

Remember, the law covenant delivered by Moses to the children of Israel was a bridge between the Abrahamic covenant and his Seed, meaning Christ. Yet that bridge, in particular the three times a year Israel was to keep a feast unto the LORD, was temporary, pointing the way to Christ's fulfilling these days. As the apostle Paul noted, "For the Law, having a shadow of the good things to come, and not the very image of the things, can never with these same sacrifices, which they offer continually year by year, make those who approach perfect."

This is another marker for Christians to know that they are indeed the lost sheep of the House of Israel in this age. These times of the feasts tell us Christ's story which has been unfolding for Christians the past 2000 years or so, "… which God ordained before the ages for our glory." [1 Cor. 2:7]. Christ came to fulfill the Law and the Prophets, and as he said, "I am sent only to the lost sheep of *the House of Israel*." If Christians are, by definition, the followers of Christ, shouldn't we be aware of what our savior actually said, and is doing for us?

The second time of the year for these feasts was the summer harvest or Pentecost. This occurred historically in the land promised to Abraham, but only after the lawgiver Moses had died, and the children of Israel passed over the river Jordan into the promised land led by Joshua, a descendant of Joseph, the kingly line of *the House of Israel.*

Christ's death and resurrection covers our debt to the law under the terms and conditions delivered by Moses. Christ established new terms. "Knowing that a man is not justified by the works of the Law but by faith in Jesus Christ, even we have believed in Christ Jesus, that we might be justified by faith in Christ and not by the works of the Law; for by the works of the Law no flesh shall be justified." [Gal. 2:16].

Fifty days from the last weekly sabbath after the second high day of unleavened bread, the Comforter, or Holy Spirit of God was sent. As Peter said on that first day of Christianity 2000 years ago, "Therefore let *all the House of Israel* know assuredly that God has made this Jesus, *whom you crucified*, both Lord and Christ... Then Peter said to them, Repent, and let every one of you [of the House of Israel] be baptized in the name of Jesus Christ for the remission of sins; and you shall receive the gift of the Holy Spirit." [Acts 2:36-38]. As the apostle John noted regarding the remission of sins, "... for sin is the transgression of the Law. And you know that he [*Christ*] was manifested to take away our sins...." [1 John 3:4, 5]. Sin being the transgression of the Law, then with who was the law covenant made, the children of Israel or gentiles? Therefore, whose sins were Christ manifested to take away, the gentiles' or Israel's? Christians are descendants of Abraham, Isaac and his son, Israel.

Christ is spiritually fulfilling the Law and the Prophets during these three times on our behalf that we might have a greater life, not of the flesh, but of the Spirit. As Paul explained it to the Christians in Rome, "For as many as are led by the Spirit of God, these are sons of God."

Now, we have a Redeemer who bought us back from the bondage to the law covenant with payment of a ransom, his life, and has taken us over the "river Jordan" to a better covenant, which was established on better promises" with a better spirit, the Spirit of God. As the prophet Isaiah wrote, "But as it is written: 'Eye has not seen, nor ear heard, nor have entered into the heart of man the things which God has prepared for those who love Him.'"

The apostle Paul wrote to the church in Rome, "But we speak the wisdom of God in a mystery, the hidden wisdom, which God ordained before the ages for our glory. For I would not, brethren, that you should be ignorant of this mystery, unless you should be wise in your own conceits; that blindness in part is happened to Israel [the House of Judah], until the fullness of the nations [Greek, *ethnos*, meaning here the nations of the House of Israel] be come in. And so*, all Israel* shall be saved." [Rom. 11:25, 26].

Paul is explaining that when the nations of the House of Israel were divorced from God, they lost their national identities and their status became the same as any gentiles before God. Therefore, no other people needed *redemption* [a buying back of something lost] except the lost sheep of the House of Israel. However, the children of the seed of Abraham are, individually in this age, which is the second feast time, restored to their place before God to a better covenant by Christ. Yet, the House of Judah will be blind to Christ as the messiah until Christ has fulfilled the second feast time for the lost sheep of the House of Israel. Then, at the third feast time, nationally *all Israel* will once again be joined in a new covenant.

Pentecost 2000 years ago marked the beginning the second of the three times of the Old Testament ordinance that was fulfilled, but it was the first to be fulfilled under the terms of the new covenant. It is the time we now live in. And it will continue until the second coming of Christ. It is a personal time of reconciliation as opposed to the third feast time which marks the national atonement of all Israel when Christ returns establishing a new national covenant.

In the New Testament we read, "For finding fault with them, he said, Behold, the days come, says the Lord, when I will make a new covenant with the House of Israel and with the House of Judah: Not according to the covenant that I made with their fathers in the day when I took them by the hand to lead them out of the land of Egypt; because they continued not in my covenant, and I regarded them not, said the Lord." [Heb. 8:8, 9]

This third feast time, which begins in early autumn, physically was commanded to Israel upon leaving Egypt. It will be fulfilled beginning with Christ's return, and includes, as well, the millennial peace and the two resurrections. Just as coming out of Egypt marked a new beginning for Israel, so too, shall Christ's second coming will mark a new time for all Israel, a spiritual fulfillment of the "Feast of Tabernacles," the third time of the year when Israel was to keep a feast unto the LORD.

"And it shall come to pass that everyone who is left of all the nations which came against Jerusalem shall go up from year to year to worship the King, the LORD of hosts, and to keep the Feast of Tabernacles." [Zec. 14:16]. This is a prophecy in Zechariah referring to the fulfilling of the third time of the feasts yet in our future, after the return of Christ.

Thus, what Christ commanded to Moses for the children of Israel to observe physically three times a year, is the blueprint for Christ's spiritual fulfillment beginning with his first coming, as a prophet and savior, and culminating in his return as king, establishing the kingdom of God on Earth. It is all one story. It's just that the characters are only part way through the story, which continues to confuse many Christians because we don't take Christ at his word when he said, "I am sent only to the lost sheep of the House of Israel." Once we fully grasp this, the pieces of our puzzle fall into place.

While Christ has fulfilled two of these three feast times on our behalf to date, Christianity hasn't a clue that he has done so, much less what this means for us. But, it's not without reason. Errantly, we participate in "times and feasts" that have been changed. "And he [*Antichrist*] shall speak great words against the most High, and shall wear out the saints of the most High, and think to change times and Laws…."

Regarding the changing of times and Laws, the JFB commentary on Daniel chapter seven, verse twenty-five says, "… **change times**--the prerogative of God alone (**Dan. 2:21**); *blasphemously assumed by Antichrist.* **The "times and Laws" here meant are those of religious ordinance;** [*three*] **stated times of feasts** [MAURER]… He [*Antichrist*] shall set himself above all that is called God (**2 Ths. 2:4**), putting his own "will" above God's times and Laws (**Dan. 11:36, 37**)," or above God's stated times of feasts.

We should ask ourselves, why would the Anti**christ** seek to change stated times and feasts of ***Israel***? Unless, of course, these stated times of feasts have great relevance for *Christ*ians? If these feasts of Israel have no spiritual significance for Christians, then, it stands to reason that Daniel's chapter seven would not reference the Antichrist, but the Antimoses.

None of the three stated times of feasts of God occur in winter, symbolically, and appropriately the dead season of the year, as does the most prominent day celebrated by "Christianity." Who is it that changed God's stated times and Laws of the feasts, thereby deceiving Christians into observing days whose roots are based in pagan traditions?

If we're too apathetic and lukewarm to care for the truth anymore, surely we are worn out. Christ warns us, the last church era before his return. "So then because you are lukewarm, and neither cold nor hot, I will spit you out of my mouth." [Rev. 3:16]. Ending up, metaphorically speaking, in the old spiritual spittoon, is more commonly known as the Apocalypse, or the time of Jacob's [Israel's] trouble. "... and there shall be a time of trouble, such as never was since there was a nation...." [Dan. 12:1].

As stated at the beginning, Christianity gives no credence to these three stated times of feasts, the dualities of God's plan fulfilled by Christ on our behalf, yet they are of greater consequence for Christians than ever before.

What Days Do Christians Need To Observe?

If there were days required of us to physically observe, it would be the days given to our ancestors of the House of Israel, and not the counterfeits Christianity blindly accepts today. However, the critical point to acknowledge is that Christ said *he* came to *fulfill* the Law and the Prophets because he broke the law covenant he made with our ancestors.

Keep in mind, *the law covenant was not made with our patriarch Israel, but with Moses* and *all the children of Israel.* The law was added 430 years *after* the promise of the Abrahamic covenant. Therefore, the covenant made with our patriarch Israel was that of Abraham, and not Moses. [See the chapter *Abraham's Seed and Heirs*]. *The two covenants are mutually exclusive of each other,* as the Apostle Paul made abundantly clear. Christians are beholden to only one of them, not bits and pieces from both. Christ, in his prerogative, has taken the entirety of the old one upon him, and given us a completely new one in its place as promised.

The Seed of Abraham, Christ, therefore, purposefully subtracted us from the law covenant equation. The observing of the holy days delivered by Moses was an integral part of the law covenant, which today is null and void, as is any previously required observance. We live in a new age, the age of faith in Christ through the Spirit rather than the age of Moses and works of the law. But this is not to say the holy days have no relevance. They do, but their relevance exists on a higher, spiritual level, which cannot be attained by our observance, but *only* by Christ spiritually fulfilling them.

When we come to realize what covenant Christ delivered to Christians upon his death and resurrection, we realize the times of *any required observance* of the holy days on our part are over.

However, there are still some people who believe that these days must physically be observed despite Christ's labor on our behalf. Under the terms of the law covenant of Moses, the children of Israel were debtors to do the *whole law*, which meant they were required to observe all holy days by sacrificing bulls and goats, etc. I doubt any churches, or even synagogues, do this. Yet under the terms of the law covenant, *these works cannot be separated from the observance of these days as written in the Law and Prophets.* The burnt sacrifices were to be offered continually on all these days. *If we must observe these days, then we must offer sacrifices as Moses commanded the children of Israel.* "Whatever I command you, observe to do it; you shall not add to it nor take away from it." [Deu. 12:32]. This is what is written in the law covenant.

Therefore, we cannot pick and choose points in the law to observe, whether they are days or other ordinances, as the apostles made abundantly clear. There is no middle ground with a little bit of this and a little bit that. We either observe the law according to the covenant made with Moses and the children of Israel or live in faith per the Abrahamic covenant of Christ. But it's totally one or the other.

In truth, however, the law covenant made with the children of Israel no longer exists. That covenant was a contract for us to fill. But we failed to do so. So much so that our ancestors were divorced from God. [Jer. 3:8].

Christ has instituted a new covenant on our behalf, the House of Israel. Christ has paid off our debt to sin. Our responsibility is to accept Christ's offer on our behalf in faith. Christ is our mediator.

So who is fulfilling the Law and the Prophets during our age: is it A) the children of Israel, B) individuals of the church, or C) Christ? Of course, it's Christ who said, "Think not that I have come to destroy the Law and the Prophets. I have not come to destroy, but to fulfill." [Mat. 5:17]. Many people read this and think because Christ said he didn't come to destroy the Law and the Prophets, he means some parts of the Mosaic law *covenant* are still binding. This is incorrect. Otherwise his death was in vain.

As we no longer are required to offer burnt sacrifices, as the children of Israel were commanded according to their legal obligations under the law covenant, we no longer are required to observe these days. *The two are explicitly tied together in the Law.* Just as Christ took it upon himself to be our sacrificial lamb, so that we no longer need offer burnt sacrifices, he has also taken it upon himself to *fulfill* the holy days so that we no longer are required to observe them. Christ is *fulfilling* the terms of the Law on our behalf.

By definition, *we cannot fulfill the holy days* by any means under any circumstances. Christ, by his sacrificial death, broke the law covenant with his people. Christ has taken it upon himself to fulfill these days, and indeed *the entire burden of the law covenant*, which is no longer binding on Christians. "And that because of *false brethren* unawares brought in, who came in secretly to spy out our liberty which we have in Christ Jesus, that they might bring us into bondage [*of the law covenant*]." [Gal. 2:4].

The prophecy concerning Christ's death and the breaking of the law covenant in Zechariah eleven is clear, "And I took my staff, Beauty, and cut it asunder, that **I might break my covenant which I had made with all the people. And <u>it was broken</u> in that day:** and so the poor of the flock that waited upon me *knew that it was the word of the LORD*. And I said unto them, If you think good, give me my price; and if not, forbear. **So they weighed for my price thirty pieces of silver.**" This is confirmed in the gospel of Matthew. [Mat. 27:9].

The Law and the Prophets, the first two divisions of the Old Testament, still stand. We need to realize, however, that **the Book of the Law *contains both* the promises of the Abrahamic covenant, and the Mosaic law covenant.** When Christ said he came to fulfill the Law and the Prophets, this includes both his breaking the law covenant, as we just read, *and* giving us a better covenant built upon better promises. This is the reason why he said *he came* to *fulfill* the Law and the Prophets.

It is the law covenant, the legal contractual obligation that required the children of Israel to keep ordinances of the law that Christ broke. As promised, Christ broke that contract and took over our responsibility to the law. Christ paid off our bad debt [sin] with his death. In place of our old debt, we have been given a new covenant by Christ, based on faith, not works of the law, which makes us debt free. How is it, then, we still are required to pay off our old debt if Christ already has paid it on our behalf and released us from all our legal obligations to do so?

Who of us, having had our home mortgage debt paid off on our behalf, would still insist we needed to make payments to the bank? In point of fact, we could not make any payments. Neither the obligation [law covenant] nor the debt [sin, "the wages of sin is death…" [Rom. 6:23a] still exist. In place of a mortgage debt [death], we have a fully paid deed [life]. "… but the gift of God is eternal life through Jesus Christ our Lord." [Rom. 6:23b]. Otherwise, our salvation is dependent upon our perfectly keeping the ordinances of the law under the terms of the old covenant.

Therefore, if we accept Christ's sacrifice as reconciliation for our sins in place of bulls and goats, then we must accept his fulfilling the holy days on our behalf as well. [Heb. 2:14-17]. Who has fulfilled the Passover, the Days of Unleavened Bread and Pentecost? Who is it that will fulfill the Day of Trumpets? The answer isn't us. The answer is Christ. If Christ is fulfilling these days, what are we doing? If we insist we have to observe the holy days, then we must observe the command to sacrifice bulls and goats. Otherwise, our actions say we trust and accept Christ's sacrifice for our sins, but we don't trust and accept him to fulfill the holy days on our behalf despite the fact he already has fulfilled two of the three appointed times.

Thus, it is important to distinguish between the Abrahamic covenant and the law covenant contained in the Book of the Law. The Abrahamic covenant was made with Abraham and his Seed, Christ. The law covenant that was later added was made with the children of Israel. "What purpose then does the law serve? It was added because of transgressions, [not forever as it had a timing factor] *until the Seed* [*Christ*] *should come* to whom the promise was made; and it was appointed through angels by the hand of a mediator." [Gal. 3:19]. Christ broke one covenant, paid our debt and gave us a better one. He is fulfilling that which is written in the Book of the Law concerning both covenants. So, which *one* do we have today?

Second, on whose terms is Christ fulfilling these days? Is it Moses or God? The correct answer is God. If it is God's, then it is according to his calendar or counting of times. Remember, when Moses received the law ordinances for the holy days, he also received the calendar to go with it. [Exd. 12:1, 2]. Prior to Moses receiving the observance of days for the children of Israel, Abib [Nisan] had been the seventh month in the civil calendar year. It was then made to be the first month in the new calendar.

Ask yourself, when Christ fulfilled the Passover, Days of Unleavened Bread and Pentecost, did he fulfill the Day of Trumpets later that same calendar year? No. The last holy day fulfilled by Christ was Pentecost when God sent the Holy Spirit in Christ's name about 2000 years ago. As there are only 150 days or so between Pentecost and Trumpets, it is very apparent God is not operating according to the holy day calendar given to Moses. Nor should we, as Christians of the Abrahamic covenant.

The calendar changed from Abraham to Moses. So we should not be surprised that the calendar is changed from Moses to Abraham's Seed, Christ. When Christ began fulfilling the holy days, he, too, began with a new calendar, which in our case defines the *spiritual* beginning and length of God's "year." As the next day to be fulfilled by Christ is his return on the Day of Trumpets, we cannot celebrate that day until it occurs as we are operating under the terms of God's calendar or year, and not that of Moses. Thus, not only is Christ spiritually fulfilling the holy days on our behalf, we don't even know when the next one will occur. "But of that day and hour no one knows, not even the angels of heaven, but my Father only." [Mat. 24:36].

Let's take a for instance. If someone came to you on a Wednesday afternoon, some time before Moses' calendar day of Trumpets and asks if you celebrate the holy days, you would answer yes.

Then that person says, "Great. I want to as well. How about I come by your house tonight and we celebrate the Passover and Days of Unleavened Bread?" You'd probably answer, "I'm sorry, but we can't do that." Why not," he'd ask? "Because according to Moses, those days occur at the beginning of spring. Not now." "Okay, then how about I come over tonight and we celebrate Trumpets?" "Well, we can't do that either. That's not for a while yet." "But I thought you guys celebrated the holy days?" "We do. It's just that they occur at *an appointed time*. It's not something we do every day."

In this *age of the Abrahamic faith covenant*, we are in the same situation theologically, rather than in the *age of the Mosaic law covenant* as in the example above, unless of course, you are bound under the terms of the law covenant, which, in reality, is not even possible for anyone. [See Zec. 11:10-13]. There are no more appointed times to observe or celebrate until the next appointed time to be *spiritually fulfilled by Christ* at his return.

For those who are led by the Spirit of God, we are on that Wednesday afternoon sometime before Trumpets in God's calendar year. No physical observing of the Day of Trumpets according to the Moses calendar, regardless of how sincere and righteous it is, will result in the return of Christ and the establishing of the kingdom of God. It's just not going to happen. Any required observance of days is of the law covenant, which no longer exists. Therefore, how can we be required to observe that which no longer exists? There is only one covenant to live by. The covenant made with Abraham and his Seed, Christ.

The children of Israel under Moses were commanded, "Three times you shall keep a feast unto me in the year." Yet the children of Israel's physical observance of these three times was just a shadow of their spiritual fulfilling by Christ, just as the spirit of man is a shadow of the Spirit of God. Yet, who of us would give up the Spirit of God within us to go back to the spirit of man? And who of us would go back to physically observing these days in the law covenant rather than have Christ spiritually fulfill them on our behalf?

In fulfilling the Law on our behalf, Christ has spiritually fulfilled the Days of Unleavened Bread, the first feast time in God's year. He has fulfilled the day of Pentecost, the second feast time. Theologically, then, in this age we are living in the second of times fulfilled by Christ. So who is it that requires us to go back to physically observing days and give up our liberty in Christ? And, for what purpose? Do we not trust Christ? Is he made perfect by our observance?

What Days Do Christians Need To Observe?

We are now living in the summer harvest of the lost sheep of the House of Israel sometime after the fulfilling of Pentecost and before the fulfilling of the third time, the Feast of Tabernacles, which begins with Trumpets. Rather than focus on physical annual observances of the holy days as delivered by Moses, we need to focus on the time we live in fulfilled by Christ, *which is the spiritual age of the summer harvest. There are no more holy days to be fulfilled until the "fullness of the children of the House of Israel be come in."* Christ was not sent except to the lost sheep of the House of Israel to whom Peter addressed his remarks on that Pentecost day, fulfilling the second feast time.

Christ has given us liberty not available under the law covenant. As Paul explained it to those in the church in Galatia, "Stand fast therefore in the liberty wherewith Christ has made us free, and be not entangled again with the yoke of bondage [*the law covenant*]." Our physical observance of any days commanded by Moses is being entangled with the yoke of bondage... again. We are not to do it. If we do, it means we do not understand what Christ meant when he said "*I have come* to fulfill the Law and the Prophets." Then, it is as Paul told the church, "Christ is become of no effect unto you." To state it colloquially, "Duh, you don't get it."

Christ is the Seed of Abraham, not the seed of Moses. This provides us with a big clue as to which covenant is for Christians. If, for any reason, we must physically observe the appointed days given by Moses, then our actions disannul the death of Christ. If we disannul the death of Christ, there is no justification by faith. And if there is no justification by faith, we are in bondage under the works of the law. As no one is perfect according to the contractual terms of the law covenant, we are all condemned before God.

It is not of the truth saying we must observe days delivered by Moses. Doing so, our actions are an expression of our lack of faith in Christ. We are essentially saying that Christ's fulfilling of these days isn't good enough, so being more righteous and knowledgeable than others, we have to return to Moses to observe these days ourselves. We can't say with our lips that we accept Christ in faith, and then physically observe days given to Moses, especially *after* Christ already has *spiritually* fulfilled the Days of Unleavened Bread and Pentecost, the first two feast times, according to God's timetable. Either we have received the Spirit of God through faith in Christ or we are children of Moses with the spirit of man through observances of the law. There is no middle ground.

This is what Paul's letter to the Galatians is all about. Remember, the physical descendants of the House of Israel in the first century very likely would have thought they would have to observe the holy days as had their forefathers. Paul had to explain to them that Christ is fulfilling these days on our behalf. Under the law, we cannot be made perfect through works of the flesh. So Paul plainly told them, "For in Jesus Christ neither circumcision avails anything, nor uncircumcision; but faith which works by love." [Gal. 5:6].

Paul also said, "Let no man therefore judge you in meat, or in drink, or in respect of an holyday, or of the new moon, or of sabbaths:" [Col. 2:16]. This is a reference to those of the circumcision [House of Judah] judging those of the uncircumcision [House of Israel; see again Gal. 2:4].

Yet neither in the flesh avails anything. The works of the flesh justifies no one. Thus, nothing is gained. It is vanity and self-righteousness. It is chasing the wind.

Paul is telling us, we are no longer required to observe any terms of the law covenant. Otherwise, "For as many as are of the works of the law are under the curse: **for it is written, Cursed is every one that continues not *in all things* which are *written in the book of the law to do them*.**" [Deu. 27:26; Gal. 3:10]. Paul makes it very clear that it's all or nothing. It's not a hybrid with bits and pieces from both. Otherwise we *are*, not might be, cursed. As Christians, why would we choose bondage and a curse rather than the liberty Christ has given us? Would we prefer living in prison or living free?

Of course, some will point out that Christ and the apostles observed the feasts according to the law. And this is correct. It was required under the law covenant *prior to his death* and resurrection. And it is correct that it probably took some time, in those pre-twitter days, for the apostles to spread this truth that Christ was fulfilling the Law and Prophets on our behalf especially as those of Judah would continue to physically observe the law covenant days throughout the Roman Empire according to the Moses calendar. There was a period of adjustment and understanding as we can read in Acts eleven regarding circumcision. However, the apostle Paul didn't feel the need to spell this out in writing until 52 CE when he wrote to the *backsliding* Christians in Galatia.

Christ fulfilled the Passover and Days of Unleavened Bread under the terms of the law covenant, which were in place until the death of the testator, Christ. "For where there is a testament, there must also of necessity be the death of the testator. For a testament is in force *after* men are dead, since it has no power at all while the testator lives." [Heb. 9:16, 17]. This is why Christ and the disciples observed these times during Christ's lifetime.

But what testament or covenant came into effect *after the crucifixion and resurrection* of Christ? The law covenant or the covenant of Abraham? Recall, Paul told the Christians in Galatia, "What purpose then does the law serve? It was added because of transgressions, *till the Seed [of Abraham] should come* to whom the promise was made...." "Wherefore the law was our schoolmaster to bring us unto Christ, that we might be justified by faith. But after that faith [*by promise to Abraham*] is come, *we are no longer* under a schoolmaster [*the law of Moses*]." [Gal. 3:19, 24, 25]. Which covenant is of Christ? Abraham's. It doesn't get much clearer than this.

It is important, theologically, to understand that Moses, the lawgiver, did not cross over the river Jordan into the land given by promise to Abraham. The first Pentecost, or summer harvest, which ultimately came to mark the first day of Christianity, could not be physically celebrated until after the children of Israel farmed the land given to them by promise to Abraham from God. And that occurred after Moses, the lawgiver, was dead. The children of Israel were led across the river Jordan by Joshua; a descendant of Ephraim, the kingly line of the House of Israel. Not coincidentally, the name Joshua means "Yehovah is salvation..." as does the name Jesus.

Christ's death under the terms of the law covenant resulted in the fulfilling of the first of the three feast times, the Days of Unleavened Bread, which historically occurred coming out of Egypt, before all Israel crossed the river Jordan. The symbolism should be clear enough. Moses, the giver of the law covenant, was dead. In this sense, he was a temporary bridge to lead the children of Israel out of Egypt. He was not the bridge to lead the children of Israel over the river Jordan into the promised land of "milk and honey."

And spiritually, neither is the Mosaic law covenant able to lead the lost sheep of the House of Israel to the kingdom of God. It is of promise and therefore it must be of faith in Christ as the Seed of Abraham. As Joshua, not Moses, physically led the children of Israel, with the spirit of man, into the promised land, so too Jesus Christ is spiritually fulfilling the days that will lead Christians, with the Spirit of God, to the coming of his kingdom. Flesh and blood cannot inherit the kingdom of God. It is of the Spirit, which is where our focus should be daily as Christians. Thus, *the covenant* of importance to Christians is not the law covenant of Moses, but the covenant made with Abraham and his Seed, Christ.

To answer the question posed, what days do Christians descended from the House of Israel need to observe, Paul states the answer very clearly.

"O foolish Galatians! Who has brought evil on you feigning praise that *you should not obey the truth*, before whose eyes Jesus Christ was clearly portrayed among you as crucified? This only I want to learn from you: Did you receive the Spirit by the works of the law, or by the hearing of faith?

Are you so foolish? Having begun in the Spirit, are you now being made perfect by the flesh?" [Gal. 1:1-3].

What is our answer to be? It really can't be any clearer than how Paul explained it to those in the church at Galatia. "Knowing that *a man is not justified by the works of the law but by faith in Jesus Christ*, even we have believed in Christ Jesus, that we might be justified by faith in Christ and *not by the works of the law*; for by the works of the law no flesh shall be justified." [Gal. 2:16].

Physically requiring the observing of days given by Moses, for any reason, are works of the law, plain and simple. What profit, then, do we gain by any works of the law? There is no profit, indeed no truth according to Paul, in returning to *any of the observances of the law covenant* when our faith is in Christ. Holy day observances are required only under the terms of the law covenant, which Christ broke. If our faith is not in Christ, then we return to the bondage of Moses. It is all one or the other.

We need to focus on the fact that Christ has fulfilled all the terms of the law covenant on our behalf. He broke the old law covenant and has given us a new covenant based on faith. And we need to fully understand that we are living, spiritually, in the second of times, according to God's calendar, the time between Christ's fulfilling Pentecost and his fulfilling Trumpets. Our faith in Christ has granted us liberty. We need not return to any yoke of bondage under the law including the observance of days delivered by Moses. Any person who does is, as Paul explained, "a debtor *to do* the whole law," which is impossible.

When we are weak in the spirit, then we return to the bondage of Moses, wherein Paul asks of us, "Who hindered you from obeying *the truth*? This persuasion does not come from Him who calls you." [Gal. 5:8]. Who does that leave then?

When we are strong in faith, we can completely accept that Christ is fulfilling the Law and Prophets on our behalf, "Standing fast in the liberty by which Christ has made us free." Lacking faith, however, we try to retreat to the law covenant, which has been broken and no longer exists. Therefore, which *one* is it, Christ or Moses who is our mediator of a better covenant established upon better promises that by faith leads us to the kingdom of God?

The Great Rebellion: A Summary

Why is First Century Christianity More Relevant Than Ever?

The simple answer is that Christ implemented major theological changes regarding the covenants, which resulted in good news for a specific group of people in our age. This group of people today is largely oblivious to the gravity of their current circumstances due to blithely ignoring their heritage despite the warnings given to them in end-time prophecies.

Having read the covenants section, you know that there is a Christian misconception today that there are two covenants in force. The Old Covenant is for the Jews and the New Covenant is for the Gentiles. There is one major theological problem with this thinking as we discovered. Only one covenant is in force for the children of Israel today.

In reference to the covenants, "For in [*the apostle*] Paul's time, according to his view, the new [*covenant*] set aside the old covenant. The Greek word for [*kaine*] New [Testament] implies that it is *of a different kind and supersedes the old*...." [A.R. Fausset, Jamieson, Fausset and Brown Commentary on Heb. 8:13].

This is absolutely correct. The Old Covenant, or the law covenant, made with Moses and the children of Israel, is no longer in existence. Christ broke it.

"And I took my staff, Beauty, and cut it in two, that *I might break the covenant which I had made with all the peoples* [Hebrew, '*am*, nations of Israel]. So **it was broken on that day**. Thus the poor of the flock, who were watching me, knew that it was the word of the LORD. And I said unto them, 'If you think good, give my price; and if not, forbear.' So they weighed for my price thirty [*pieces*] of silver. And the LORD said to me, "Throw it to the potter"— that princely price they set on me. So I took the thirty [*pieces*] of silver and threw them into the house of the LORD for the potter." [Zec. 11:10-13].

Zechariah, one of the restoration prophets, wrote this prophecy more than five centuries before Christ's first coming. And as we know, it came to came to pass. "What are you [*chief priests*] willing to give me [*Judas*] if I deliver Him [*Christ*] to you?" And they counted out to him thirty pieces of silver." [Mat. 26:15].

Just as the prophet Zechariah wrote, Christ being delivered to the chief priests to be crucified for thirty pieces of silver resulted in the breaking of the law covenant *on that day*. It is no longer in force and hasn't been for nearly two millennia. [See Gal. 3:24, 25].

The now defunct law covenant *was* for all Israel, both the House of Israel and the House of Judah. But as the House of Israel was divorced more than 700 years before Christ's first coming, the law covenant is erroneously perceived today as being only for the Jews. And although the Jews do not recognize Christ, nor that the law covenant was broken long ago, it is null and void along with all its ordinances. [See Gal. 3:10, 11].

However, neither the House of Judah nor Christians, nee the House of Israel, realize this. It is understandable for those descended from Judah for they are blinded to this intentionally. But for those descended from the House of Israel to believe the Old Covenant *is* for the Jews and the New Covenant *is* for the Gentiles totally misses the mark on both counts! We've been duped big time.

And the reason why we've been duped is that we don't understand the theological changes Christ made in the first century regarding the covenants. And the reasons why we today don't understand these changes is that the vast majority of Christians think we are Gentiles despite Christ's very clear and plain statement to a non-Israelite, Gentile woman, "I am not sent but unto the lost sheep of the House of Israel." Instead, end-times Christianity tells Christ, "You're wrong. Read John 3:16." Small wonder Christ and the truth have so little credibility today.

And because we choose to rebel against this basic fact of who we are, in spite of it being hidden in plain sight, Christianity is merrily following the Antichrist, riding those rogue ponies, mindlessly headed right into the teeth of the Apocalypse. And despite the furor about the "end-times," most Christians today could care less about rectifying any of this, exactly as the prophecies tell us.

Of course, this will change rapidly once the pony apples hit the fan. But by then, even the proverbial "pound of cure" will be too little too late. Or as the prophet Jeremiah quoted our LORD saying to both Judah and Israel in the end-times, "All your lovers have forgotten you; they care nothing for you; for *I have dealt you the blow of an enemy*, the punishment of a merciless foe, because *your guilt is great*, because *your sins are flagrant*. Why do you cry about your affliction? *Your sorrow is <u>incurable</u>.* Because of the multitude of your iniquities, your sins have increased, *I have done these things to you.*" [Jer. 30:14, 15].

The net result is essentially the same as what end-times Christians are told by Christ in Revelation, "So, because you are lukewarm, and neither hot nor cold, *I will spit you out of my mouth*. For you say, 'I am rich, I have prospered, and I need nothing,' not realizing that you are wretched, pitiable, poor, blind, and naked." [Rev. 3:16, 17 ESV]. Ignorance and apathy has its price. But, looking on the bright side, our beloved Santa Claus and Easter Bunny will save us from the mean old Jesus Christ... *right*?! [See Jer. 10:1, 11].

If we took Christ at his word, paid attention to first century Christianity as delivered by Christ and the apostles, and acted accordingly, 21st century Christianity would still be relevant, especially to so many of our young men and women who are driven to atheism. Instead, we invent convoluted arguments to support our errant ways, self-righteously justifying our ends, which theologically make us, politely speaking, pony patooties.

However, once we understand the role of the covenants, what they mean for us, and that Christ was correct in telling us he was sent only to the lost sheep of the House of Israel, then we can correctly understand the gospel, the good news.

Christ had to redeem us from our divorce from God because of our forefathers' rebellion against the word of God nearly 3000 years ago. His death on our behalf and resurrection allowed us to be redeemed into our new covenant relationship with God exactly as it was intended. Only the

House of Israel, therefore, is in the covenant relationship with God in this age.

The Light has come into the kosmos. The plan of God, the new covenant is that we are restored to our place before God according to the promises made with Abraham, and his Seed, Christ. [See Gal. 3:18]. This is the good news given to the lost sheep of the House of Israel. *This* is the gospel.

Once we understand this, we no longer sit in darkness. Not understanding this, we remain in the dark. Gullibly, we believe the fictitious tale that Abraham's covenant was made with many seeds as in the Gentiles of the world. Hoodwinked by the Antichrist, we resist the plain words of Christ about our rightful inheritance, riding the rogue ponies back into the shadow of death from which our forefathers were delivered twenty centuries ago.

"Now when Jesus heard that John [*the baptist*] had been put in prison, He departed to Galilee. And leaving Nazareth, He came and dwelt in Capernaum, which is by the sea, in the regions of Zebulun and Naphtali, that it might be *fulfilled which was spoken by Isaiah* the prophet [*of Israel*], saying: "The land of Zebulun and the land of Naphtali [*sons of the House of Israel*], by the way of the sea, beyond the Jordan, Galilee of the nations: The people [*of the House of Israel*] who sat in darkness [*divorced from God, outside the covenant relationship,* Jer. 3:8] have seen a great light, And upon those who sat in the region and shadow of death, Light has dawned. And from that time Jesus began to preach, "Repent [*change your ways*] for the kingdom [*basileia,* royal power and authority; see John 3:5] of heaven is at hand." [Mat. 4: 12-17; Isa. 9:1, 2].

This is why it makes sense that Christ began preaching *in the synagogues* in the traditional homeland of Zebulun and Naphtali. A remnant of those descended from the scattered sheep of the House of Israel, taken captive by the Assyrians more than seven centuries earlier, had returned into their historical lands of Israel. It was to them that Christ sent out the apostles. "These twelve Jesus sent out, instructing them, "Go *nowhere among the Gentiles* and enter no town of the Samaritans, but *go rather to the lost sheep of the House of Israel.*" [Mat. 10:5, 6, ESV].

Why did Christ instruct his apostles, who were to preach *the gospel*, to go nowhere among the Gentiles? Because *the House of Israel* was to be redeemed, but into the new covenant relationship with God as promised to Abraham and his Seed [Greek, *sperma*], Christ. The children of Abraham's covenant are literally children of the freewoman, Sarah. [See Gal. 4:31].

And to the rest of the House of Israel still scattered all over the Roman Empire, the apostle Paul was sent to preach the same good news or gospel to them as well. "Paul, a servant of Christ Jesus, called to be an apostle and set apart for *the gospel of God.*" [Rom. 1:1].

There are some, however, not understanding for whom the gospel is meant, that claim Paul was the apostle to the Gentiles. "For this cause, I Paul, the prisoner of Christ Jesus for you the nations..." [Eph. 3:1, YNG]. Many Bible translations, including the KJV use the word Gentiles in place of nations here. But this is incorrect and misleading. The word is *ethnos* in Greek. And correctly it is translated as nations because the gospel, the good news was meant for the ten nations of the House of Israel, the seed of Abraham through Christ. And we can see evidence of this in Paul's writings made all the clearer when we understand the role of the Abrahamic covenant.

"Paul, an apostle of Jesus Christ by the will of God, and Timothy our brother, To the church of God which is at Corinth, with all the saints who are in all Achaia…." [2 Cor. 1:1]. Now if any church in first century Christianity could be characterized as "Gentile" due to the backsliding of some members for their lasciviousness and fornication as noted by Paul, it would be the church in Corinth. [See 1 Cor. 5:1; 2 Cor. 12:21]. Yet, the gospel preached to the House of Israel in Palestine by the twelve apostles was the same good news Paul preached to these descendants of the House of Israel in Asia Minor.

"For I want you to know, brothers, that *our fathers* were all under the cloud, and all passed through the sea, and *all were baptized into Moses* in the cloud and in the sea and all ate the same spiritual food, and all drank the same spiritual drink. For they drank from the spiritual Rock that followed them, and the *Rock was Christ*." [1 Cor. 10:1-4, ESV].

Paul, a descendant of Benjamin, a son of the House of Israel, explained that even when our fathers of Israel came out of Egypt, Christ, the Seed of Abraham, was right there with them. "So God heard their groaning [*in Egypt*], and *God remembered His covenant with Abraham, with Isaac, and with Jacob*. And God looked upon the children of Israel, and God acknowledged them." [Exd. 2:24, 25]. Understanding the relevancy of the covenant made with Abraham, what we call the new covenant, allows us to understand the gospel, the good news that is meant for the House of Israel in our age.

Now once we understand the role of the covenant made with Abraham and his Seed, Christ, we can readily understand that Christ was correct in saying he was sent only to the lost sheep of the House of Israel. Knowing this, we can see the true gospel, or good news, that all the apostles were sent to preach to the House of Israel. They were specifically instructed by Christ not to go among the Gentiles because the covenant has no relevancy for them. They are not *the seed* [Greek, *sperma*] of Abraham through Christ. [See Mat. 1:1-16].

When we blatantly mistrust the explicit word of Christ about being sent only to the House of Israel, we will never truly understand the gospel either. A cavalier attitude towards the truth leads us away from Christ.

Taking Christ at his word, however, understanding the meaning of the Abrahamic covenant for Christians, we can clearly see the meaning of the gospel. And understanding what the good news is for us, we can understand the bad news for us in the prophecies of the Old Testament and in Revelation in particular.

When we deny our true heritage, the light of the gospel, and discount Christ's plain words while declaring we are Gentiles and that we are not in Biblical end-time prophecies, we walk in the darkness of fables, draped in the lies of deceit.

"And this is the condemnation, that the Light has come into the world [*kosmos*], and men [*anthropos*] loved darkness rather than light, because their deeds were evil." [John 3:19].

But not to worry. If Christ was wrong about being sent only to the House of Israel, he has to be wrong about sending the apostles only to the House of Israel too. And therefore, he can't be right that men love darkness and as a result their deeds are evil. And certainly this can't apply to 21st century Christianity.

But it does. We've lost our spiritual purity. And it is clear in the prophecies. In Isaiah 63 we read that Christ will turn to be our enemy in the end-times because we, the House of Israel, "*have rebelled and vexed his Holy Spirit.*" But we don't take note of these warning prophecies because we don't know our Biblical identity. And refusing to acknowledge our true Biblical identity means we can never heed the warning in the prophecies meant for us. It's a lethal Catch-22.

We have denied our heritage, the covenant made with Abraham, and Christ's plain words. We have denied his true gospel. The very great majority of the 30,000 plus denominations, comprised of one and a half to two billion Christians today, have followed after false gods and celebrated days rooted in pagan tradition thinking we are Gentiles. We've fallen out of love with the truth. How blind we have become.

While no one knows when this age will come to an end, there is a sequence of events that will transpire that will let us know these events are near. [See Mat. 24:30-33]. There are many events still needing to occur before the end of the world [Greek, *aion*, meaning age]. Nevertheless, we should be mindful of what the apostle Paul wrote to the ekklesia in Thessalonica in the first century.

"And now, brothers and sisters, let us tell you about the coming again of our Lord Jesus Christ and how we will be gathered together to meet him. Please don't be so easily shaken and troubled by those who say that the day of the Lord has already begun. Even if they claim to have had a vision, a revelation, or a letter supposedly from us, don't believe them. Don't be fooled by what they say. For that day will not come until there is *a great rebellion* [Greek, *apostasia,* a falling away] against God...." [2 Ths. 2:1-3, NLT].

Discounting the trending move towards atheism, Christianity certainly doesn't recognize their apostasia when myopically seeking divine direction from within their Gentile house of mirrors. By riding our rogue ponies away from our covenant inheritance as the House of Israel, dismissing the plain words of the gospel delivered by Christ, and following the trail of darkness by celebrating pagan traditions in the name of Christ, rather than diligently holding fast the Light delivered to us, we are rebelling against God and vexing the Holy Spirit that was given to the House of Israel on the very first day of Christianity nearly two millennia ago. [See Acts 2:36-38].

Paul expounded about the apostasia in a letter to Timothy, "*For the time will come* when they will not endure sound doctrine, but according to their own desires, because they have itching ears [*wanting to hear what they want rather than the truth*], they will heap up for themselves teachers; and they will turn their ears away from the truth, and be turned aside to fables." [2 Tim. 4:3, 4].

Believing we are Gentiles rather than descendants of the House of Israel is a fable. Believing Christ was born on

The Great Rebellion: A Summary
Why is First Century Christianity More Relevant Than Ever?

December 25th is a fable. Santa Claus is a fable. The Easter Bunny is a fable. Believing Christ, as Abraham's Seed, was sent to all the Gentiles of the world is a fable. Teaching that the US is not in end-times prophecy is a fable. Just about every chapter in this book, and the previous two Elephant books, addresses a fable in one form or another. If you are a lover of the fables, you probably won't have reached this far in the book.

The events of the Apocalypse that will come upon Christians are set to occur after our rebellion against God. And why are we rebelling against God? According to God, regardless of the words that pass over our lips, we turn our back to God because *we no longer love the truth*. The fear of the LORD is the beginning of knowledge. [See Pro. 1:17, Rom. 3:18]. The fear of the truth is the fruit of deceit. And so it is with our itching ears that love the fables.

Paul continues, "… and the man of lawlessness is revealed— the one who brings destruction. He will exalt himself and defy every god there is and tear down every object of adoration and worship. He will position himself in the temple of God, claiming that he himself is God. Don't you remember that I told you this when I was with you?

"And you know what is holding him back, for he can be revealed only when his time comes. For this lawlessness is already at work secretly [*in the first century*. Read chapter six in *The Blind Man's Elephant*], and it will remain secret until the one who is holding it back steps out of the way. Then the man of lawlessness will be revealed, whom the Lord Jesus will consume with the breath of his mouth and destroy by the splendor of his coming." [See Rev. 17:14].

"This evil man [666] will come to do the work of Satan with counterfeit power and signs and miracles. He will use *every kind of wicked deception* to fool those who are **on their way to destruction because they refuse to believe the truth that would save them.** So God will send great deception upon them, and they will believe all these lies. Then, *they will be condemned for not believing the truth* and for *enjoying* the evil they do." [2 Ths. 2:4-12, NLT; see Rev. 13:4-8].

Christians enjoy Christmas probably more than anything else. *Joyeux Noel*. However, it is based on a lie. It is a pagan tradition and is not the birth date of Christ. Even atheists recognize this. The president of the American Atheists organization was quoted as saying, "Christianity is one of over a dozen religions that named the winter solstice as their god's birthday. This is not original." Regarding these pagan Christmas traditions so eagerly pursued by "Christians," we are told by the prophet Jeremiah, "Thus says the LORD, Learn not the way of the heathen, and be not dismayed at the signs of heaven." This is a reference to the winter solstice. Jeremiah continues, "But they [*Christians today*] are altogether brutish [*stupid*] and foolish: the tree is a doctrine of vanities." [Jer. 10:1, 8].

We've already been deceived about our covenant heritage, our Biblical identity as the lost sheep of the House of Israel and the true gospel. Where does this "wicked deception" put us in the grand scheme of things according to Paul? In about the same predicament that the House of Israel found itself with the Assyrians 700 years or so before the coming of Christ. Sanctimoniously, disregarding the warnings given to them, their national identities were destroyed, the people scattered as slaves among the Assyrian Empire. Our modern day analogy means there will be no more "good 'ol US of A." But if we think for a moment that God would never let this happen to us because after all, we are a God-fearing nation, it will be deja vu for the House of Israel.

Why? Because we've rebelled against the spiritual liberty and truth that Christ has granted us by the sacrifice of his life on our behalf as the Seed of Abraham. No wonder the prophecies tell us, "... *your guilt is great*, ... *your sins are flagrant*" and that our Lord says to us, "*I have done these things to you.*" Our destiny, for those who choose to continue on this path, is found in the events of the Apocalypse. We need to return to the love of the truth that will save us. We need to be earnest doers of our faith, full of power of the Spirit of God as was the Assyrian period prophet Micah in his prophetic words of warning to the House of Israel.

"But truly I am full of power by the Spirit of the LORD, and of justice and might, to declare to Jacob his transgression and to [*the House of*] Israel his sin. Now hear this, you *heads of the House of Jacob* and *rulers of the House of Israel*, who abhor justice and pervert all equity... Her heads [*our executive, legislative and judicial leaders*] judge for a bribe, her priests teach for pay, and her prophets divine for money. Yet they lean on the LORD, and say, "Is not the LORD among us? No harm can come upon us." [Micah 3:8, 9, 11]. Deja vu.

The prophecies tell us our historical amnesia and love of fables is terminal unless we make changes to our current modus operandi. Therefore, we need to garner a passionate love of the truth set forth for us in both Testaments, following the apostle James' advice, "... *be doers* of the word, and not hearers [*and readers*] only, deceiving yourselves."

When we ignore our heritage, and decline to make the needed major changes in our lives, we are refusing to learn from history. And when through our actions we refuse to learn from history, we are doomed to repeat it. It is for this reason that first century Christianity is more relevant than ever before.

The Great Britain-US Flow Chart

Biblical Overview:
Great Britain & United States

As **The Curious Elephant**, **Holy Curiosity: Factoids From the First Century** is a compendium of articles supporting and expanding upon points in the chapters of both **The Blind Man's Elephant** and **The Hijacked Elephant** books, readers have requested a flow chart or someway to keep track of our history from Abraham to present day and beyond. In just a few pages, the storyline of the Biblical record's big picture can be easily understood. It is included here.

Please keep in mind that it is a *flow* chart and not a timeline. As such, the length of the connecting lines do not represent any amount of time nor are they in proportion. They merely connect significant events in sequence.

The Great Britain-US Flow Chart

House of Israel Flow Chart

See chapter *Is The US In End-times Bible Prophecy?*

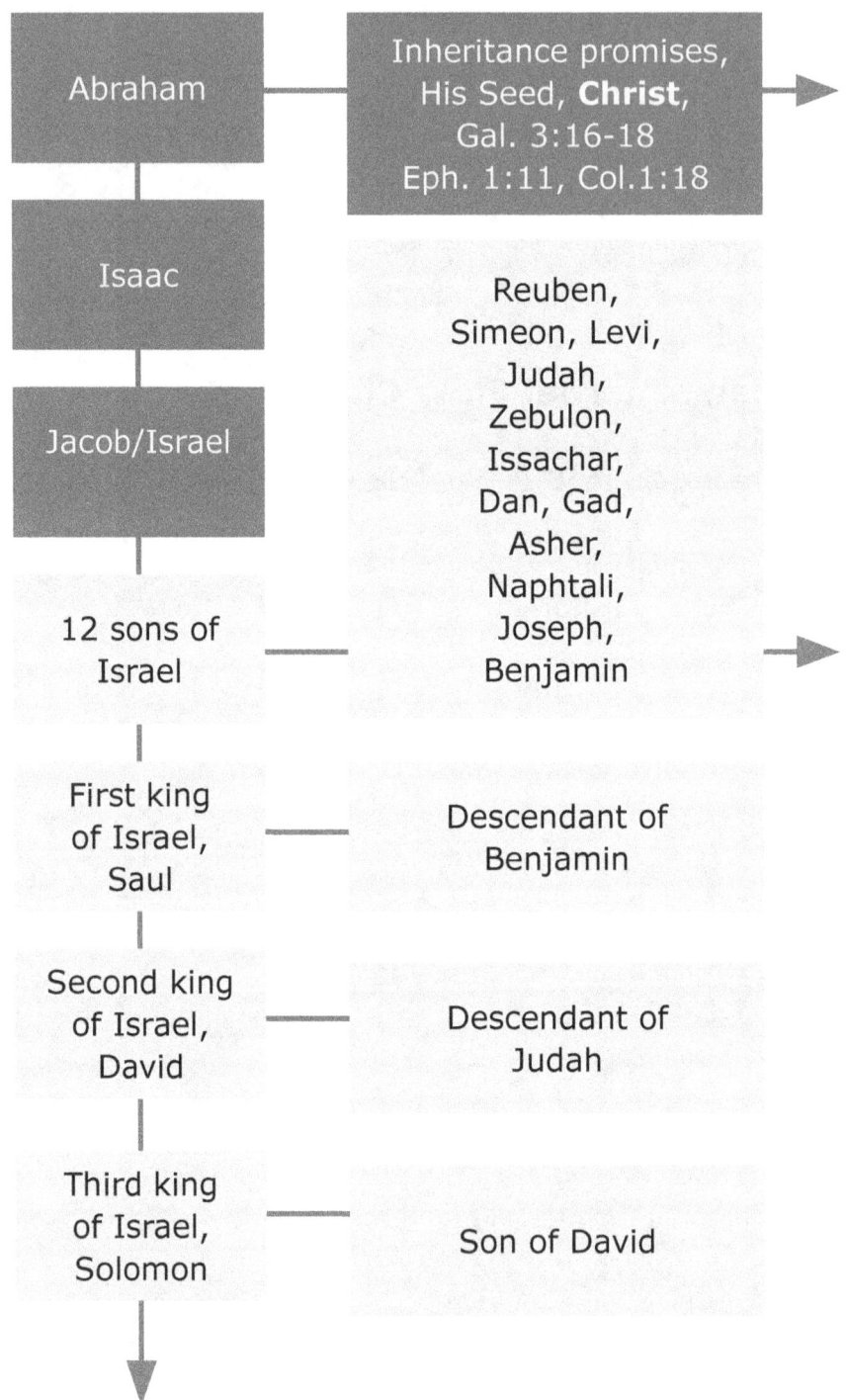

The Great Britain-US Flow Chart
House of Israel Flow Chart 1/4

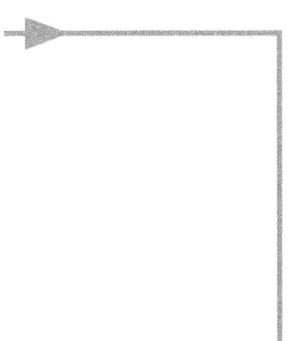

Joseph's sons,
birthright
inheritance:
1 Chr. 5:1
Col. 3:24
Ephraim, GB
Manasseh, US
Gen. 48

```
                    Rehoboam,                    Jeroboam,
                   grandson of                 descendant of
                   David, king of              Joseph, king of
                  House of Judah,             House of Israel,
                     one nation                  ten nations
                  1 Kng. 12:20-24             1 Kng. 11:29-32
                          │                          │
                          │          Levi,           │
                          │    priesthood for        │
                          │      all Israel,         │
                          │       one nation         │
                          │                          │
                          │              House of Israel divorced
                          │              from God, broken off from
                          │              the inheritance promises,
                          │              1 Kng. 12:26-33  Jer. 3:6-8
                          │
                   House of Judah
                 Babylonian captivity,
                        70 years
                          │
                 Christ's first coming
                          │
                          ▼
```

The Great Britain-US Flow Chart
House of Israel Flow Chart 2/4

```
                │
                ▼
```

Christ's death & resurrection, major changes

House of Israel redeemed
Christ sent only to lost sheep House of Israel, *Mat. 15:24*;
Levi priesthood passes away, Christ is high priest, *Heb. 3:1, 4:14*

House of Judah broken off until second coming
Isa. 29:10
Rom. 11:8-10

Christ fulfills Passover, Days of Unleavened Bread, Pentecost for **House of Israel, receives Holy Spirit,** *Acts 2:36-38*

Events of apocalypse

Christ's return fulfilling Day of Trumpets, first resurrection
Rev. 19, 20

The Great Britain-US Flow Chart
House of Israel Flow Chart 3/4

Law covenant broken by Christ; Brotherhood of Judah & Israel broken
Zec. 11:10-14, Rom. 11

Christ opens first five seals, false prophets, wars, famine, pestilence, martyrs
Rev. 6:1-11

The falling away from the love of the truth
2 Ths. 2:3, 10

144,000 sealed, 12,000 from each nation of Israel except Dan; Manasseh [US], of Joseph, replaces Dan as twelfth nation,
Rev. 7:4-8

Christ opens seals six and seven, **events of apocalypse**, time of Jacob's/Israel's *trouble*
Jer. 30:4-15
Rev. 6:12-17, 8:1ff;

Christ's return fulfills Day of Atonement, New covenant with House of Israel and House of Judah,
Heb. 8:8

House of Judah and House of Israel joined again as one nation, Israel
Eze. 37:16-28
Rom. 11:25, 26

Christ fulfills Feast of Tabernacles, Millennium, 1000 years of peace.
Rev. 20:4-7

Last Great Day, Great Resurrection, New heaven and Earth
Rev. 21

Biblical Book Abbreviations

Biblical Book Abbreviations
Old Testament

Genesis	Gen.
Exodus	Exd.
Leviticus	Lev.
Numbers	Num.
Deuteronomy	Deu.
Joshua	Jos.
Judges	Jdg.
Samuel	Sam.
Kings	Kng.
Isaiah	Isa.
Jeremiah	Jer.
Ezekiel	Eze.
Hosea	Hos.
Joel	Joel
Amos	Amos
Obadiah	Oba.
Jonah	Jon.
Micah	Mic.
Nahum	Nah.
Habakkuk	Hab.
Zephaniah	Zep.
Haggai	Hag.
Zechariah	Zec.
Malachi	Mal.

Psalms   Psa.
Proverbs   Pro.
Job   Job

Solomon's Song   Sgs.
Ruth   Ruth
Lamentations   Lam.
Ecclesiastes   Ecc.
Esther   Est.

Daniel   Dan.
Ezra   Ezra
Nehemiah   Neh.
Chronicles   Chr.

Biblical Book Abbreviations
New Testament

Matthew	Mat.
Mark	Mark
Luke	Luke
John	John
Acts	Acts
James	Jam.
Peter	Pet.
Jude	Jude
Romans	Rom.
Corinthians	Cor.
Galatians	Gal.
Ephesians	Eph.
Philippians	Php.
Colossians	Col.
Thessalonians	Ths.
Hebrews	Heb.
Timothy	Tim.
Titus	Tts.
Philemon	Phi.
Revelation	Rev.

Bible Version Abbreviations

American Standard Version	ASV
English Standard Version	ESV
King James Version	KJV
New American Standard Bible	NASB
New International Version	NIV
New King James Version	NKJV
New Living Translation	NLT
Revised Standard Version	RSV
Young's Literal Translation	YNG

About the author, Michael J. Miller

For more than four decades the author has written numerous articles for newspapers and magazines, as well as television documentaries and award winning educational films on varied topics including local, national and international politics, economics, medicine, history, marine environment and theology among others. He has degrees in poitical science, history and theology. He is the author of the "Elephant book trilogy," *The Blind Man's Elephant*, *The Hijacked Elephant* and *The Curious Elephant*.

www.ingramcontent.com/pod-product-compliance
Lightning Source LLC
LaVergne TN
LVHW051822080426
835512LV00018B/2687